Directory
to
Collections
of
New York
Vital Records

1726–1989

with
Rare Gazetteer

Fred Q. Bowman and Thomas J. Lynch

HERITAGE BOOKS
2015

HERITAGE BOOKS
AN IMPRINT OF HERITAGE BOOKS, INC.

Books, CDs, and more—Worldwide

For our listing of thousands of titles see our website
at
www.HeritageBooks.com

Published 2015 by
HERITAGE BOOKS, INC.
Publishing Division
5810 Ruatan Street
Berwyn Heights, Md. 20740

International Standard Book Numbers
Paperbound: 978-0-7884-5630-5
Clothbound: 978-0-7884-0275-3

TABLE OF CONTENTS

ACKNOWLEDGEMENTS

The information here reflected was obtained by me through repeated on-site searches at the New York State Library, the New York Genealogical and Biographical Society Library, the Brooklyn Historical Society Library, the Loudonville (NY) branch of the Latter Day Saints (Mormon) Family History Library and the National Society of the Daughters of the American Revolution Library. Without the always cheerful assistance of both library and society staff members in each setting, this project would never have been completed.

James Lane, Associate Librarian at the New York State Library, and Arthur C.M. Kelly, book publisher at Kinship in Rhinebeck, New York, have both made substantial suggestions that have been here included. David K. Martin, editor of *Tree Talks*, published by the Central New York Genealogical Society (P.O. Box 104, Colvin Station, Syracuse, NY 13205), has steered me to a large number of here-reported collections from that publication. I am especially grateful to Henry B. Hoff, editor of the *New York Genealogical and Biographical Record*, not only for his self-initiated mailings to me of supplementary information but also for his constant encouragement.

Undoubtedly this report is incomplete. None of the five libraries has a master list identifying all of its newspaper vital record collections. I have spent limited time in the on-site searches at each of these libraries. Responsibility for any record lacks or errors is solely mine.

Fred Q. Bowman

PREFACE

This is a three-part book. Part 1 (pages 1-31), the main part, contains the county centered directory. Part 2 (pages 41-78) contains a specialized county-centered gazetteer. Part 3 (pages 79-84) provides, among other things, the date of formation of each of New York's present-day counties. Many persons will need to turn to the contents of Part 2 before consulting Part 1. Details in this regard and others as well are found cumulatively in the discussions under the three sub-headings which follow.

Concerning Part 1 - The County-Centered Directory

In New York, town-filed vital records prior to 1880 are scarcely available. Fortunately, from the early 1700's newspapers have continually featured marriage and death notices. Over the years collections of these records have appeared in book or article form. Unfortunately, directories identifying what collections are available where are generally lacking.

Residence places of persons identified in newspaper marriage and death columns are by no means confined to the counties within which the newspapers are published. Communities in the rest of New York as well as New England and the mid-west are frequently specified. Occasionally found are residence places in East Florida, California, Burma, Surinam, China, and Malta to name a few of the more distant regions. Frequently these newspaper postings contain specific detail lacking in more commonly sought cemetery, church and town record books. Illustrations in the above two regards (the span in residence place reportings and the power of specific detail) are furnished in Appendix A.

Co-author Thomas J. Lynch, in Appendix B, furnishes additional background information. Most particularly he offers suggestions which enable the searcher to make maximum progress through use of these specialized newspaper vital records of New York.

This book identifies in Part 1, several hundred collections of these newspaper-published records and specifies in which of five large genealogical libraries each of these collections is presently available. The newspapers here identified were published, 1726 through 1989, in 92 cities and villages spread across 54 of New York's 62 present-day counties. The collections of report vary greatly in length with the smallest one reflecting three records. Those collections drawn from the New York State Daughters of the American Revolution Society's 630 volume series modestly titled *Cemetery, Church and Town Records* (full series reportedly available in only three settings nationwide*) span cumulatively 10,300 pages of typescript vital record copy. Joseph Gavit's collection, handwritten on 3 x 5 cards (microfilm copy at the NY State Library), reflects 40,000 records, 1784-1829, drawn from 65 newspapers. Gertrude A. Barber's 1801-1890 collection from the *New York Evening Post* (published in New York County) fills 78 volumes typescript. My four books and an article (Thomas J. Lynch co-author) contain cumulatively more than 39,000 pre-1851 records spread across New York state.**

---

* New York State Library, New York City Public Library (not complete) and the NSDAR Library.
** These four books and others are identified in Appendix C.

Identified in Part 1 initially are statewide and regional collections. Following this is a listing of counties and towns within which the newspapers were published, together with the date spans of the individual collections and thirdly, the newspapers' titles.

In Part 1, unless otherwise indicated, each collection reflects both marriages and deaths. The bold-faced numerals **1** through **5** within brackets identify the library or libraries which hold each collection of reference within the following pattern:

1 - **New York State Library** (Cultural Education Center, Empire Plaza, Albany, NY 12230)

2 - **New York Genealogical and Biographical Society Library** (122 East 58th St., NY, NY 12230)

3 - **Brooklyn Historical Society Library** (128 Pierrepont Street, Brooklyn, NY 11201)

4 - **Latter-Day Saints (Mormon) Family History Library** (35 NW Temple St., Salt Lake City, UT 84103) Collections are available through any LDS branch library.

5 - **National Society of the Daughters of the American Revolution Library** (1776 D St., NW, Washington, DC 20006)

The code D-Cem stands for NYS DAR's *Cemetery, Church and Town Records* of earlier reference and D-Bible stands for this same society's 255 volume series titled *Bible Records*. The seven-digit number frequently found following bold-faced **4** postings is the number for ordering in microform at LDS libraries the applicable collections. The code [*NYG&B RECORD*] identifies the *New York Genealogical and Biographical Record*, a 124 volume series published continuously since 1869. Partial or full sets of this series are available in many genealogical libraries in all sections of the United States. *Tree Talks*, a 34 volume periodical of frequent reference here, contains varied records spread across most of New York (lower Hudson Valley, New York City and Long Island excepted).

<u>Concerning Part 2 - The County-Centered Gazetteer</u>

In Part 1 the collections are grouped under the alphabetically-listed present-day <u>counties</u> within which the newspapers of reference were published. Many persons know the names of communities within which the marriages and deaths of their concerns occurred but lack information as to the names of the present-day counties within which these communities lie. For these persons, unless some accommodation is made, the contents of Part 1 are practically useless. Part 2 with its alphabetical list of New York cities, villages and hamlets (6710 in number with obsolete communities included) showing their locations by <u>present-day</u> <u>counties</u> and <u>towns</u> (called townships in some states) bridges the community-county gap. Since the U.S. census indexes reflect solely the towns (not the cities, villages or hamlets) of residence of all persons listed, this <u>town-related</u> information found in Part 2 - although not directly useful here - can prove extremely helpful in regard to New York family searches in general.

<u>Concerning Part 3 - The Formation and Origins of New York's Present-Day 62 Counties</u>

It took New York (first settled in 1624 in today's Albany area) no fewer than 232 years (1683-1914) to form its present-day sixty-two counties. In 1683 this colony was divided into ten counties with Albany being by far the largest one. Within the interval 1683 through census-time 1790 five additional counties were formed from within Albany's original bounds. Between 1791 and 1854 forty-five additional counties were struck off from within the existing ones statewide. The final two counties, Bronx and Nassau, were formed in 1899 and 1914 respectively.

[Although not of primary concern in this book, New York's slow rate of town formations merits mention here. It was not until 1788 that for the first time all land in this state was carved into towns - 120 in number with many of these being extremely large in size. For example, Whitestown, the largest one, as of 1788 covered all of present-day New York lying to the west of the present-day city of Utica. Within the interval 1788 through 1860 several hundred towns were struck off from within those previously formed with relatively few new ones formed after the latter date. John H. French's *Historical and Statistical Gazetteer of New York State*, Syracuse, 1860* reflects not only the dates of formations and origins of New York's counties formed prior to 1860 but also the same information concerning its towns. Included in this gazetteer which contains detail concerning the pioneer settlers in most of the towns listed is a relatively complete place-name index identifying 6200 cities, villages, hamlets and towns formed prior to 1860.]

This part contains details concerning the formation, origin and other significant information pertaining to each of New York's present-day sixty-two counties.

---

* Reprints of this book are available from either of these publishers: Heart of the Lakes, Interlaken, NY or Genealogical Publishing Company, Baltimore, MD.

Part One

Directory to Collections of New York Vital Records, 1726-1989

(with a county outline map of New York on page 2 and Appendices A, B, and C and Table 1)

Codes

1 - New York State Library

2 - New York Genealogical and Biographical Society Library

3 - Brooklyn Historical Society Library

4 - Latter-Day Saints (Mormon) Family History Library

5 - National Society of the Daughters of the American Revolution Library

BRONX
NEW YORK
QUEENS
KINGS
RICHMOND

NASSAU

SUFFOLK

NEW YORK'S SIXTY-TWO PRESENT-DAY COUNTIES

(SCHEN. for SCHENECTADY)

CHAUTAUQUA
CATTARAUGUS
ALLEGANY
ERIE
NIAGARA
WYOMING
GENESEE
ORLEANS
MONROE
LIVINGSTON
STEUBEN
ONTARIO
WAYNE
YATES
SENECA
SCHUY-LER
CHEMUNG
TOMP-KINS
CAYUGA
SENECA
TIOGA
CORTLAND
ONONDAGA
OSWEGO
JEFFERSON
BROOME
CHENANGO
MADISON
ONEIDA
LEWIS
ST. LAWRENCE
DELAWARE
OTSEGO
HERKIMER
HAMILTON
FRANKLIN
SULLIVAN
SCHOHARIE
MONTGOMERY
FULTON
ESSEX
CLINTON
ORANGE
ULSTER
GREENE
ALBANY
SCHEN.
SARATOGA
WARREN
WASHINGTON
ROCK-LAND
PUTNAM
WEST-CHESTER
DUTCHESS
COLUMBIA
RENSSELAER

(see inset)

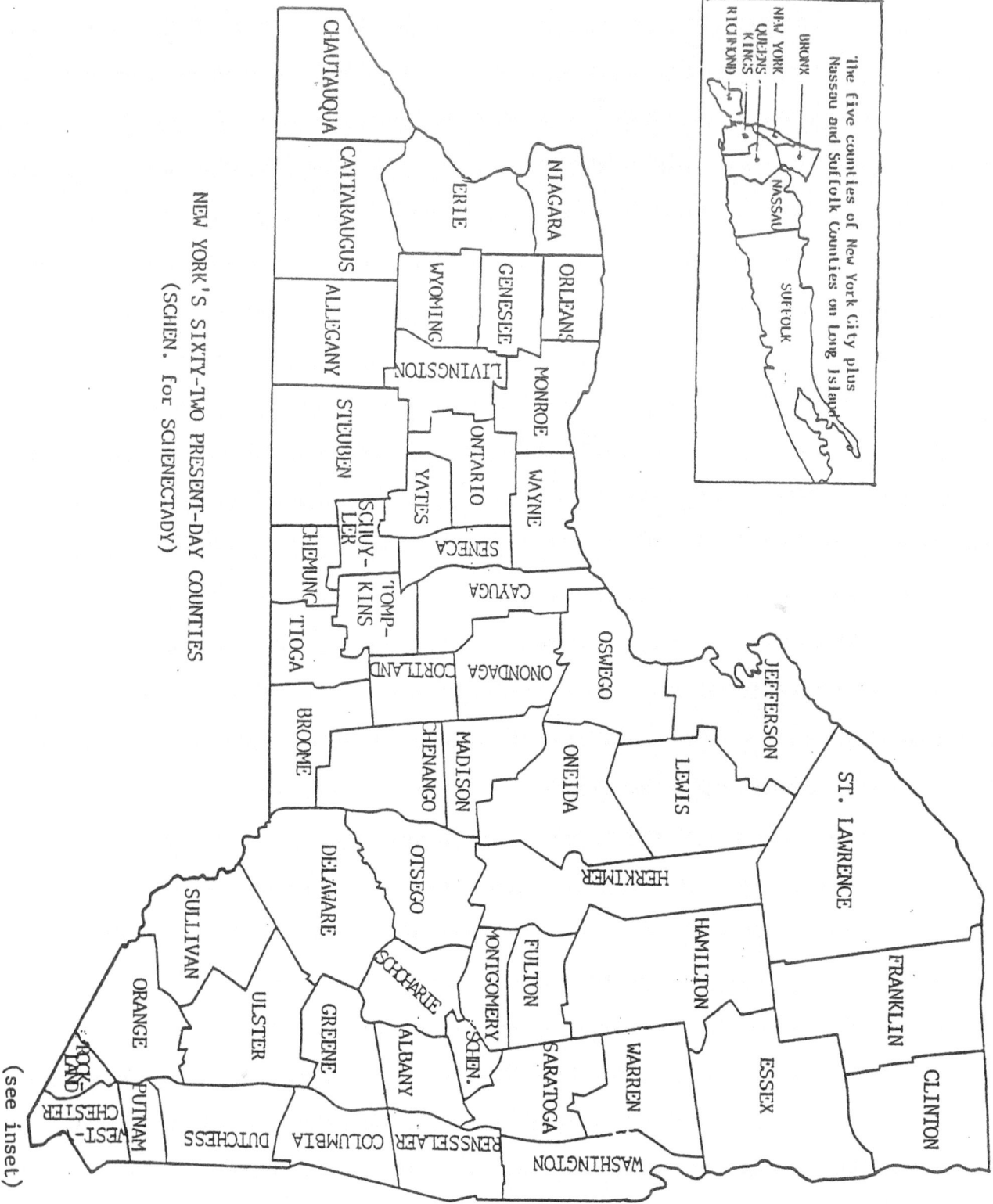

Adapted with permission of JIMAPCO, Inc. copyright 1993

2

NEW YORK STATE
Regional

????-????	Misc. newspapers (central New York). [4 #0924459]
????-????	Misc. newspapers (central and southern tier). [4 #0017837 items 2-7]
1777-1834	Misc. newspapers, *10,000 Vital Records of Eastern New York, 1777-1834*, Fred Q. Bowman. Genealogical Publishing Co., Baltimore, MD, 1987. (book) [**1,2,3,4,5**]
1782-1866	Misc. newspapers, Edna Huntington. [**3**]
1784-1829	*American Deaths and Marriages, 1784-1829*, Joseph Gavit, microfilm, 1976. [**1,3**]
1784-1829	*Index to Non-Principals in Joseph Gavit's American Deaths and Marriages, 1784-1829*, Kenneth Scott. Polyanthos Press, New Orleans, LA 1976. (book) [**1**]
1785-1794	*Marriage Notices from the Whole United States*, Charles K. Bolton, 1900 (scattered NY records, mostly New England, found in the *Massachusetts Centinel* and the *Columbian Centinel* published in Boston, Mass.) reprint available: Kinship, Rhinebeck, NY, 1989. (book) [**1**]
1798-1817	Misc. newspapers [**1,2,3,4,5**, *NYG&B RECORD* 113:210-212]
1790-1902	Misc. newspapers [**3**]
1800-1816	Misc. newspapers, marriages. [**1,2,3,4,5**, *NYG&B RECORD* 114:16-17]
1804-1850	Misc. newspapers, *8,000 More Vital Records of Eastern New York State, 1804-1850*, Fred Q. Bowman. Kinship, Rhinebeck, NY. (book) [**1,2,3,4,5**]
1804-1869	Misc. newspapers, deaths. [**1,5**, D-Cem 133:1-225]
1806-1869	Misc. newspapers, deaths. [**1,5**, D-Cem 132:1-213]
1808-1881	Misc. newspapers [**3**]
1809-1850	Misc. newspapers, *10,000 Vital Records of Western New York, 1809-1850*, Fred Q. Bowman. Genealogical Publishing Co., Baltimore, MD, 1985. (book) [**1,2,3,4,5**]
1813-1850	Misc. newspapers, *10,000 Vital Records of Central New York, 1813-1850*, Fred Q. Bowman. Genealogical Publishing Co., Baltimore, MD, 1988. (book) [**1,2,3,4,5**]
1815-1853	*Early Marriages from Newspapers Published in Central New York*, 1992 (from scrap-book of William Beauchamp, b.1830, d.1925; edited by Mary Keysor Meyer). (book) [**1**]
1826-1865	Misc. newspapers (central New York). [4 #0017610 item 8]
1830-1831	Janet Wethy Foley's *Early Settlers of New York State*, 2:20-23 (book); *Gospel Advocate* (newspaper published in Utica, Oneida Co., NY). [**1**]
1835-1841	*Western NY Genealogical Journal*, vols. 10-12. [**1**]
1835-1850	Misc. newspapers, surnames A-Cr. [**1,2,3,4,5**, *NYG&B RECORD* 118:135-142 - see pg. 135 for newspaper towns]
1835-1850	Misc. newspapers, surnames Cr-Hen. [**1,2,3,4,5**, *NYG&B RECORD* 118:203-209 - see pg. 135 for newspaper towns]
1835-1850	Misc. newspapers, surnames Her-Pit. [**1,2,3,4,5**, *NYG&B RECORD* 119:35-43 - see 118:135 for newspaper towns]
1835-1850	Misc. newspapers, surnames Po-T. [**1,2,3,4,5**, *NYG&B RECORD* 119:91-98 - see 118:135 for newspaper towns]
1835-1850	Misc. newspapers, surnames V-Y. [**1,2,3,4,5**, *NYG&B RECORD* 119:166-170 - see 118:135 for newspaper towns]
1855-1856	Moore's *Rural New Yorker* (central and western NY) in Janet Wethy Foley's *Early Settlers of New York State*, 5:201-202, 217-219. (book) [**1**]

ALBANY COUNTY
Albany

1806-1834	Misc. newspapers, *The Annals of Albany*, J. Munsell, 5 vols., scattered deaths but names indexed within each volume; Vol. 5, Jan. 1, 1806-Aug. 15, 1813; Vol. 6, May 24, 1813-Sept. 4, 1818; Vol. 7, Nov. 16, 1816-April 29, 1822; Vol. 8, May 4, 1822-Dec. 26, 1869; Vol. 9, Jan. 1, 1827-June 30, 1834. (book) [1]
1818-1825	*Albany Argus* (from ms. collection NYG&B). [4 #0017508 item 6]
1829-1831	*Albany Argus*; *10,000 Vital Records of Eastern New York, 1777-1834*, Fred Q. Bowman. Genealogical Publishing Co., Baltimore, MD, 1987. (book) [1,2,3,4,5]
1830-1831	*Albany Argus* [1,5, D-Cem 185:146-154]
1830-1831	*Albany Argus*, marriages and deaths. [1,2,4,5, *Tree Talks* 20:23-24; Albany Co. pp. 55-56]
1832-1834	*Albany Argus*; *8,000 More Vital Records of Eastern New York State, 1804-1850*, Fred Q. Bowman. Kinship, Rhinebeck, NY. (book) [1,2,3,4,5]
1841	*Weekly Argus*, deaths, from *The Capital* (Kinship, Rhinebeck, NY), Vol. 1, #1 through Vol. 2, #3. [1,2,4,5]
1878	*Albany Argus* [1,5, D-Cem 134:1-5]

ALLEGANY COUNTY
Cuba

1895-1915	Misc. newspapers [4 #1321385]

BROOME COUNTY

????-????	Misc. newspapers [4 #1421864]
1825	Misc. newspapers (pioneers who died in 1825). [4 #1035592 item 15]
1827-1865	Misc. newspapers [4 #0017610 item 8]
1850-1900	Misc. newspapers [4 #0896899]
1859-1889	Misc. newspapers [1,5, D-Cem 523:27-44]
1859-1889	Misc. newspapers [4 #1036357 item 18]

Binghamton

1815-1816	*The Phoenix* [1,5, D-Cem 541:1-6]
1815-1816	*The Phoenix* [4 #1035592 item 9]
1821-1823	*Republican Herald* [1,5, D-Cem 543:178-180]
1821-1823	*Republican Herald* [4 #1035592 item 13]
1828-1830	*Broome Republican* [1,5, D-Cem 543:70-75]
1828-1832	*Broome Republican* [4 #1035592 items 10-12]
1830-1832	*The Broome County Republican* [1,5, D-Cem 541:13-29]
1831-1837	*Broome County Courier*, marriages. [1,2,4,5, *Tree Talks* 5:115-7:185; Broome Co., pp. 16-25]
1831-1837	*Broome County Courier*, deaths. [1,2,4,5, *Tree Talks* 8:19-9:213; Broome Co., pp. 26-33]
1831-1841	Misc. newspapers [1,5, D-Cem 104:20-61]
1831-1857	*Broome County Republican*, marriages. [3]
1831-1870	*Broome County Republican*, deaths. [3]
1842	*Broome County Iris*, deaths. [1,2,4,5, *Tree Talks* 27:85-86; Broome Co. pp. 101-102]
1842-1843	*Broome County Iris* [1,5, D-Cem 442:80-94]
1842-1845	*Broome County Republican* [1,5, D-Cem 112:68-95]
1842-1845	*Broome County Republican*; *10,000 Vital Records of Central New York, 1813-1850*, Fred Q. Bowman. Genealogical Publishing Co., Baltimore, MD, 1988. (book) [1,2,3,4,5]
1843-1853	*The Iris* [1,5, D-Cem 543:86-155]
1843-1853	*The Iris* [4 #1035592 items 4-8]

1846-1847   *The Iris* [**1,5**, D-Cem 543:86-155]
1846-1850   *Broome County Republican* [**1,5**, D-Cem 145:159-197]
1847-1849   *The Iris* [**1,5**, D-Cem 560:145-173]
1851-1853   *The Iris* [**1,5**, D-Cem 543:86-155]
pre-1857   *Binghamton Democrat* (deaths of Broome Co. pioneers). [**1,5**, D-Cem 543:186-188]
1858-1870   *Broome County Republican*, marriages. [**3**]

Union
1851-1897   *Union News* [**1,5**, D-Cem 442:54-63, 83-99]
1857-1860   *Union News*, marriages and deaths. [**1,2,4,5**, *Tree Talks* 33:86-34:88; Broome Co. pp. 136-142]
1873-1875   *Union Weekly News* [**4** #1036357 item 7]

CATTARAUGUS COUNTY
Allegany
1886-1947   *Allegany Citizen*, deaths. [**1,5**, D-Cem 188:166-184]

CAYUGA COUNTY
1805-1835   Misc. newspapers [**1,5**, D-Cem 412:1-214]
1818-1880?   Misc. newspapers (with church records of Auburn and Fleming interspersed). [**1,5**, D-Cem 349:1-174]

Auburn
1816-1824   *Auburn Gazette* and *Cayuga Republican*, deaths. [**1,2,4,5**, *Tree Talks* 4:182-8:21; Cayuga Co. pp. 16-29]
1816-1880   *Auburn Gazette* and *Cayuga Republican*, marriages. [**1,2,4,5**, *Tree Talks* 8:81-17:26; Cayuga Co. pp. 30-85]
1817   *Auburn Gazette*, marriages and deaths. [**1,2,4,5**, *Tree Talks* 23:89-90; Cayuga Co. pp. 120-121]
1825-1834   *Cayuga Patriot*, typescript. [**3**]
1828-1880   Misc. newspapers, deaths. [**1,2,4,5**, *Tree Talks*, 17:79-21:91; 25:33-26:148 Cayuga Co. pp. 86-110; 128-139]
1849-1854   *Cayuga Chief* and *Auburn Daily Advertiser* [**1,5**, D-Cem 516:1-151]
1855-1860   *Auburn Daily Advertiser* [**1,5**, D-Cem 519:1-192]
1861-1865   *Auburn Daily Advertiser* [**1,5**, D-Cem 559:1-287]

CHAUTAUQUA COUNTY
1797-1939   Misc. newspapers [**4** #1381728 item 34]
1826-1880   Misc. newspapers, surnames A-B. [**1,5**, D-Cem 490:1-227]
1826-1880   Misc. newspapers, surnames C-DePew. [**1,5**, D-Cem 509:1-193]
1826-1880   Misc. newspapers, surnames Deak-Flynt. [**1,5**, D-Cem 517:1-134]
1826-1880   Misc. newspapers, surnames Fogle-Hewitt. [**1,5**, D-Cem 521:1-205]
1826-1880   Misc. newspapers, surnames Heyn-Irwin. [**1,5**, D-Cem 571:113-212]

Fredonia
????-????   *NY Censor* [**4** #0895184 item 2]
1823-1840   *Fredonia Censor* [**1,5**, D-Cem 209:276-428]
1826-1828   *Fredonia Censor*, marriages and deaths. [**1,2,4,5**, *Tree Talks* 25:158; Chautauqua Co. p. 82]

Jamestown
1826-1830   *Jamestown Journal*, marriages. [**1,2,4,5**, *Tree Talks* 27:89-28:30; Chautauqua Co. pp. 89-92]
1826-1830   *Jamestown Journal*, deaths. [**1,2,4,5**, *Tree Talks* 28:30-90; Chautauqua Co. pp. 92-94]
1826-1850   *Jamestown Journal*; *10,000 Vital Records of Western New York, 1809-1850*, Fred Q. Bowman. Genealogical Publishing Co., Baltimore, MD, 1985. (book) [**1,2,3,4,5**]

1832-1834   *Jamestown Journal*, deaths. [**1,5**, D-Cem 266:65]
1832-1835   *Jamestown Journal*, marriages. [**1,2,4,5**, *Tree Talks* 4:183-5:118; Chautauqua Co. pp. 3-6]
1833-1835   *Jamestown Journal*, deaths. [**1,2,4,5**, *Tree Talks* 4:74-183; Chautauqua Co. pp. 1-3]
1857-1858   *Chautauqua Democrat* [**4** #0895184 item 2]
1953   *Jamestown Post Journal*, obituaries. [**1,5**, D-Cem 201:169-181]
Westfield
1830   *The Pantheon* [**1,5**, D-Cem 289:50-54]

CHEMUNG COUNTY
Elmira
1847-1850   *Elmira Republican; 10,000 Vital Records of Central New York, 1813-1850*, Fred Q. Bowman. Genealogical Publishing Co., Baltimore, MD, 1988. (book) [**1,2,3,4,5**]

CHENANGO COUNTY
1818-1886   Misc. newspapers [**1,5**, D-Cem 219:1-235]
1829   Misc. newspapers [**1,2,4,5**, *Tree Talks* 18:93; Chenango Co. p. 65]
1845   Misc. newspapers [**1,2,4,5**, *Tree Talks* 18:93; Chenango Co. p. 65]
Norwich
1816-1830   *Norwich Journal; 10,000 Vital Records of Central New York, 1813-1850*, Fred Q. Bowman. Genealogical Publishing Co., Baltimore, MD, 1988. (book) [**1,2,3,4,5**]
1847-1855   *Chenango Union* [**1,5**, D-Cem 171:251]
1848-1850   *Chenango Union*, marriages. [**1,2,4,5**, *Tree Talks* 1:pages not here noted-8:200; Chenango Co. pp. 1-29]
1856-1858   Misc. newspapers [**1,5**, D-Cem 184:1-142]
Oxford
1813-1826   *Oxford Gazette; 10,000 Vital Records of Central New York, 1813-1850*, Fred Q. Bowman. Genealogical Publishing Co., Baltimore, MD, 1988. (book) [**1,2,3,4,5**]
1826-1830   *Chenango Republican; 10,000 Vital Records of Central New York, 1813-1850*, Fred Q. Bowman. Genealogical Publishing Co., Baltimore, MD, 1988. (book) [**1,2,3,4,5**]
1829-1830   *Chenango Republican* [**1,2,4,5**, *Tree Talks* 17:83-144; Chenango Co. pp. 61-64]
1833-1847   *Oxford Republican; 10,000 Vital Records of Central New York, 1813-1850*, Fred Q. Bowman. Genealogical Publishing Co., Baltimore, MD, 1988. (book) [**1,2,3,4,5**]
1842-1845   *Oxford Republican* [**1,2,4,5**, *Tree Talks* 17:83-144; Chenango Co. pp. 61-64]
1845   *Oxford Times; 10,000 Vital Records of Central New York, 1813-1850*, Fred Q. Bowman. Genealogical Publishing Co., Baltimore, MD, 1988. (book) [**1,2,3,4,5**]
Sherburne
1864-1900   Misc. newspapers, marriages. [**1,5**, D-Cem 255 and 256:1-230]
1864-1900   Misc. newspapers, marriages. [**4** #0851116 item 5]
1864-1900   Misc. newspapers, deaths. [**1,5**, D-Cem 241:1-238]
1864-1900   Misc. newspapers, deaths. [**4** #0851119 item 6]

CLINTON COUNTY
Keeseville
1828-1834   *Keeseville Herald; 10,000 Vital Records of Eastern New York, 1777-1834*, Fred Q. Bowman. Genealogical Publishing Co., Baltimore, MD, 1987. (book) [**1,2,3,4,5**]

1833-1834   *Keeseville Argus; 10,000 Vital Records of Eastern New York, 1777-1834*, Fred Q. Bowman. Genealogical Publishing Co., Baltimore, MD, 1987. (book) [**1,2,3,4,5**]

1835-1837   *Keeseville Argus*, surnames A-Cr. [**1,2,3,4,5**, *NYG&B RECORD* 118:135-142]

1835-1837   *Keeseville Argus*, surnames Cr-Hen. [**1,2,3,4,5**, *NYG&B RECORD* 118:203-209]

1835-1837   *Keeseville Argus*, surnames Her-Pit. [**1,2,3,4,5**, *NYG&B RECORD* 119:35-43]

1835-1837   *Keeseville Argus*, surnames Po-T. [**1,2,3,4,5**, *NYG&B RECORD* 119:91-98]

1835-1837   *Keeseville Argus*, surnames V-Y. [**1,2,3,4,5**, *NYG&B RECORD* 119:166-170]

1835-1838   *Keeseville Herald*, surnames A-Cr. [**1,2,3,4,5**, *NYG&B RECORD* 118:135-142]

1835-1838   *Keeseville Herald*, surnames Cr-Hen. [**1,2,3,4,5**, *NYG&B RECORD* 118:203-209]

1835-1838   *Keeseville Herald*, surnames Po-T. [**1,2,3,4,5**, *NYG&B RECORD* 119:91-98]

1835-1838   *Keeseville Herald*, surnames V-Y. [**1,2,3,4,5**, *NYG&B RECORD* 119:166-170]

1842-1846   *Essex County Republican*, surnames A-Cr. [**1,2,3,4,5**, *NYG&B RECORD* 118:135-142]

1842-1846   *Essex County Republican*, surnames Cr-Hen. [**1,2,3,4,5**, *NYG&B RECORD* 118:203-209]

1842-1846   *Essex County Republican*, surnames Her-Pit. [**1,2,3,4,5**, *NYG&B RECORD* 119:35-43]

1842-1846   *Essex County Republican*, surnames Po-T. [**1,2,3,4,5**, *NYG&B RECORD* 119:91-98]

1842-1846   *Essex County Republican*, surnames V-Y. [**1,2,3,4,5**, *NYG&B RECORD* 119:166-170]

Plattsburgh

1811-1834   *Plattsburgh Republican; 10,000 Vital Records of Eastern New York, 1777-1834*, Fred Q. Bowman. Genealogical Publishing Co., Baltimore, MD, 1987. (book) [**1,2,3,4,5**]

COLUMBIA COUNTY

Hudson

1801-1808   *The Balance; 10,000 Vital Records of Eastern New York, 1777-1834*, Fred Q. Bowman. Genealogical Publishing Co., Baltimore, MD, 1987. (book) [**1,2,3,4,5**]

1802-1851   *Deaths and Marriages and Miscellaneous from Hudson, NY Newspapers*, Arthur C.M. Kelly, deaths, Vol. 1, Rhinebeck, NY (from *The Balance* and *The Columbia Repository, 1802-1811* and *The Rural Repository or Bower of Literature, 1824-1851*). (book) [**1**]

1802-1851   *Deaths and Marriages and Miscellaneous from Hudson, NY Newspapers*, Arthur C.M. Kelly, marriages, Vol. 2, Rhinebeck, NY (from *The Balance* and *The Columbia Repository, 1802-1811* and *The Rural Repository or Bower of Literature, 1824-1851*). (book) [**1**]

1807   *The Balance* and *The Columbia Repository* [**1,5**, D-Cem 42:261-265]

1809-1820   *The Northern Whig; 10,000 Vital Records of Eastern New York, 1777-1834*, Fred Q. Bowman. Genealogical Publishing Co., Baltimore, MD, 1987. (book) [**1,2,3,4,5**]

1823-1828   *The Northern Whig* [**3**]

1824-1837   *The Rural Repository*, deaths. [**3**]

1828-1829   *The Rural Repository* [**1,5**, D-Cem 99:320-326]

1828-1832   *The Rural Repository*, marriages. [**3**]

1832-1837   *The Rural Repository*, marriages. [**3**]

1834   *The Rural Repository*, marriages and deaths. [**1,2,4,5**, *Tree Talks* 11:151-12:146; Columbia Co. pp. 2-9]

1837-1842   *The Rural Repository*, marriages. [**3**]

1837-1842   *The Rural Repository*, deaths. [**3**]

1840-1846   *The Rural Repository*, marriages. [**3**]

1840-1846	*The Rural Repository*, deaths. [3]
1840-1846	*The Rural Repository* [4 #0234580]
1841-1843	*The Rural Repository* [1,5, D-Cem 134:289-333]
1845-1851	*The Rural Repository*, marriages. [3]
1845-1851	*The Rural Repository*, deaths. [3]

Kinderhook

| 1836-1850 | *Kinderhook Sentinel; 8,000 More Vital Records of Eastern New York State, 1804-1850*, Fred Q. Bowman. Kinship, Rhinebeck, NY. (book) [1,2,3,4,5] |

CORTLAND COUNTY

1815-1840	*Historical Records of Cortland County*, Cortland Co. Historical Society, Vol. 22. (book) [1]
1815-1840	Misc. newspapers (typescript from *NYG&B RECORD*). [4 #0017610 item 6]
1815-1882	*Historical Records of Cortland County*, Cortland Co. Historical Society, Vol. 23. (book) [1]
1826-1879	Misc. newspapers (typescript from *NYG&B RECORD*). [4 #0017610 item 7]
1827	*Historical Records of Cortland County*, Cortland Co. Historical Society, Vol. 15. (book) [1]

Cortland

| 1826-1827 | *Cortland Observer*, marriages. [4 #0017610 item 8] |
| 1827-1865 | Misc. newspapers [4 #0017610 item 8] |

DELAWARE COUNTY
Delhi

1819-1844	*Delhi Gazette*, Gertrude A. Barber, deaths (1819-July 31, 1844). (book) [1,3]
1819-1879	*Delhi Gazette*, deaths. [4 #0017622 item 4]
1819-1820	*Delaware Gazette*, marriages and deaths. [1,2,4,5, *Tree Talks* 4:27 and 6:75, 117; Delaware Co. pp. 2, 7-8]
1819-1895	*Delaware Gazette*, Gertrude A. Barber, marriages. (book) [1]
1844-1868	*Delhi Gazette*, Gertrude A. Barber, deaths (Aug. 7, 1844-1868). (book) [1,3]
1868-1879	*Delhi Gazette*, Gertrude A. Barber, deaths (June 17, 1868-1879). (book) [1,3]
1880-1895	*Delhi Gazette*, Gertrude A. Barber, marriages. (book) [1,3]
1880-1895	*Delhi Gazette*, Gertrude A. Barber, deaths. (book) [1,3]

Stamford

| 1789-1880 | *Stamford Recorder*, marriages. [1,2,4,5, *Tree Talks* 31:40-34:95; Delaware Co. pp. 82-95] |

DUTCHESS COUNTY

1826-1851	*Marriage Notices from Dutchess Co., NY Newspapers, 1826-1851*, Arthur C.M. Kelly, Rhinebeck, NY, 1983. (book) [1,2]
1826-1875	Misc. newspapers, deaths, from *The Dutchess* (Kinship, Rhinebeck, NY), Vol. 7, #1 through Vol. 21. [1,2]
1865-1890	Misc. newspapers, deaths. [4 #0823867 item 3]
1865-1890	Misc. newspapers, deaths. [4 #0529190 item 3]
1865-1890	Misc. newspapers, deaths. [4 #0514684 item 5]

Fishkill

| 1777-1783 | *New York Packet; 10,000 Vital Records of Eastern New York, 1777-1834*, Fred Q. Bowman. Genealogical Publishing Co., Baltimore, MD, 1987. (book) [1,2,3,4,5] |
| 1893-1894 | *The Fishkill Weekly Times* [1,5, D-Cem 134:262-265] |

Poughkeepsie

????-????	Misc. newspapers (deaths from newspapers published in California). [4 #1421878]
1778-1825	Misc. newspapers [4 #1206459 item 25]
1778-1825	Misc. newspapers [4 #0940250]

1778-1825	Misc. newspapers, Dutchess County Historical Society Collections, Vol. 4, 1982; Society address: Box 88, Poughkeepsie, NY, 12602 [1,2]
1785-1834	*Poughkeepsie Journal*; *10,000 Vital Records of Eastern New York, 1777-1834*, Fred Q. Bowman. Genealogical Publishing Co., Baltimore, MD, 1987. (book) [1,2,3,4,5]
1806	*The Poughkeepsie Farmer* [1,5, D-Cem 54:282-283]
1840-1867	*Poughkeepsie Eagle* [1,5, 54:280-281]

Red Hook

1859-1918	Misc. newspapers, compiled by Margaret Herrick, deaths, Kinship, Rhinebeck, NY (book) [1,2,4]
1859-1936	Misc. newspapers, compiled by Margaret Herrick, marriages, Kinship, Rhinebeck, NY (book) [4]
1919-1936	Misc. newspapers, compiled by Margaret Herrick, deaths, Kinship, Rhinebeck, NY (book) [1,2,4]

Rhinebeck

1846-1899	*Deaths, Marriages and Much Miscellaneous from Rhinebeck Newspapers, 1846-1899*, Arthur C.M. Kelly, deaths, Vol. 1, Rhinebeck, NY, 1978. (book) [1,2,4]
1846-1899	*Deaths, Marriages and Much Miscellaneous from Rhinebeck Newspapers, 1846-1899* Arthur C.M. Kelly, marriages, Vol. 2, Rhinebeck, NY, 1978. (book) [1,2,4]

ERIE COUNTY

????-????	Misc. newspapers (contact LDS library for details re: surnames). [4 #1432315 to #1432323]
1812-1985	Misc. newspapers, surnames A-Bez, deaths. [4 #1419935]
1812-1985	Misc. newspapers, surnames Bi-Choa, deaths. [4 #1419936]
1812-1985	Misc. newspapers, surnames Choa-Doz, deaths. [4 #1419937]
1812-1985	Misc. newspapers, surnames Dra-Get, deaths. [4 #1419938]
1812-1985	Misc. newspapers, surnames Geth-Hills, deaths. [4 #1432339]
1812-1985	Misc. newspapers, surnames Hills, C-Kraft, B, deaths. [4 #1432340]
1812-1985	Misc. newspapers, surnames Kraft, C-McK, deaths. [4 #1432341]
1812-1985	Misc. newspapers, surnames McL-Paul, P, deaths. [4 #1432342]
1812-1985	Misc. newspapers, surnames Paul, R-Sawtelle, A, deaths. [4 #1432343]
1812-1985	Misc. newspapers, surnames Sawtelle, H-Stor, deaths. [4 #1432344]
1812-1985	Misc. newspapers, surnames Stot-Whaley, Fred, deaths. [4 #1432345]
1812-1985	Misc. newspapers, surnames Whaley, Frederick-Z, deaths. [4 #1432346]

Buffalo

1811-1816	*Buffalo Gazette* [1,5, D-Cem 69:247-295]
1819-1820	*Niagara Journal* [1,5, D-Cem 49:261-268]

ESSEX COUNTY

Elizabethtown

1833-1834	*Essex County Times*; *10,000 Vital Records of Eastern New York, 1777-1834*, Fred Q. Bowman. Genealogical Publishing Co., Baltimore, MD, 1987. (book) [1,2,3,4,5]
1835-1844	*Essex County Times*, surnames A-Cr. [1,2,3,4,5, *NYG&B RECORD* 118:135-142]
1835-1844	*Essex County Times*, surnames Cr-Hen. [1,2,3,4,5, *NYG&B RECORD* 118:203-209]
1835-1844	*Essex County Times*, surnames Her-Pit. [1,2,3,4,5, *NYG&B RECORD* 119:35-43]
1835-1844	*Essex County Times*, surnames Po-T. [1,2,3,4,5, *NYG&B RECORD* 119:91-98]
1835-1844	*Essex County Times*, surnames V-Y. [1,2,3,4,5, *NYG&B RECORD* 119:166-170]
1849	*Essex County Reporter*, surnames A-Cr. [1,2,3,4,5, *NYG&B RECORD* 118:135-142]

1849   *Essex County Reporter*, surnames Cr-Hen. [**1,2,3,4,5**, *NYG&B RECORD* 118:203-209]

1849   *Essex County Reporter*, surnames Her-Pit. [**1,2,3,4,5**, *NYG&B RECORD* 119:35-43]

1849   *Essex County Reporter*, surnames Po-T. [**1,2,3,4,5**, *NYG&B RECORD* 119:91-98]

1849   *Essex County Reporter*, surnames V-Y. [**1,2,3,4,5**, *NYG&B RECORD* 119:166-170]

Essex

1831-1832   *Essex Republican; 10,000 Vital Records of Eastern New York, 1777-1834*, Fred Q. Bowman. Genealogical Publishing Co., Baltimore, MD, 1987. (book) [**1,2,3,4,5**]

Keeseville

1828-1834   *Keeseville Herald; 10,000 Vital Records of Eastern New York, 1777-1834*, Fred Q. Bowman. Genealogical Publishing Co., Baltimore, MD, 1987. (book) [**1,2,3,4,5**]

1833-1834   *Keeseville Argus; 10,000 Vital Records of Eastern New York, 1777-1834*, Fred Q. Bowman. Genealogical Publishing Co., Baltimore, MD, 1987. (book) [**1,2,3,4,5**]

1835-1837   *Keeseville Argus*, surnames A-Cr. [**1,2,3,4,5**, *NYG&B RECORD* 118:135-142]

1835-1837   *Keeseville Argus*, surnames Cr-Hen. [**1,2,3,4,5**, *NYG&B RECORD* 118:203-209]

1835-1837   *Keeseville Argus*, surnames Her-Pit. [**1,2,3,4,5**, *NYG&B RECORD* 119:35-43]

1835-1837   *Keeseville Argus*, surnames Po-T. [**1,2,3,4,5**, *NYG&B RECORD* 119:91-98]

1835-1837   *Keeseville Argus*, surnames V-Y. [**1,2,3,4,5**, *NYG&B RECORD* 119:166-170]

1835-1838   *Keeseville Herald*, surnames A-Cr. [**1,2,3,4,5**, *NYG&B RECORD* 118:135-142]

1835-1838   *Keeseville Herald*, surnames Cr-Hen. [**1,2,3,4,5**, *NYG&B RECORD* 118:203-209]

1835-1838   *Keeseville Herald*, surnames Her-Pit. [**1,2,3,4,5**, *NYG&B RECORD* 119:35-43]

1835-1838   *Keeseville Herald*, surnames Po-T. [**1,2,3,4,5**, *NYG&B RECORD* 119:91-98]

1835-1838   *Keeseville Herald*, surnames V-Y. [**1,2,3,4,5**, *NYG&B RECORD* 119:166-170]

1842-1846   *Essex County Republican*, surnames A-Cr. [**1,2,3,4,5**, *NYG&B RECORD* 118:135-142]

1842-1846   *Essex County Republican*, surnames Cr-Hen. [**1,2,3,4,5**, *NYG&B RECORD* 118:203-209]

1842-1846   *Essex County Republican*, surnames Her-Pit. [**1,2,3,4,5**, *NYG&B RECORD* 119:35-43]

1842-1846   *Essex County Republican*, surnames Po-T. [**1,2,3,4,5**, *NYG&B RECORD* 119:91-98]

1842-1846   *Essex County Republican*, surnames V-Y. [**1,2,3,4,5**, *NYG&B RECORD* 119:166-170]

FRANKLIN COUNTY
Malone

1820-1829   *Franklin Telegraph; 8,000 More Vital Records of Eastern New York State, 1804-1850*, Fred Q. Bowman. Kinship, Rhinebeck, NY. (book) [**1,2,3,4,5**]

1849-1850   *Frontier Palladium; 8,000 More Vital Records of Eastern New York State, 1804-1850*, Fred Q. Bowman. Kinship, Rhinebeck, NY. (book) [**1,2,3,4,5**]

1852-1861   *Frontier Palladium* [**1,2,4,5**, *Tree Talks* 30:41-34:48; Franklin Co. pp. 46-57]

FULTON COUNTY

????-????   Misc. newspaper clippings, surnames A-C. [**4** #1276120] (original in Johnstown, NY Public Library)

????-????   Misc. newspaper clippings, surnames D-R. [**4** #1276121] (original in Johnstown, NY Public Library)

????-????   Misc. newspaper clippings, surnames S-Z. [**4** #1276122] (original in Johnstown, NY Public Library)

Johnstown

1830-1831	*Montgomery Republican* [**4** #1298602 item 6]
1834	*Montgomery Republican* [**4** #1298602 item 6]

GENESEE COUNTY
Batavia

1822-1850	*Republican Advocate*; *10,000 Vital Records of Western New York, 1809-1850*, Fred Q. Bowman. Genealogical Publishing Co., Baltimore, MD, 1985. (book) [**1,2,3,4,5**]
1825-1838	*The Advocate* [**1,5**, D-Cem 104:87-88]

GREENE COUNTY
Catskill

1793-1799	*The Catskill Packett* [**1,5**, D-Cem 98:201-212]
1832-1841	*The Catskill Examiner*, deaths. [**1,5**, D-Cem 71:229-243a]

Windham

1857	*Windham Journal* [**1,5**, D-Cem 362:1-96]
1860-1862	*Windham Journal* [**1,5**, D-Cem 365:96a-211]
1863-1865	*Windham Journal* [**1,5**, D-Cem 366:212-279]
1866-1868	*Windham Journal* [**1,5**, D-Cem 367:280-361]
1869-1871	*Windham Journal* [**1,5**, D-Cem 416:128-158]

HERKIMER COUNTY
Ilion

1855	*Ilion Independent* [**4** #0982411 item 1]

Little Falls

1823-1825	*The Gospel Inquirer*, marriages and deaths. [**1,2,4,5**, *Tree Talks* 33:97-34:98; Herkimer Co. pp. 106-109]

JEFFERSON COUNTY
Adams

1855-1876	*Jefferson County News*, deaths. [**1,5**, D-Cem 74:1-194]
1855-1878	*Jefferson County News*, marriages. [**1,5**, D-Cem 58:1-302]
1877-1882	*Jefferson County News*, deaths. [**1,5**, D-Cem 75:195-469]
1879-1885	*Jefferson County News*, marriages. [**1,5**, D-Cem 59:303-525]
1882-1887	*Jefferson County News*, deaths. [**1,5**, D-Cem 76:470-742]
1887-1895	*Jefferson County News*, deaths. [**1,5**, D-Cem 112:1-67]

Carthage

1861	*Carthage Republican* [**1,2,4,5**, *Tree Talks* 26:104-27:53; Jefferson Co. pp. 77-80]

Watertown

1826-1828	*Thursday Post* [**1,5**, D-Cem 188:185-189]
1832-1833	*Watertown Eagle* [**1,5**, D-Bible 86:218-221]
1874-1951	Misc. newspapers [**1,5**, D-Cem 263:26-54]

KINGS COUNTY
Brooklyn

1791-1886	Misc newspapers, abstracts of marriages and deaths, indexed. [**3**]
1800-1886	Misc. newspapers, Edna Huntington. [**3**]
1807-1846	*Long Island Star*, card file index to vital records. [**3**]
1809-1811	*Long Island Star* [**1,2,3,4,5**, *NYG&B RECORD* 48:411-413]
1809-1846	*Long Island Star* and *Brooklyn Evening Star*, Josephine C. Frost, vital records (index cards, 66 drawers), manuscript. [**3**]
1821-1833	*Long Island Patriot*, Edna Huntington. [**3**]
1833	*Long Island Patriot*, Edna Huntington. [**3**]

1841-1880	*Brooklyn Eagle*, abstracts of marriages and deaths, indexed. [3]
1841-1845	*Brooklyn Eagle*, Gertrude A. Barber, deaths, Vol. 1. (book) [3]
1841-1846	*Brooklyn Daily Eagle*, abstracts of vital statistics, excluding marriages and deaths. [3]
1841-1848	*Brooklyn Eagle*, Gertrude A. Barber, marriages, Vol. 1. (book) [3]
1844-	*Long Island Star*, marriages and deaths, in *Suffolk County Historical Society Register* 16:51-59, 81-89, 99-102 (in progress). [2]
1844-1846	*Brooklyn Eagle* [3]
1846-1850	*Brooklyn Eagle*, Gertrude A. Barber, deaths, Vol. 2. (book) [3]
1849-1851	*Brooklyn Eagle*, Gertrude A. Barber, marriages, Vol. 2. (book) [3]
1851-1852	*Brooklyn Eagle*, Gertrude A. Barber, deaths, Vol. 3. (book) [3]
1852-1854	*Brooklyn Eagle*, Gertrude A. Barber, marriages, Vol. 3. (book) [3]
1853-1855	*Brooklyn Eagle*, Gertrude A. Barber, deaths, Vol. 4, (Mar. 14,1853-1855). (book) [3]
1855-1858	*Brooklyn Eagle*, Gertrude A. Barber, marriages, Vol. 4. (book) [3]
1856-1858	*Brooklyn Eagle*, Gertrude A. Barber, deaths, Vol. 5. (book) [3]
1859-1861	*Brooklyn Eagle*, Gertrude A. Barber, deaths, Vol. 6. (book) [3]
1859-1862	*Brooklyn Eagle*, Gertrude A. Barber, marriages, Vol. 5, (Feb. 9, 1859-1862). (book) [3]
1861-1862	*Brooklyn5 Eagle*, Gertrude A. Barber, deaths, Vol. 7, (May 18, 1861-1862). (book) [3]
1863-1864	*Brooklyn Eagle*, Gertrude A. Barber, marriages, Vol. 6. (book) [3]
1863-1864	*Brooklyn Eagle*, Gertrude A. Barber, deaths, Vol. 8, (1863-April 30, 1864). (book) [3]
1864-1865	*Brooklyn Eagle*, Gertrude A. Barber, deaths, Vol. 9, (May 2, 1864-July 10, 1865). (book) [3]
1865-1866	*Brooklyn Eagle*, Gertrude A. Barber, deaths, Vol. 10, (July 11, 1865-Aug. 18, 1866). (book) [3]
1865-1867	*Brooklyn Eagle*, Gertrude A. Barber, marriages, Vol. 7, (Jan. 1, 1865-June 30,1867). (book) [3]
1866-1867	*Brooklyn Eagle*, Gertrude A. Barber, deaths, Vol. 11, (Aug. 19, 1866-Sept. 21, 1867). (book) [3]
1867-1868	*Brooklyn Eagle*, Gertrude A. Barber, deaths, Vol. 12, (Sept. 23, 1867-Oct. 19, 1868). (book) [3]
1867-1869	*Brooklyn Eagle*, Gertrude A. Barber, marriages, Vol. 8, (July 1, 1867-Sept. 17, 1869). (book) [3]
1868-1869	*Brooklyn Eagle*, Gertrude A. Barber, deaths, Vol. 13, (Oct. 24, 1868-Mar., 1869). (book) [3]
1869-1870	*Brooklyn Eagle*, Gertrude A. Barber, deaths, Vol. 14, (April, 1869-Nov. 19, 1870). (book) [3]
1869-1871	*Brooklyn Eagle*, Gertrude A. Barber, marriages, Vol. 9, (Sept. 18, 1869-Oct. 19, 1871). (book) [3]
1870-1871	*Brooklyn Eagle*, Gertrude A. Barber, deaths, Vol. 15, (Nov. 21, 1870-Oct. 31, 1871). (book) [3]
1871-1872	*Brooklyn Eagle*, Gertrude A. Barber, deaths, Vol. 16, (Nov. 1, 1871-Aug. 3, 1872). (book) [3]
1871-1873	*Brooklyn Eagle*, Gertrude A. Barber, marriages, Vol. 10, (Oct. 20, 1871-Oct. 1, 1873). (book) [3]
1872-1873	*Brooklyn Eagle*, Gertrude A. Barber, deaths, Vol. 17, (Aug. 5, 1872-June 2, 1873). (book) [3]
1873-1874	*Brooklyn Eagle*, Gertrude A. Barber, deaths, Vol. 18, (June 3, 1873-April 10, 1874). (book) [3]
1873-1875	*Brooklyn Eagle*, Gertrude A. Barber, marriages, Vol. 11, (Oct. 2, 1873-July 30, 1875). (book) [3]

1874-1875	*Brooklyn Eagle*, Gertrude A. Barber, deaths, Vol. 19, (April 11, 1874-Jan. 20, 1875). (book) [3]
1875	*Brooklyn Eagle*, Gertrude A. Barber, deaths, Vol. 20, (Jan. 21, 1875-Oct. 16, 1875). (book) [3]
1875-1876	*Brooklyn Eagle*, Gertrude A. Barber, deaths, Vol. 21, (Oct. 18, 1875-July 16, 1876). (book) [3]
1875-1877	*Brooklyn Eagle*, Gertrude A. Barber, marriages, Vol. 12 (Aug. 2, 1875-July 26, 1877) (book) [3]
1876-1877	*Brooklyn Eagle*, Gertrude A. Barber, deaths, Vol. 22, (July 19, 1876-April 24, 1877). (book) [3]
1877-1878	*Brooklyn Eagle*, Gertrude A. Barber, deaths, Vol. 23, (April 25, 1877-Jan. 28, 1878). (book) [3]
1877-1879	*Brooklyn Eagle*, Gertrude A. Barber, marriages, Vol. 13, (July 27, 1877-June 30, 1879). (book) [3]
1878	*Brooklyn Eagle*, Gertrude A. Barber, deaths, Vol. 24, (Jan. 29, 1878-Oct. 21, 1878). (book) [3]
1878-1879	*Brooklyn Eagle*, Gertrude A. Barber, deaths, Vol. 25, (Oct. 22, 1878-June 14, 1879). (book) [3]
1879-1880	*Brooklyn Eagle*, Gertrude A. Barber, marriages, Vol. 14, (July 2, 1879-Dec. 31, 1880). (book) [3]
1879-1880	*Brooklyn Eagle*, Gertrude A. Barber, deaths, Vol. 26, (June 15, 1879-Feb. 15, 1880). (book) [3]
1880-1880	*Brooklyn Eagle*, Gertrude A. Barber, deaths, Vol. 27, (Feb. 16, 1880-Dec. 31, 1880). (book) [3]
1891-1902	*Brooklyn Daily Eagle*, obituaries. [3]
1903-1912	*Brooklyn Daily Eagle Almanac* (deaths for prior year under "Local Necrology", no index). [2]
1907	*Index to Vital Statistics from the Brooklyn Daily Eagle*, Vol. 1. [3]
1909	*Index to Vital Statistics from the Brooklyn Daily Eagle*, Vol. 1. [3]

LEWIS COUNTY
Lowville
1831-1832	*Marriage and Death Records from The Black River Gazette, 1831-32 and The Northern Journal, 1838-45, 1847-53, 1855-59*, Anna E. Crawford. (book) [1]
1831-1832	*Black River Gazette* [4 #0017738]
1838-1845	*Marriage and Death Records from The Black River Gazette, 1831-32 and The Northern Journal, 1838-45, 1847-53, 1855-59*, Anna E. Crawford. (book) [1]
1838-1859	*Northern Journal* [4 #0017738]
1847-1853	*Marriage and Death Records from The Black River Gazette, 1831-32 and The Northern Journal, 1838-45, 1847-53, 1855-59*, Anna E. Crawford. (book) [1]
1855-1859	*Marriage and Death Records from The Black River Gazette, 1831-32 and The Northern Journal, 1838-45, 1847-53, 1855-59*, Anna E. Crawford. (book) [1]

MADISON COUNTY
1818-1886	Misc. newspapers [1,5, D-Cem 219:1-235]
1818-1886	Misc. newspapers [4 #1294966 item 2]
1825-1847	Misc. newspapers, deaths. [1,2,4,5, *Tree Talks* 24:108-25:47; Madison Co. pp. 130-131]

Cazenovia
1843	*Madison County Eagle*, marriages and deaths. [1,2,4,5, *Tree Talks* 12:201; Madison Co. p. 56]
1845	*Madison County Whig*, marriages and deaths. [1,2,4,5, *Tree Talks* 1:pages not here noted, 9:102+; Madison Co. pp. 1-4, 34-36]
1863-1893	Misc. newspapers [3]

Chittenango

1834-1844   *Chittenango Herald; 10,000 Vital Records of Central New York, 1813-1850*, Fred Q. Bowman. Genealogical Publishing Co., Baltimore, MD, 1988. (book) [1,2,3,4,5]

1831-1854   Misc. newspapers [4 #1294966 item 1]

Morrisville

1814-1878   *Madison/Morrisville Observer* [4 #1036659 item 3]

1840-1844   *Madison Observer*, deaths. [4 #0017769 item 1]

MONROE COUNTY

Rochester

1818-1850   Misc. newspapers [1,5, D-Cem 19:187-301]

1840-1841   *Rochester Gem and Ladies Amulet* [1,5, D-Cem 24:260-265]

1841-1842   *Rochester Gem and Ladies Amulet*, marriages. [4 #0017885 item 3]

1857   *Moore's Rural New Yorker*, marriages and deaths. [1,2,4,5, *Tree Talks* 32:109-34:108; Monroe Co. pp. 94-99]

1862   *Moore's Rural New Yorker* [1,5, D-Cem 363:177-187]

1866-1867   *Moore's Rural New Yorker* [1,5, D-Cem 211:185-186]

MONTGOMERY COUNTY

1863-1884   Misc. newspapers, deaths. [4 #1298602 item 3]

Amsterdam

1855-1867   Misc. newspapers [4 #1298602 item 4]

1858-1861   *Amsterdam Recorder* [4 #1298602 item 5]

Fort Plain

1854-1862   *Mohawk Valley Register* [4 1298602 item 7]

1891-1896   *Mohawk Valley Register* [4 1298602 item 7]

NEW YORK COUNTY

Manhattan

1726-1736   *Zenger's New York Journal*, deaths. [1,2,3,4,5, *NYG&B RECORD* 47:393-394]

1726-1744   *New York Gazette*, misc. data. [1,2,3,4,5, *NYG&B RECORD* 95:220-232]

1726-1783   *Genealogical Data from Colonial New York Newspapers* (from articles in the *NYG&B RECORD*), Kenneth Scott. Genealogical Publishing Co., Baltimore, MD, 1977. (book) [1,2]

1726-1804   *The Arts and Crafts in New York...Advertisements and News Items from New York City Newspapers*, Rita Susswein Guttesman, 3 vols., Collections of New York Historical Society, 1936, 1948-49. (book) [2]

1730-1790   *Old New York and Trinity Church*, Collections of New York Historical Society, 1870:147-408. [2]

1733-1751   *Zenger's New York Weekly Journal*, misc. data. [1,2,3,4,5, *NYG&B RECORD* 96:1-15]

1736-1738   *Zenger's New York Weekly Journal*, misc. data. [1,2,3,4,5, *NYG&B RECORD* 48:304-305]

1739-1744   *Zenger's New York Weekly Journal*, misc. data. [1,2,3,4,5, *NYG&B RECORD* 49:343-345]

1743-1773   *Genealogical Data from the New York Post-Boy, 1743-1773*, Kenneth Scott. National Genealogical Society, Washington D.C., 1970. (book) [1,2]

1752   *New York Mercury*, misc. data. [1,2,3,4,5, *NYG&B RECORD* 96:77-90]

1755-1784   *New York Mercury* in *Journal of American Genealogy*, 1:66-70; 160-161;255-260;325-329, 1921. (book) [1]

1756-1758   *New York Mercury*, misc. data. [1,2,3,4,5, *NYG&B RECORD* 96:144-156; 232-239]

1756-1829   Misc. newspapers, Edna Huntington. [3]

1758-1762	*New York Mercury*, misc. data. [**1,2,3,4,5**, *NYG&B RECORD* 97:22-28; 86-90; 150-157; 246-250]
1762-1765	*New York Mercury*, misc. data. [**1,2,3,4,5**, *NYG&B RECORD* 98:47-50; 104-108; 168-175; 246-252]
1766-1768	*New York Mercury*, misc. data. [**1,2,3,4,5**, *NYG&B RECORD* 99:10-20; 69-73; 206-212]
1768-1770	*New York Gazette and Weekly Mercury*, misc. data. [**1,2,3,4,5**, *NYG&B RECORD* 100:96-102; 221-224]
1770-1772	*New York Gazette and Weekly Mercury*, misc. data. [**1,2,3,4,5**, *NYG&B RECORD* 101:104-111; 212-218]
1772-1773	*New York Gazette and Weekly Mercury*, misc. data. [**1,2,3,4,5**, *NYG&B RECORD* 102:95-101; 231-234]
1773	*New York Gazette and Weekly Mercury*, misc. data. [**1,2,3,4,5**, *NYG&B RECORD* 103:103-106; 150-154]
1773-1783	*Rivington's New York Newspapers, Excerpts from Loyalist Press, 1773-1783*, Kenneth Scott. New York Historical Society, 1973. (book) [**1**]
1774-1775	*New York Gazette and Weekly Mercury*, misc. data. [**1,2,3,4,5**, *NYG&B RECORD* 104:42-46; 76-82; 150-156]
1776	*New York Gazette and Weekly Mercury*, misc. data. [**1,2,3,4,5**, *NYG&B RECORD* 105:32-36; 76-77]
1777-1779	*New York Gazette and Weekly Mercury*, misc. data. [**1,2,3,4,5**, *NYG&B RECORD* 106:27-32; 82-84; 152-156]
1780-1783	*New York Gazette and Weekly Mercury*, misc. data. [**1,2,3,4,5**, *NYG&B RECORD* 107:20-25; 90-96; 146-150; 218-222]
1784-1810	Misc. newspapers, Edna Huntington and Theresa Swezey. [**3**]
1785-1787	"Vital Records from Old New York Newspapers: Deaths and Marriages from McClean's *Independent Journal*", Wharton Dickinson in *Journal of American Genealogy* 2:313-318. [**2**]
1787-1788	*American Magazine*, C.J. Stevens in *National Genealogical Society Quarterly* 63:284-290, death notices. [**2**]
1788-1817	*New York Weekly Museum* (index of marriages and deaths), manuscript published by American Antiquarian Society, 1952. [**2**]
1789-1796	*Marriage and Death Notices from the New York Weekly Museum*, typescript, Consuela and Robert Furman, 1950. (book) [**2**]
1789-1799	"Old Time Marriage and Death Notices", A.J. Wohlhagen in Valentine's *Manual of the City of New York*, new series, 1916-1927, 1:19-22, 222-256; 2:306-314; 3:341-353; 4:401-434; 5:250-255. [**2**]
1790-1797	*The New York Magazine Marriages and Deaths, 1790-1797*, Kenneth Scott. Polyanthos Press, New Orleans, LA, 1975. (book) [**1,2**]
1790-1799	*New York Weekly Museum* [**1,5**, D-Cem 41:55-139]
1792-1793	*The Weekly Museum* [**1,5**, D-Bible 80:169-176]
1794	*Monthly Register, NY Magazine and/or Literary Repository* (Oct. 1794 from manuscript at NYS Library). [**4** #001737 item 3]
1800-1806	*New York Weekly Museum*, marriages. [**1,5**, D-Bible 34:49-143]
1800-1806	*New York Weekly Museum*, deaths. [**1,5**, D-Bible 34:1-48]
1800-1810	*New York Evening Post* in *Ancestral Notes from Chedwato*, 14:85-87. [**1**]
1800-1925	Marriage Notice Clippings from New York City newspapers, May King Van Rensselaer, 9 vols., manuscript. [**2**]
1801-1802	*New York Evening Post* [**1,5**, D-Cem 42:218-260]
1801-1804	*New York Weekly Museum* and *The Telescope*, marriages and deaths. [**1,2,3,4,5**, *NYG&B RECORD* 49:345-352]
1801-1811	*New York Evening Post*, Gertrude A. Barber, marriages, Vol. 1. (book) [**2**]
1801-1811	*New York Evening Post*, Gertrude A. Barber, deaths, Vol. 1, 1933. (book) [**2**]
1801-1890	*New York Evening Post*, abstracts of marriages and deaths, indexed. [**3**]

1802-1816	*New York Herald*, Edna Huntington. (book) [3]
1802-1806	*New York Evening Post* [1,5, D-Cem 54:176-279]
1803-1806	*New York Spectator* [1,5, D-Cem 41:140-169]
1804	*New York Evening Post* [1,5, D-Cem 42:218-260]
1807	New York City Marriages and Deaths, Oct., Nov. and Dec. 1807, manuscript. [2]
1807-1809	*New York Weekly Museum*, deaths. [1,5, D-Cem 99:1-116]
1807-1812	*New York Evening Post* [1,5, D-Cem 41:170-275]
1808-1816	*New York Evening Post* in *Ancestral Notes from Chedwato*, deaths, 14:143-144, 1967. [1]
1808-1816	*New York Evening Post*, Gertrude A. Barber, deaths, Vol. 2, 1933. (book) [2]
1809-1811	*New York Journal*, Edna Huntington. (book) [3]
1810	*New York Weekly Museum* [1,5, D-Cem 153:12-36]
1810-1814	*Commercial Advertiser*, Marie K. Pidgeon, marriages, typescript. [2]
1810-1814	*Commercial Advertiser*, marriages. [4 #0017785 item 4]
1811-1818	*New York Evening Post*, Gertrude A. Barber, marriages, Vol. 2. (book) [2]
1812-1818	*New York Evening Post* in *Ancestral Notes from Chedwato*, marriages, 13:77-81. [1]
1814-1816	*Longworth's American Almanac*, Edna Huntington, May 1, 1814-June 1, 1816. (book) [3]
1816-1819	*New York Evening Post*, Gertrude A. Barber, deaths, Vol. 3, 1933. (book) [2]
1818-1822	*New York Evening Post*, Gertrude A. Barber, marriages, Vol. 3, 1934. (book) [2]
1819-1822	*New York Evening Post*, Gertrude A. Barber, deaths, Vol. 4, 1933. (book) [2]
1820-1824	*The Minerva*; Janet Wethy Foley's *Early Settlers of New York State*, 7:123, 139, 154, 170, 186; 8:202, 218, 235. (book) [1]
1822-1824	*New York Evening Post*, Gertrude A. Barber, deaths, Vol. 5, 1933. (book) [2]
1822-1825	*New York Evening Post*, Gertrude A. Barber, marriages, Vol. 4, 1934. (book) [2]
1823-1824	*The Minerva* [1,5, D-Cem 54:167-175]
1823-1824	*The New York Minerva*; Robert Morris Terry Collection in Janet Wethy Foley's *Early Settlers of New York State* 7:123, 129, 154, 170, 186; 8:202, 218, 235. (book) [1,2]
1824	"Vital statistics from *The Telescope*", Hopper Striker Mott. [1,2,3,4,5, *NYG&B RECORD* 49:350-352]
1824-1825	*New York Evening Post*, Gertrude A. Barber, deaths, Vol. 6, 1933. (book) [2]
1825-1827	*New York Evening Post*, Gertrude A. Barber, deaths, Vol. 7, 1933. (book) [2]
1825-1829	*New York Evening Post*, Gertrude A. Barber, marriages, Vol. 5, 1935. (book) [2]
1827	"Vital records from *The Telescope*", National Genealogical Society Quarterly 29:15-17. [2]
1827-1829	*New York Evening Post*, Gertrude A. Barber, deaths, Vol. 8, 1934. (book) [2]
1827-1831	*Gleanings from the "Christian Advocate and Journal and Zion's Herald", September 1827-1831* (Methodist), Dolores Haller and Marilyn Robinson. Heritage Books, Inc., Bowie, MD, 1989. [2]
1829-1831	*New York Evening Post*, Gertrude A. Barber, deaths, Vol. 9, 1936. (book) [2]
1829-1833	*New York Evening Post*, Gertrude A. Barber, marriages, Vol. 6, 1935. (book) [2]
1830-1866	Misc. newspapers, Edna Huntington. [3]
1830-1870	Marriages published in the *Christian Intelligencer* of the Reformed Dutch Church, Ray C. Sawyer, 10 vols., typescript, 1931-1933. (book) [2,3]
1830-1870	Deaths published in the *Christian Intelligencer* of the Reformed Dutch Church, Ray C. Sawyer, 7 vols., typescript, 1932-1933. (book) [2,3]
1831-1832	*New York Evening Post*, Gertrude A. Barber, deaths, Vol. 10, 1936. (book) [2]
1832-1834	*New York Evening Post*, Gertrude A. Barber, deaths, Vol. 11, 1936. (book) [2]
1832-1844	*New York Observer* [1,5 D-Cem 134:266-278]
1833-1837	*New York Evening Post*, Gertrude A. Barber, marriages, Vol. 7, 1935. (book) [2]
1834-1835	*New York Evening Post*, Gertrude A. Barber, deaths, Vol. 12, 1937. (book) [2]

1834-1835	*New York Messenger and Phildelphia Universalist* in *Detroit Society for Genealogical Research Magazine* 21:29-33 [1]
1835-1837	*New York Evening Post*, Gertrude A. Barber, deaths, Vol. 13, 1939. (book) [2]
1835-1855	*Index to Marriages and Deaths in the "New York Herald" 1835-1855*, James P. Maher, Genealogical Publishing Co., Baltimore, MD, 1987. (book) (reportedly a volume 2 for the above is now available - date spans not here known) [2,4]
1836	*Marriage records from "The Herald" and "Morning Herald"*, DeWitt Van Buren, typescript. [2]
1836-1841	*Marriages and Deaths from "The New Yorker", 1836-1841*, Kenneth Scott. National Genealogical Society, Washington D.C., 1980, Pub. #46. (book) [1,2,4]
1837-1838	*New York Evening Post*, Gertrude A. Barber, marriages, Vol. 8, 1935. (book) [2]
1837-1838	*New York Evening Post*, Gertrude A. Barber, deaths, Vol. 14, 1939. (book) [2]
1838	*Marriage records from "The Herald" and "Morning Herald"*, DeWitt Van Buren, typescript. [2]
1838-1839	*New York Evening Post*, Gertrude A. Barber, deaths, Vol. 15, 1939. (book) [2]
1838-1840	*New York Evening Post*, Gertrude A. Barber, marriages, Vol. 9, 1935. (book) [2]
1839-1840	*New York Evening Post*, Gertrude A. Barber, deaths, Vol. 16, 1939. (book) [2]
1840-1841	*New York Evening Post*, Gertrude A. Barber, deaths, Vol. 17, 1939. (book) [2]
1840-1842	*New York Evening Post*, Gertrude A. Barber, marriages, Vol. 10, 1935. (book) [2]
1841-1842	*New York Evening Post*, Gertrude A. Barber, deaths, Vol. 18, 1939. (book) [2]
1841-1842	*Vital records from "The New York Weekly Tribune" in the "Boston Evening Transcript"*, microfiche. From Part 1, Note 2691, Oct. 26, 1934, through Part 40, Note 2691, Sept. 14, 1936. [2]
1842-1844	*New York Evening Post*, Gertrude A. Barber, marriages, Vol. 11, 1935. (book) [2]
1842-1844	*New York Evening Post*, Gertrude A. Barber, deaths, Vol. 19, 1939. (book) [2]
1843	*New York Daily Tribune*, deaths. [1,5, D-Cem 134:282]
1843	*Marriages and Deaths from "The New World", January 1, 1843 to July 1, 1843*. Harriett M. Wiles, typescript. [2]
1843	*New York Tribune* [1,5, D-Cem 134:283-285]
1843-1849	*Nation-Wide Marriage Notices as Gleaned from "The New York Weekly Tribune"*, Judith Rush, 1978. (book) [2]
1843-1864	*News Articles in "The New York Weekly Tribune"*, Judith Rush, deaths, 1979. (book) [2]
1844-1845	*New York Evening Post*, Gertrude A. Barber, deaths, Vol. 20, 1940. (book) [2]
1845-1846	*New York Evening Post*, Gertrude A. Barber, deaths, Vol. 21, 1940. (book) [2]
1845-1849	*New York Evening Post*, Gertrude A. Barber, marriages, Vol. 12, 1935. (book) [2]
1846	*New York Evening Post*, Gertrude A. Barber, deaths, Vol. 22, 1940. (book) [2]
1846-1847	*New York Evening Post*, Gertrude A. Barber, deaths, Vol. 23, 1940. (book) [2]
1847-1848	*New York Evening Post*, Gertrude A. Barber, deaths, Vol. 24, 1940. (book) [2]
1848-1849	*New York Evening Post*, Gertrude A. Barber, deaths, Vol. 25, 1940. (book) [2]
1849-1850	*New York Evening Post*, Gertrude A. Barber, deaths, Vol. 26, 1940. (book) [2]
1849-1852	*New York Evening Post*, Gertrude A. Barber, marriages, Vol. 13, 1936. (book) [2]
1850-1851	*New York Evening Post*, Gertrude A. Barber, deaths, Vol. 27, 1940. (book) [2]
1851-1852	*New York Evening Post*, Gertrude A. Barber, deaths, Vol. 28, 1940. (book) [2]
1851-1989	*Personal Name Index to the New York Times Index*, (1976-83 with later supplements through 1989). [2]
1852-1853	*New York Evening Post*, Gertrude A. Barber, deaths, Vol. 29, 1940. (book) [2]
1852-1854	*New York Evening Post*, Gertrude A. Barber, marriages, Vol. 14, 1937. (book) [2]
1853-1854	*New York Evening Post*, Gertrude A. Barber, deaths, Vol. 30, 1941. (book) [2]
1854-1855	*New York Evening Post*, Gertrude A. Barber, deaths, Vol. 31, 1941. (book) [2]
1854-1856	*New York Evening Post*, Gertrude A. Barber, marriages, Vol. 15, 1937. (book) [2]
1855-1856	*New York Evening Post*, Gertrude A. Barber, deaths, Vol. 32, 1941. (book) [2]
1856-1857	*New York Evening Post*, Gertrude A. Barber, deaths, Vol. 33, 1941. (book) [2]
1856-1859	*New York Evening Post*, Gertrude A. Barber, marriages, Vol. 16, 1937. (book) [2]

1857-1858	*New York Evening Post*, Gertrude A. Barber, deaths, Vol. 34, 1941. (book) [2]
1858	*New York Speculator* [1,5 D-Cem 134:279-281]
1858-1859	*New York Evening Post*, Gertrude A. Barber, deaths, Vol. 35, 1941. (book) [2]
1858-1968	*New York Times Obituary Index 1858-1968*, New York Times, New York, NY, 1970. (book) [1]
1858-1978	*New York Times Obituaries Index 1858-1978*, New York Times, New York, NY, 1970-80, 2 vols. (book) [2]
1859-1860	*New York Evening Post*, Gertrude A. Barber, deaths, Vol. 36, 1941. (book) [2]
1859-1863	*New York Evening Post*, Gertrude A. Barber, marriages, Vol. 17, 1937. (book) [2]
1859	*The Examiner*, marriages. [1,5 D-Cem 237:68-69]
1860-1861	*New York Evening Post*, Gertrude A. Barber, Vol. 37, 1941. (book) [2]
1861-1862	*New York Evening Post*, Gertrude A. Barber, deaths, Vol. 38, 1941. (book) [2]
1862-1863	*New York Evening Post*, Gertrude A. Barber, deaths, Vol. 39, 1941. (book) [2]
1863-1864	*New York Evening Post*, Gertrude A. Barber, deaths, Vol. 40, 1941. (book) [2]
1863-1866	*New York Evening Post*, Gertrude A. Barber, marriages, Vol. 18, 1938. (book) [2]
1864-1866	*New York Evening Post*, Gertrude A. Barber, deaths, Vol. 41, 1941. (book) [2]
1866-1868	*New York Evening Post*, Gertrude A. Barber, deaths, Vol. 42, 1941. (book) [2]
1866-1870	*New York Evening Post*, Gertrude A. Barber, marriages, Vol. 19, 1938. (book) [2]
1868-1869	*New York Evening Post*, Gertrude A. Barber, deaths, Vol. 43, 1941. (book) [2]
1869-1871	*New York Evening Post*, Gertrude A. Barber, deaths, Vol. 44, 1941. (book) [2]
1870-1874	*New York Evening Post*, Gertrude A. Barber, marriages, Vol. 20, 1938. (book) [2]
1870-1891	New York Death Notices, 2 vols., clippings. [2]
1871-1873	*New York Evening Post*, Gertrude A. Barber, deaths, Vol. 45, 1941. (book) [2]
1873-1875	*New York Evening Post*, Gertrude A. Barber, deaths, Vol. 46, 1942. (book) [2]
1874-1879	*New York Evening Post*, Gertrude A. Barber, marriages, Vol. 21, 1938. (book) [2]
1875-1877	*New York Evening Post*, Gertrude A. Barber, deaths, Vol. 47, 1942. (book) [2]
1877-1879	*New York Evening Post*, Gertrude A. Barber, deaths, Vol. 48, 1942. (book) [2]
1878-1879	"Marriages and deaths from the *New York Tribune*", untitled manuscript, no index. [2]
1879-1880	*New York Evening Post*, Gertrude A. Barber, deaths, Vol. 49, 1942. (book) [2]
1879-1883	*New York Evening Post*, Gertrude A. Barber, marriages, Vol. 22, 1938. (book) [2]
1880-1882	*New York Evening Post*, Gertrude A. Barber, deaths, Vol. 50, 1942. (book) [2]
1882-1884	*New York Evening Post*, Gertrude A. Barber, deaths, Vol. 51, 1942. (book) [2]
1884-1885	*New York Evening Post*, Gertrude A. Barber, deaths, Vol. 52, 1942. (book) [2]
1884-1890	*New York Evening Post*, Gertrude A. Barber, marriages, Vol. 23, 1948. (book) [2]
1885-1887	*New York Evening Post*, Gertrude A. Barber, deaths, Vol. 53, 1942. (book) [2]
1887-1889	*New York Evening Post*, Gertrude A. Barber, deaths, Vol. 54, 1947. (book) [2]
1889-1890	*New York Evening Post*, Gertrude A. Barber, deaths, Vol. 55, 1947. (book) [2]
1897	*New York Herald* (scrapbook June and July 1897). [3]

NIAGARA COUNTY

????-????	Misc. newspapers (contact LDS library for details). [4 #1411831 to 1411848]
1823-1868	Misc. newspapers and records, marriages. [1,2,4,5, *Tree Talks* 8:99-18:108, 24:111-30:111; Niagara Co. pp. 15-56, 67-79]

ONEIDA COUNTY

1837-1871	*Detroit Society for Genealogical Research Magazine*, "Deaths and Marriages from Fifteen Oneida Co. Newspapers having a Michigan Reference," 40:163-166. [1]
1847-1848	*Temperance Advocate* [1,2,4,5, *Tree Talks* 28:57-29:58; Oneida Co. pp. 110-117]

Camden

1851-1853	Misc newspapers [4 #1435189 item 5]

Rome

1835-1838	*Rome Telegram*, marriages and deaths. [1,2,4,5, *Tree Talks* 6:88-7:149; Oneida

	Co. pp. 18-23]
1840	*Roman Citizen*, marriages and deaths. [**1,2,4,5**, *Tree Talks* 3:92-4:39; Oneida Co. pp. 7-9]

Utica

1824-1834	*Utica Western Recorder*; *10,000 Vital Records of Central New York, 1813-1850*, Fred Q. Bowman. Genealogical Publishing Co., Baltimore, MD, 1988. (book) [**1,2,3,4,5**]
1825-1826	*Abstracts of Utica Sentinel and Gazette* (June 14, 1825-June 6, 1826), Vol. 1. [**2,3**]
1825-1826	*Oneida Sentinel and Gazette*, misc. data, Vol. 1, Hanson Heritage Publishers, Sauk Village, IL. (book) [**2**]
1825-1842	*Utica Sentinel and Gazette* (handwritten records), Vol. 1. [**3**]
1825-1842	*Utica Sentinel and Gazette* (handwritten records), Vol. 2. [**3**]
1826-1827	*Abstracts of Utica Sentinel and Gazette* (June 13, 1826-June 8, 1827), Vol. 2. [**2,3**]
1826-1827	*Oneida Sentinel and Gazette*, misc. data, Vol. 2, Hanson Heritage Publishers, Sauk Village, IL. (book) [**2**]
1827-1849	Misc. newspapers [**4** #1435189 item 1]
1827-1880	Misc. newspapers [**4** #1435189 item 2]
1828-1829	*Abstracts of Utica Sentinel and Gazette* (June 10, 1828-Dec. 29, 1829). [**3**]
1828-1829	*Oneida Sentinel and Gazette*, misc. data, Vol. 3, Hanson Heritage Publishers, Sauk Village, IL. (book) [**2**]
1830-1831	*Oneida Sentinel and Gazette*, misc. data, Vol. 4, Hanson Heritage Publishers, Sauk Village, IL, 1982. (book) [**2**]
1831	*Gospel Advocate* [**1,5**, D-Cem 477:109-124]
1831	*Evangelical Magazine* [**4** #1435189 item 7]
1832	*Oneida Sentinel and Gazette*, misc. data, Vol. 5, Hanson Heritage Publishers, Sauk Village, IL, 1982. (book) [**2**]
1833-1834	*Oneida Sentinel and Gazette*, misc. data, Vol. 6, Hanson Heritage Publishers, Sauk Village, IL, 1983. (book) [**2**]
1836-1839	*Evangelical Magazine and Gospel Advocate*, typescript. [**4** #0017990]
1837-1838	*Utica Observer*, deaths of Rev. soldiers and wives. [**1,5**, D-Cem 167:202]
1839-1840	*Friend of Man* (anti-slavery publication). [**3**]
1840-1845	*Utica Democrat* [**4** #1435189 item 3]
1842-1850	*Utica Daily Gazette*; *10,000 Vital Records of Central New York, 1813-1850*, Fred Q. Bowman. Genealogical Publishing Co., Baltimore, MD, 1988. (book) [**1,2,3,4,5**]
1850	*Utica Daily Gazette* [**4** #1435189 item 6]

Waterville

1884-1896	*Waterville Times* [**1,5**, D-Cem 378:39-44]

ONONDAGA COUNTY

1814-1850	Misc. newspapers, births, marriages, deaths. [**1,2,4,5**, *Tree Talks* 1:pages not here noted, 2:77-4:40, 6:89-179; Onondaga Co. pp. 1-5, 8-13, 22-24]
1818-1880?	Misc. newspapers (with church records of Auburn and Fleming interspersed). [**1,5**, D-Cem 349:1-174]
1828-1860	Misc. newspapers, deaths (in Lester Card's *Deaths in Onondaga County, Vol. 1*, also scattered in Vols. 5 and 6). [**3**]
1842	*The Methodist Reformer*, marriages and deaths. [**1,2,4,5**, *Tree Talks* 33:115-116; Onondaga Co. pp. 176-177]

Baldwinsville

1846-1850	*Onondaga Gazette*; *10,000 Vital Records of Central New York, 1813-1850*, Fred Q. Bowman. Genealogical Publishing Co., Baltimore, MD, 1988. (book) [**1,2,3,4,5**]
1846-1850	*Onondaga Gazette*, deaths. [**1,2,4,5**, *Tree Talks* 21:118-24:50; Onondaga Co. pp. 109-121]

1846-1869   *Onondaga Gazette* [**1,5**, D-Cem 78:1-42 and 101-130]
1886-1893   *Baldwinsville Gazette and Farmers Journal* [**1,5**, D-Cem 78:43-99 and 131-255]
Fayetteville
1840-1842   *The Fayetteville Luminary and Reformed Methodist Intelligencer*, marriages and deaths. [**1,2,4,5**, *Tree Talks* 26:118-27:160; Onondaga Co. pp. 135-143]
1871   *Weekly Recorder* and *The Examiner and Chronicler* [**1,5**, D-Cem 77:257-258]
Syracuse
1835-1842   *Onondaga Standard*, marriages and deaths. [**1,2,4,5**, *Tree Talks* 12:174-19:175; Onondaga Co. pp. 55-100]
1873-1875   *Syracuse Daily Journal*, deaths. [**4** #0973008 item 3]

ONTARIO COUNTY
1803-1809   Misc. newspapers, marriages. [**1,2,4,5**, *Tree Talks* 31:118-34:118; Ontario Co. pp. 80-90]
1803-1810   Misc. newspapers, deaths. [**1,2,4,5**, *Tree Talks* 29:161-31:117; Ontario Co. pp. 73-79]
1803-1847   Misc. newspapers [**4** #0547077]
1803-1878   Misc. newspapers, deaths. [**1,5**, D-Cem 538:1-360 + index]
1803-1879   Misc. newspapers, marriages. [**1,5**, D-Cem 539:1-115 + index]
1807-1908   Misc. newspapers [**4** #0833158]
1888   Misc. newspapers, deaths. [**1,2,4,5**, *Tree Talks* 22:47-48; Ontario Co. pp. 49-50]
Geneva
1809-1827   *Geneva Gazette*; *10,000 Vital Records of Western New York, 1809-1850*, Fred Q. Bowman. Genealogical Publishing Co., Baltimore, MD, 1985. (book) [**1,2,3,4,5**]
1818   *Geneva Courier*, marriages. [**1,2,4,5**, *Tree Talks* 3:127-5:32; Ontario Co. pp. 4-9]
1830-1849   *Geneva Gazette*; *10,000 Vital Records of Central New York, 1813-1850*, Fred Q. Bowman. Genealogical Publishing Co., Baltimore, MD, 1988. (book) [**1,2,3,4,5**]
1850   *Geneva Courier*, marriages. [**1,2,4,5**, *Tree Talks* 3:127-5:32; Ontario Co. pp. 4-9]
1850   *Geneva Courier*, deaths. [**1,2,4,5**, *Tree Talks* 4:41; Ontario Co. p. 5]

ORANGE COUNTY
Florida
1778-1803   Misc. newspapers [**4** #0363878 item 4]
Goshen
1809-1819   *Marriages and Deaths from the "Orange County Patriot"*, Eric V.D. Schweser, Newton, NJ, 1973. (book) [**2**]
1828-1831   *Marriages and Deaths from the "Orange County Patriot", 1828-1831*, Gertrude A. Barber. (book) [**1**]
1828-1831   *Orange County Patriot*, Gertrude Barber, 1939. (book) [**3**]
1828-1831   *Orange County Patriot* [**4** #0017833 item 2]
Middletown
1851-1865   *The Whig Press*, marriages. [**2**]
1851-1865   *The Whig Press*, deaths. [**2**]
1851-1865   *Death Notices from the "Whig Press", 1851-65*, George and Virginia Gardner, Middletown, 1978. (book) [**1**]
1851-1865   *Death Notices from the "Whig Press", 1851-65*, George and Virginia Gardner, Middletown, 1978. (book) [**4**]
Newburgh
1836-1837   *The Newburgh Telegraph* [**1,5**, D-Cem 71:244-268]

OSWEGO COUNTY
1820-1845   Misc. newspapers [**1,2,4,5**, *Tree Talks* 10:260; Oswego Co. p. 41]

1842-1844	*Western Luminary*, marriages and deaths. [1,2,4,5, *Tree Talks* 33:165; Oswego Co. p. 184]
1858	Misc. newspapers [1,2,4,5, *Tree Talks* 11:57; Oswego Co. p. 42]

Fulton
1851	*Fulton Patriot*, marriages and deaths. [1,2,4,5, *Tree Talks* 33:165-33:126; Oswego Co. pp. 184-186]

Mexico
1930-1935	*Mexico Independent*, deaths. [1,5, D-Cem 89:160-219]

Oswego
1819-1839	*The Palladium* [1,5, D-Cem 146:1-37]

OTSEGO COUNTY
1808-1875	Misc. newspapers, abstracts from obituaries. [2]

Cherry Valley
1818-1834	*Cherry Valley Gazette*, marriages. [1,5, D-Cem 416:10-34]
1818-1908	*Cherry Valley Gazette* [1,5, D-Cem 153:1-11]
1818-1908	*Cherry Valley Gazette* [3]
1818-1825	*Cherry Valley Gazette* [4 #0017604 item 3]
1851-1858	*Cherry Valley Gazette* [4 #0017604 item 3]
1862-1863	*Cherry Valley Gazette* [4 #0017604 item 3]
1867	*Cherry Valley Gazette* [4 #0017604 item 3]
1908	*Cherry Valley Gazette* [4 #0017604 item 3]

Cooperstown
1795-1820	*Otsego Herald*; *10,000 Vital Records of Eastern New York, 1777-1834*, Fred Q. Bowman. Genealogical Publishing Co., Baltimore, MD, 1987. (book) [1,2,3,4,5]
1821-1826	*Freemen's Journal*; *10,000 Vital Records of Eastern New York, 1777-1834*, Fred Q. Bowman. Genealogical Publishing Co., Baltimore, MD, 1987. (book) [1,2,3,4,5]
1823-1824	*Freeman's Journal*, deaths. [1,2,4,5, *Tree Talks* 31:165-33:126; Otsego Co. pp. 88-93]

Oneonta
1853-1860	*Oneonta Herald* [1,5, D-Cem 436:1-56]
1882-1942	Misc. Oneonta newspapers [1,5, D-Bible 190:7-18]
1900+	Misc. Oneonta newspapers [1,5, D-Cem 386:1-32]

Otsego
1795-1840	*Otsego Herald and Western Advertiser* and *Freeman's Journal*, Gertrude A. Barber, Vol 1. (book) [3]
1795-1840	*Otsego Herald and Western Advertiser* and *Freeman's Journal* [4 #0908217 item 2]
1841-1862	*Otsego Herald and Western Advertiser* and *Freeman's Journal*, Gertrude A. Barber, Vol. 2. (book) [3]
1862-1875	*Otsego Herald and Western Advertiser* and *Freeman's Journal*, Gertrude A. Barber, Vol. 3. (book) [3]

Worcester
1877-1915	*Worcester Times* [1,5, D-Cem 386:1-22]

PUTNAM COUNTY
Carmel
1849-1873	*Putnam Co. Democrat Courier* and *Putnam Co. Courier* [4 #0908046 item 1]

QUEENS COUNTY
????-1832	*Queens County in Olden Times*, Henry Onderdonk, Jr., 1865, marriages and deaths, manuscript. [2]

????-1863	"Notes on the History of Queens County", Henry Onderdonk, Jr. in *Journal of Long Island History* 7:1:53-70; 7:2:36-53. [2]
1847-1870	Misc. newspapers, *Church Records [sic] of Long Island: Marriages 1847-1870, Deaths 1847-1870*, Josephine C. Frost, typescript. [2]
1858-1878	*Queens County Sentinel, Queens County, New York: Index of Birth, Marriage and Death Announcements, 1858-1878*, Anthony Hood, 1991. (book) [2]

Jamaica

1821-1829	*Long Island Farmer and Queens County Advertiser*, Edna Huntington, Vol. 1. (book) [3]
1830-1834	*Long Island Farmer and Queens County Advertiser*, Edna Huntington, Vol. 2 (book) [3]
1835-1841	*Long Island Farmer and Queens County Advertiser*, Harriet Stryker-Rodda, Vol. 3 (scrapbook April 29, 1835-Dec. 28, 1841). [2,3]
1835-1850	*Long Island Democrat*, Ann-B Moorhouse, marriages (July 8, 1835-Dec. 31, 1850) (book) [3]
1835-1850	*Long Island Democrat*, Harriet Stryker-Rodda, marriages (scrapbook July 8, 1835-Dec. 31, 1850). [3]
1835-1850	*Long Island Democrat*, Ann-B Moorhouse, deaths (July 8, 1835-Dec. 31, 1850). (book) [3]
1835-1850	*Long Island Democrat*, Harriet Stryker-Rodda, deaths (scrapbook July 8, 1835-Dec. 31, 1850). [3]
1851-1856	*Long Island Democrat*, Ann-B Moorhouse, marriages (Jan. 7, 1851-Dec. 30, 1856). (book) [3]
1851-1856	*Long Island Democrat*, Harriet Stryker-Rodda, marriages (scrapbook Jan. 7, 1851-Dec. 30, 1856). [3]
1851-1856	*Long Island Democrat*, Harriet Stryker-Rodda, deaths (scrapbook Jan. 7, 1851-Dec. 30, 1856). [3]
1861-1885	*Long Island Democrat*, Harriet Stryker-Rodda, marriages (scrapbook). [3]
1861-1885	*Long Island Democrat*, Harriet Stryker-Rodda, deaths (scrapbook). [3]
1861-1885	*Long Island Democrat*, Harriet Stryker-Rodda, marriages and deaths (index to above scrapbooks), typescript, 1960. [2]

Newtown

1877-1882	*Newtown Register*, Harriet Stryker-Rodda (scrapbook). [3]

RENSSELAER COUNTY
Lansingburgh

1787-1850	Misc. newspapers, deaths. [1,2,4,5, *Tree Talks* 8:43-11:220, 20:57-21:53, 25:181-33:168; Rensselaer Co. pp. 15-31, 60-64, 78-95]
1787-1850	Misc. newspapers, marriages. [1,2,4,5, *Tree Talks* 11:220-19:54; Rensselaer Co. pp. 31-59]
1787-1895	Misc. newspapers, marriages. [4 #1437398 item 13]
1787-1895	Misc. newspapers, deaths. [4 #1437398 items 11, 12]
1798-1803	*Lansingburgh Gazette*; *10,000 Vital Records of Eastern New York, 1777-1834*, Fred Q. Bowman. Genealogical Publishing Co., Baltimore, MD, 1987. (book) [1,2,3,4,5]

Troy

????-????	*Troy Daily Whig* [4 #1035941 item 4]
1797-1820	Misc. newspapers, deaths. [1,2,4,5, *Tree Talks* 4:44-6:41; Rensselaer Co. pp. 1-9]
1797-1860	Misc. newspapers, marriages. [4 #1437397 items 1, 2]
1797-1860	Misc. newspapers, deaths. [4 #1437397 item 3]
1803-1828	*Troy Budget*; *10,000 Vital Records of Eastern New York, 1777-1834*, Fred Q. Bowman. Genealogical Publishing Co., Baltimore, MD, 1987. (book) [1,2,3,4,5]

1812-1823	*Troy Post*, Doris R. Sheridan. (book) [**1,5**, D-Cem 500:51-98]
1812-1823	*Troy Post*, surnames A-B, from *The Capital* (Kinship, Rhinebeck, NY), Vol.1, #1. [**1,2,4,5**]
1812-1823	*Troy Post*, surnames B, from *The Capital* (Kinship, Rhinebeck, NY), Vol. 1, #2. [**1,2,4,5**]
1812-1823	*Troy Post*, surnames B-C, from *The Capital* (Kinship, Rhinebeck, NY), Vol. 1, #3. [**1,2,4,5**]
1812-1823	*Troy Post*, surnames C-D, from *The Capital* (Kinship, Rhinebeck, NY), Vol. 1, #4. [**1,2,4,5**]
1812-1823	*Troy Post*, surnames D-F, from *The Capital* (Kinship, Rhinebeck, NY), Vol. 2, #1. [**1,2,4,5**]
1812-1823	*Troy Post*, surnames F-H, from *The Capital* (Kinship, Rhinebeck, NY), Vol. 2, #2. [**1,2,4,5**]
1812-1823	*Troy Post*, surnames H-K, from *The Capital* (Kinship, Rhinebeck, NY), Vol. 2, #3. [**1,2,4,5**]
1812-1823	*Troy Post*, surnames K-M, from *The Capital* (Kinship, Rhinebeck, NY), Vol. 2, #4. [**1,2,4,5**]
1812-1823	*Troy Post*, surnames M, from *The Capital* (Kinship, Rhinebeck, NY), Vol. 3, #1. [**1,2,4,5**]
1812-1823	*Troy Post*, surnames M-P, from *The Capital* (Kinship, Rhinebeck, NY), Vol. 3, #2. [**1,2,4,5**]
1812-1823	*Troy Post*, surnames P-R, from *The Capital* (Kinship, Rhinebeck, NY), Vol. 3, #3. [**1,2,4,5**]
1812-1823	*Troy Post*, surnames R-S, from *The Capital* (Kinship, Rhinebeck, NY), Vol. 3, #4. [**1,2,4,5**]
1812-1823	*Troy Post*, surnames S-V, from *The Capital* (Kinship, Rhinebeck, NY), Vol. 4, #1. [**1,2,4,5**]
1812-1823	*Troy Post*, surnames V-W, from *The Capital* (Kinship, Rhinebeck, NY), Vol. 4, #2. [**1,2,4,5**]
1812-1823	*Troy Post*, surnames W-Z, from *The Capital* (Kinship, Rhinebeck, NY), Vol. 4, #3. [**1,2,4,5**]
1812-1834	Misc. newspapers [**4** #1437397 item 4]
1823-1832	*Troy Sentinel*, Doris R. Sheridan. (book) [**1,5**, D-Cem 500:99-167]
1832-1834	*Troy Press*, Doris R. Sheridan. (book) [**1,5**, D-Cem 500:168-185]
1834-1843	*Weekly Whig*, Doris R. Sheridan. (book) [**1,5**, D-Cem 514:102-110]
1834-1835	*Troy Daily Whig*, Doris R. Sheridan. (book) [**1,5**, D-Cem 493:1-183]
1834-1863	*Troy Daily Whig* [**4** #1437398 items 18, 19]
1836	*Troy Whig*, Doris R. Sheridan. (book) [**1,5**, D-Cem 495:103-116]
1837-1844	*Troy Daily Whig*, Doris R. Sheridan. (book) [**1,5**, D-Cem 493:1-183]
1845-1853	*Daily Whig*, Doris R. Sheridan. (book) [**1,5**, D-Cem 492:1-182]
1846-1847	*Troy Post*, Doris R. Sheridan. (book) [**1,5**, D-Cem 495:2-42]
1846-1885	Misc. newspapers [**4** #1437397 item 5]
1848-1851	*Troy Post*, Doris R. Sheridan. (book) [**1,5**, D-Cem 479:1-81]
1848-1851	*Troy Post* [**4** #1035941 item 5]
1854-1863	*Troy Daily Whig*, Doris R. Sheridan. (book) [**1,5**, D-Cem 494:1-179]
1861-1865	Misc. newspapers, Doris R. Sheridan. (book) [**1,5**, D-Cem 507:1-139]
1861-1881	*Troy Daily Times* [**4** #1437397 items 6-8]
1864-1873	*Troy Daily Whig*, Doris R. Sheridan. (book) [**1,5**, D-Cem 499:1-179]
1864-1878	*Troy Daily Whig* [**4** #1437398]
1866-1867	Misc newspapers, Doris R. Sheridan. (book) [**1,5**, D-Cem 508:1-124]
1868-1873	*Troy Budget*, Doris R. Sheridan. (book) [**1,5**, D-Cem 506:1-163]
1870-1873	*Daily Times*, Doris R. Sheridan. (book) [**1,5**, D-Cem 514:2-101]
1874-1875	*Troy Daily Whig*, Doris R. Sheridan. (book) [**1,5**, D-Cem 500:2-50]
1875-1876	*Troy Daily Times*, Doris R. Sheridan. (book) [**1,5**, D-Cem 473:1-170]

1875-1881   *Troy Daily Times* [4 #1035941 item 6]
1876-1878   Misc newspapers, Doris R. Sheridan. (book) [1,5, D-Cem 508:1-124]
1877   *Troy Daily Times* Doris R. Sheridan. (book) [1,5, D-Cem 476:1-83]
1878   *Troy Daily Times*, Doris R. Sheridan. (book) [1,5, D-Cem 491:1-109]
1879   *Troy Daily Times*, Doris R. Sheridan. (book) [1,5, D-Cem 479:82-138]
1880   *Troy Daily Times*, Doris R. Sheridan. (book) [1,5, D-Cem 495:43-102]
1881   *Troy Daily Times*, Doris R. Sheridan. (book) [1,5, D-Cem 491:1-109]
1884-1885   *Troy Budget*, Doris R. Sheridan. (book) [1,5, D-Cem 506:1-163]

RICHMOND COUNTY
1726-1890   Misc. newspapers (indexed). [4 #0509189]
1790-1797   *NY Magazine or Literary Depository* [4 #0509186]
1833-1866   Misc. newspapers, Edna Huntington. [3]
1838-1866   Misc. newspapers [3]
Staten Island
1838-1839   *Richmond County Mirror*, (9 records), Harriet Stryker-Rodda. [3]

ST. LAWRENCE COUNTY
Ogdensburgh
1826-1830   *St. Lawrence Gazette*; *8,000 More Vital Records of Eastern New York State, 1804-1850*, Fred Q. Bowman. Kinship, Rhinebeck, NY. (book) [1,2,3,4,5]
1827-1852   Misc. newspapers, marriages and deaths. [1,2,4,5, *Tree Talks* 4:80-6:120; St. Lawrence Co. 1-6]
1831-1833   *Northern Lights*; *8,000 More Vital Records of Eastern New York State, 1804-1850*, Fred Q. Bowman. Kinship, Rhinebeck, NY. (book) [1,2,3,4,5]
1833-1843   *St. Lawrence Republican*; *8,000 More Vital Records of Eastern New York State, 1804-1850*, Fred Q. Bowman. Kinship, Rhinebeck, NY. (book) [1,2,3,4,5]
Potsdam
1845-1846   *The Northern Cabinet and Literary Repository*, marriages and deaths. [1,2,4,5, *Tree Talks* 11:104-12:102; St. Lawrence Co. pp. 27-31]

SARATOGA COUNTY
Ballston Spa
1808-1812   *Independent American; Ballston Spa Republican; Ballston Journal*, from *The Saratoga* (Kinship, Rhinebeck, NY), Vol. 5, #4. [1,2,4,5]
1812-1814   *Independent American; Ballston Spa Republican; Ballston Journal*, from *The Saratoga* (Kinship, Rhinebeck, NY), Vol. 6, #1. [1,2,4,5]
1813-1814   *Independent American; Ballston Spa Republican; Ballston Journal*, from *The Saratoga* (Kinship, Rhinebeck, NY), Vol. 1, #2. [1,2,4,5]
1814-1818   *Independent American; Ballston Spa Republican; Ballston Journal*, from *The Saratoga* (Kinship, Rhinebeck, NY), Vol. 6, #2. [1,2,4,5]
1821-1825   *Ballston Spa Gazette*; *10,000 Vital Records of Eastern New York, 1777-1834*, Fred Q. Bowman. Genealogical Publishing Co., Baltimore, MD, 1987. (book) [1,2,3,4,5]
1836-1839   *Independent American; Ballston Spa Republican; Ballston Journal*, from *The Saratoga* (Kinship, Rhinebeck, NY), Vol. 1, #2. [1,2,4,5]
1847   *Independent American; Ballston Spa Republican; Ballston Journal*, from *The Saratoga* (Kinship, Rhinebeck, NY), Vol. 1, #2. [1,2,4,5]
1847-1848   *Independent American; Ballston Spa Republican; Ballston Journal*, from *The Saratoga* (Kinship, Rhinebeck, NY), Vol. 1, #3. [1,2,4,5]
1848   *Independent American; Ballston Spa Republican; Ballston Journal*, from *The Saratoga* (Kinship, Rhinebeck, NY), Vol. 1, #4. [1,2,4,5]
1848-1849   *Independent American; Ballston Spa Republican; Ballston Journal*, from *The Saratoga* (Kinship, Rhinebeck, NY), Vol. 2, #1. [1,2,4,5]

1849-1850   *Independent American; Ballston Spa Republican; Ballston Journal*, from *The Saratoga* (Kinship, Rhinebeck, NY), Vol. 2, #2. **[1,2,4,5]**

1850   *Independent American; Ballston Spa Republican; Ballston Journal*, from *The Saratoga* (Kinship, Rhinebeck, NY), Vol. 2, #3. **[1,2,4,5]**

1855   *Independent American; Ballston Spa Republican; Ballston Journal*, from *The Saratoga* (Kinship, Rhinebeck, NY), Vol. 2, #3. **[1,2,4,5]**

1855-1856   *Independent American; Ballston Spa Republican; Ballston Journal*, from *The Saratoga* (Kinship, Rhinebeck, NY), Vol. 2, #4. **[1,2,4,5]**

1856-1858   *Independent American; Ballston Spa Republican; Ballston Journal*, from *The Saratoga* (Kinship, Rhinebeck, NY), Vol. 3, #1. **[1,2,4,5]**

1858-1859   *Independent American; Ballston Spa Republican; Ballston Journal*, from *The Saratoga* (Kinship, Rhinebeck, NY), Vol. 3, #2. **[1,2,4,5]**

1859-1860   *Independent American; Ballston Spa Republican; Ballston Journal*, from *The Saratoga* (Kinship, Rhinebeck, NY), Vol. 3, #3. **[1,2,4,5]**

1860-1861   *Independent American; Ballston Spa Republican; Ballston Journal*, from *The Saratoga* (Kinship, Rhinebeck, NY), Vol. 3, #4. **[1,2,4,5]**

1861   *Independent American; Ballston Spa Republican; Ballston Journal*, from *The Saratoga* (Kinship, Rhinebeck, NY), Vol. 4, #1. **[1,2,4,5]**

1861-1862   *Independent American; Ballston Spa Republican; Ballston Journal*, from *The Saratoga* (Kinship, Rhinebeck, NY), Vol. 4, #2. **[1,2,4,5]**

1862-1863   *Independent American; Ballston Spa Republican; Ballston Journal*, from *The Saratoga* (Kinship, Rhinebeck, NY), Vol. 4, #3. **[1,2,4,5]**

1863   *Independent American; Ballston Spa Republican; Ballston Journal* **[1,2,4,5**, *The Saratoga* (Kinship, Rhinebeck, NY) Vol. 4 #4**]**

1863-1864   *Independent American; Ballston Spa Republican; Ballston Journal*, from *The Saratoga* (Kinship, Rhinebeck, NY), Vol. 5 #1. **[1,2,4,5]**

1864   *Independent American; Ballston Spa Republican; Ballston Journal*, from *The Saratoga* (Kinship, Rhinebeck, NY), Vol. 5, #1 through Vol. 5, #4. **[1,2,4,5]**

Saratoga Springs

1819   *Saratoga Sentinel*, marriages and deaths **[1,2,4,5**, *Tree Talks* 8:44-163; Saratoga Co. pp. 22-24**]**

1819-1837   *Marriage and Death Notices in the Saratoga Sentinel, 1819-1837*, Cornelius E. Durkee. (book) **[1]**

1819-1837   *Marriage and Death Notices in the Saratoga Sentinel, 1819-1837*, Cornelius E. Durkee. **[4 #0017954 items 1, 2]**

1819-1837   *Marriage and Death Notices in the Saratoga Sentinel, 1819-1837*, Cornelius E. Durkee. **[4 #0532966 item 3]**

1839-1853   *Saratoga Daily Whig (Saratoga County Press)* **[1,2,4,5**, *Tree Talks* 8:223-9:113; Saratoga Co. pp. 25-27**]**

1876   *Daily Saratogian*, marriage and deaths, (from *The Patents*, the newsletter of the Northeastern NY Genealogical Society) Vols. 5 and 6. **[1,2,4]**

1876   *Saratoga Sentinel*, marriage and deaths, (from *The Patents*, the newsletter of the Northeastern NY Genealogical Society) Vol. 6. **[1,2,4]**

SCHENECTADY COUNTY
Schenectady

1800's   Misc. newspapers **[4 #1304632; #1304633 items 1-3]**

1812-1819   *Schenectady Cabinet* and *Schenectady Whig*, marriages and deaths, from *The Mohawk* (Kinship, Rhinebeck, NY), Vol. 1, #1. **[1,2,4,5]**

1812-1823   Misc. newspapers, marriages **[1,2,4,5**, *Tree Talks* 11:105-223, 12:103-16:195; Schenectady Co. pp. 23-25, 27-33**]**

1819-1825   *Schenectady Cabinet* and *Schenectady Whig*, marriages and deaths, from *The Mohawk* (Kinship, Rhinebeck, NY), Vol. 1, #2. **[1,2,4,5]**

1825	*Schenectady Cabinet* and *Schenectady Whig*, marriages and deaths, from *The Mohawk* (Kinship, Rhinebeck, NY), Vol. 1, #3. [**1,2,4,5**]
1825-1826	*Schenectady Cabinet* and *Schenectady Whig*, marriages and deaths, from *The Mohawk* (Kinship, Rhinebeck, NY), Vol. 1, #4. [**1,2,4,5**]
1826-1827	*Schenectady Cabinet* and *Schenectady Whig*, marriages and deaths, from *The Mohawk* (Kinship, Rhinebeck, NY), Vol. 2, #1. [**1,2,4,5**]
1826-1840	*Vital Statistics of Marriages and Deaths from Schenectady Newspapers, Vol. 1*, Marie Noll Cormack. (book) [**1**]
1827-1828	*Schenectady Cabinet* and *Schenectady Whig*, marriages and deaths, from *The Mohawk* (Kinship, Rhinebeck, NY), Vol. 2, #2. [**1,2,4,5**]
1828	*Schenectady Cabinet* and *Schenectady Whig*, marriages and deaths, from *The Mohawk* (Kinship, Rhinebeck, NY), Vol. 2, #3. [**1,2,4,5**]
1828-1829	*Schenectady Cabinet* and *Schenectady Whig*, marriages and deaths, from *The Mohawk* (Kinship, Rhinebeck, NY), Vol. 2, #4. [**1,2,4,5**]
1829	*Schenectady Cabinet* and *Schenectady Whig*, marriages and deaths, from *The Mohawk* (Kinship, Rhinebeck, NY), Vol. 3, #1. [**1,2,4,5**]
1829-1830	*Schenectady Cabinet* and *Schenectady Whig*, marriages and deaths, from *The Mohawk* (Kinship, Rhinebeck, NY), Vol. 3, #2. [**1,2,4,5**]
1830	*Schenectady Cabinet* and *Schenectady Whig*, marriages and deaths, from *The Mohawk* (Kinship, Rhinebeck, NY), Vol. 3, #3 and #4. [**1,2,4,5**]
1830-1831	*Schenectady Cabinet* and *Schenectady Whig*, marriages and deaths, from *The Mohawk* (Kinship, Rhinebeck, NY), Vol. 4, #1. [**1,2,4,5**]
1831	*Schenectady Cabinet* and *Schenectady Whig*, marriages and deaths, from *The Mohawk* (Kinship, Rhinebeck, NY), Vol. 4, #2. [**1,2,4,5**]
1831-1832	*Schenectady Cabinet* and *Schenectady Whig*, marriages and deaths, from *The Mohawk* (Kinship, Rhinebeck, NY), Vol. 4, #3. [**1,2,4,5**]
1831-1834	*Schenectady Cabinet* and *Schenectady Whig*, marriages and deaths, from *The Mohawk* (Kinship, Rhinebeck, NY), Vol. 5, #1. [**1,2,4,5**]
1832	*Schenectady Cabinet* and *Schenectady Whig*, marriages and deaths, from *The Mohawk* (Kinship, Rhinebeck, NY), Vol. 4, #4 and Vol. 5, #1. [**1,2,4,5**]
1833	*Schenectady Cabinet* and *Schenectady Whig*, marriages and deaths, from *The Mohawk* (Kinship, Rhinebeck, NY), Vol. 5, #1 and #2. [**1,2,4,5**]
1833-1834	*Schenectady Cabinet* and *Schenectady Whig*, marriages and deaths, from *The Mohawk* (Kinship, Rhinebeck, NY), Vol. 5, #3. [**1,2,4,5**]
1835	*Schenectady Cabinet* and *Schenectady Whig*, marriages and deaths, from *The Mohawk* (Kinship, Rhinebeck, NY), Vol. 6, #1. [**1,2,4,5**]
1835-1836	*Vital Statistics of Marriages and Deaths from Schenectady Newspapers, Vol. 2*, Marie Noll Cormack. (book) [**1**]
1835-1836	*Schenectady Cabinet* and *Schenectady Whig*, marriages and deaths, from *The Mohawk* (Kinship, Rhinebeck, NY), Vol. 6, #2. [**1,2,4,5**]
1836	*Schenectady Cabinet* and *Schenectady Whig*, marriages and deaths, from *The Mohawk* (Kinship, Rhinebeck, NY), Vol. 6, #3 and #4. [**1,2,4,5**]
1836-1837	*Schenectady Cabinet* and *Schenectady Whig*, marriages and deaths, from *The Mohawk* (Kinship, Rhinebeck, NY), Vol. 7, #1. [**1,2,4,5**]
1837-1838	*Schenectady Cabinet* and *Schenectady Whig*, marriages and deaths, from *The Mohawk* (Kinship, Rhinebeck, NY), Vol. 7, #2. [**1,2,4,5**]
1838-1839	*Schenectady Cabinet* and *Schenectady Whig*, marriages and deaths, from *The Mohawk* (Kinship, Rhinebeck, NY), Vol. 7, #3. [**1,2,4,5**]
1839-1840	*Schenectady Cabinet* and *Schenectady Whig*, marriages and deaths, from *The Mohawk* (Kinship, Rhinebeck, NY), Vol. 1, #4. [**1,2,4,5**]
1839-1849	*Vital Statistics of Marriages and Deaths from Schenectady Newspapers, Vol. 2*, Marie Noll Cormack [**1**]
1840	*Schenectady Cabinet* and *Schenectady Whig*, marriages and deaths, from *The Mohawk* (Kinship, Rhinebeck, NY), Vol. 8, #1. [**1,2,4,5**]

1840-1841	*Schenectady Cabinet* and *Schenectady Whig*, marriages and deaths, from *The Mohawk* (Kinship, Rhinebeck, NY), Vol. 8, #2. [1,2,4,5]
1841-1842	*Schenectady Cabinet* and *Schenectady Whig*, marriages and deaths, from *The Mohawk* (Kinship, Rhinebeck, NY), Vol. 8, #3. [1,2,4,5]
1842	*Schenectady Cabinet* and *Schenectady Whig*, marriages and deaths, from *The Mohawk* (Kinship, Rhinebeck, NY), Vol. 8, #4. [1,2,4,5]
1842-1843	*Schenectady Cabinet* and *Schenectady Whig*, marriages and deaths, from *The Mohawk* (Kinship, Rhinebeck, NY), Vol. 9, #1. [1,2,4,5]
1843-1844	*Schenectady Cabinet* and *Schenectady Whig*, marriages and deaths, from *The Mohawk* (Kinship, Rhinebeck, NY), Vol. 9, #2. [1,2,4,5]
1844	*Schenectady Cabinet* and *Schenectady Whig*, marriages and deaths, from *The Mohawk* (Kinship, Rhinebeck, NY), Vol. 9, #3 and #4. [1,2,4,5]
1844-1845	*Schenectady Cabinet* and *Schenectady Whig*, marriages and deaths, from *The Mohawk* (Kinship, Rhinebeck, NY), Vol. 10, #1. [1,2,4,5]
1845	*Schenectady Cabinet* and *Schenectady Whig*, marriages and deaths, from *The Mohawk* (Kinship, Rhinebeck, NY), Vol. 10, #2. [1,2,4,5]
1845-1846	*Schenectady Cabinet* and *Schenectady Whig*, marriages and deaths, from *The Mohawk* (Kinship, Rhinebeck, NY), Vol. 10, #3. [1,2,4,5]
1846	*Schenectady Cabinet* and *Schenectady Whig*, marriages and deaths, from *The Mohawk* (Kinship, Rhinebeck, NY), Vol. 10, #4. [1,2,4,5]
1867	*Vital Statistics of Marriages and Deaths from Schenectady Newspapers, Vol. 2,* Marie Noll Cormack. (book) [1]

SCHOHARIE COUNTY
Schoharie
????-????	*Schoharie Co. Republican*, deaths. [4 #1298603 item 7]
1830-1879	*Schoharie Republican*, deaths, two drawer card file. [1]
1838-1839	*Schoharie Patriot*, marriages. [1,2,4,5, *Tree Talks* 4:155-5:90; Schoharie Co. pp. 1-4]
1838-1839	*Schoharie Patriot*, deaths. [1,2,4,5, *Tree Talks* 5:143-6:186; Schoharie Co. pp. 5-7]
1838-1863	*Schoharie Patriot* [4 #1298603 item 6]

SENECA COUNTY
1807-1908	Misc. newspapers [4 #0833158]
1817-1963	Misc. newspapers [4 #0812842]
Ovid
1822-1869	Vital records from *The Ovid Bee*, Jesse H. Finch. [2]

STEUBEN COUNTY
1797-1868	*Marriages and Deaths from Steuben County, NY Newspapers*, Yvonne E. Martin. (book) [2]
1797-1868	Misc. newspapers [4]
1847-1865	Misc. newspapers [4 #0219412 and #0219413]
Bath
1831-1850	*Steuben Farmers Advocate*; *10,000 Vital Records of Western New York, 1809-1850*, Fred Q. Bowman. Genealogical Publishing Co., Baltimore, MD, 1985. (book) [1,2,3,4,5]
Canisteo
1880	*Canisteo Times* [1,5, D-Cem 336:12-13]
1883-1942	*Canisteo Times* (plus village records). [1,5, D-Cem 336:14-16]
Corning
1840-1842	*Corning and Blossburg Advocate*, marriages. [1,2,4,5, *Tree Talks* 5:197; Steuben Co. p. 11 also by mistake under Broome County 5:61 (Broome Co. p. 15)]

1840-1843   *Corning Weekly Journal; 10,000 Vital Records of Central New York, 1813-1850*,
               Fred Q. Bowman. Genealogical Publishing Co., Baltimore, MD, 1988. (book)
               [1,2,3,4,5]
1847-1850   *Corning Weekly Journal; 10,000 Vital Records of Central New York, 1813-1850*,
               Fred Q. Bowman. Genealogical Publishing Co., Baltimore, MD, 1988. (book)
               [1,2,3,4,5]

SUFFOLK COUNTY
????-????   Misc. newspapers, deaths. [4]
1791-1898   Misc. Long Island Newspapers, Edna Huntington. [3]
1871-1901   Misc. newspapers, marriages. [4 #1033836 items 5-8]
Babylon
1890-1900   *The South Side Signal* and *The Republican Watchman*, marriages and deaths, loose
               clippings. [2]

Greenport
1816-1832   *Marriages and Deaths from Various Newspapers* [titles vary], Louis Tooker Vail,
               typescript. [2]
1859-1900   *Republican Watchman*, Gertrude A. Barber, 5 vols. (book) [2]
1890-1900   *The South Side Signal* and *The Republican Watchman*, marriages and deaths, loose
               clippings. [2]

Huntington
1826-1827   *Portico; 8,000 More Vital Records of Eastern New York State, 1804-1850*, Fred Q.
               Bowman. Kinship, Rhinebeck, NY. (book) [1,2,3,4,5]
1839-1850   *The Long Islander; 8,000 More Vital Records of Eastern New York State, 1804-
               1850*, Fred Q. Bowman. Kinship, Rhinebeck, NY. (book) [1,2,3,4,5]
1839-1857   *The Index to the Long Islander*, Irene G. Sniffen, 3 vols., 1977-1981, (all names,
               not just marriages and death notices). [2]
1839-1864   *The Long Islander*, deaths. [4 #0982340 item 1]
1839-1864   *An Index to the Long Islander, 1839-1864*, Marian F. Stevens, Huntington Histori-
               cal Society, 1974. (book) [2,3]
1847-1870   *The Long Islander*, Harriet Stryker-Rodda (from a scrapbook). (book) [3]
1861-1881   *An Index to the Long Islander*, Robert L. Simpson. (book) [2,3]
1865-1881   Index to *The Long Islander* [2,4 #136078 item 8]
1871-1879   *The Long Islander*, Harriet Stryker-Rodda (from a scrapbook). (book) [3]

Sag Harbor
????-1827   "Suffolk County in Olden Times", Henry Onderdonk, Jr. in *Journal of Long Island
               History*, 5:4:13-38; 6:15-36; 6:2:23-41. [2]
1791-1798   *Frothingham's Long Island Herald*, "Glimpses of Long Island Life in the 1790's",
               Journal of Long Island History, 8:26-56, Joan B. Peyer and Kenneth Scott,
               marriages and deaths. [2]
1804-1805   *Suffolk Gazette; 8,000 More Vital Records of Eastern New York State, 1804-1850*,
               Fred Q. Bowman. Kinship, Rhinebeck, NY. (book) [1,2,3,4,5]
1804-1808   *Suffolk Gazette*, Rufus King, marriages and deaths. [1,2,3,4,5, *NYG&B RECORD*
               25:6-8; 89-92; 137-139; 161-164]
1807-1808   *Suffolk Gazette*, Rufus King, marriages. [1,2,3,4,5, *NYG&B RECORD* 24:86-88;
               159-161]
1816-1832   *Marriages and Deaths from Various Newspapers* [titles vary], Louis Tooker Vail,
               typescript. [2]
1822-1826   *The Corrector; 8,000 More Vital Records of Eastern New York State, 1804-1850*,
               Fred Q. Bowman. Kinship, Rhinebeck, NY. (book) [1,2,3,4,5]
1854-1855   *The Corrector Marriage and Death Notices*, Josephine C. Frost, manuscript. [2]

TIOGA COUNTY
1841-1855   Misc. newspapers [4]

1864-1865	Misc. newspapers, marriages. [4 #0017610 item 8]

Owego

1814-1832	*Owego Gazette* [4 #1421864 item 10]
1821-1823	*Owego Gazette* [1,5, D-Cem 543:161-175]
1837-1843	*Owego Gazette* [4 #1421864 item 10]
1842-1843	*Owego Gazette* [1,5, D-Cem 543:161-175]
1848-1850	*Owego Gazette* [1,5, D-Cem 520:52-69]
1848-1850	*Owego Gazette* [4 #1421864 item 10]
1852	*Owego Gazette* [1,5, D-Cem 520:76-89]
1853	*Owego Gazette* [4 #1035592 item 21]

TOMPKINS COUNTY

1807-1908	Misc. newspapers [4 #0833158]
1827-1847	Misc. newspapers, marriages and deaths. [1,2,4,5 *Tree Talks* 8:169-10:186; Tompkins Co. pp. 26-34]

Ithaca

1826-1829	Misc. newspapers [1,5, D-Cem 285:106-117]
1827-1829	*Ithaca Journal and General Advertiser*, marriages and deaths. [1,2,4,5 *Tree Talks* 3:135-6:48; Tompkins Co. pp. 8-16]

Trumansburg

1827-1840	Misc. newspapers, 285:96-102. [1,5]
1832	*Trumansburg Advertiser*, marriages and deaths. [1,2,4,5, *Tree Talks* 3:100-135; Tompkins Co. pp. 7-8]
1845-1846	Misc. newspapers, 285:96-102. [1,5]

ULSTER COUNTY

1842-1890	Misc. newspapers [4 #0514684 item 6]
1865-1890	Misc. newspapers, *Scrap book of Elmirah Freer*, Kenneth Hasbrouck. (book) [1]

Kingston

1820-1830	Misc. newspapers [3]
1820-1830	Misc. newspapers [4 #0823832 item 6]
1826-1847	*Death Notices of Revolutionary Veterans and Men and Women of the Revolutionary Period from Kingston, New York Newspapers, 1826-1847*, Louise Hasbrouck Zimm, (10 page typescript). (booklet) [1,3]
1826-1847	*Death Notices of Revolutionary Veterans and Men and Women of the Revolutionary Period from Kingston, New York Newspapers, 1826-1847*, Louise Hasbrouck Zimm, (10 page typescript) [4 #0973035 item 10]
1830-1839	Misc. newspapers [3]
1837-1845	*Ulster Republican* [1,5, D-Cem 533:1-150]
1846-1848	*The Ulster Republican* [1,5, D-Cem 544:1-199]
1849-1850	*The Ulster Republican* [1,5, D-Cem 548:1-80]
1895	*Weekly Freeman and Journal* [1,5, D-Bible 159:136-138]

Saugerties

1848-1852	*Obituaries and Death Notices and Genealogical Gleanings from "The Saugerties Telegraph"*, Audrey M. Klinkenberg, Vol. 1. (book) [1]
1849-1858	Misc. newspapers [1]
1853-1860	*Obituaries and Death Notices and Genealogical Gleanings from "The Saugerties Telegraph"*, Audrey M. Klinkenberg, Vol. 1. (book) [1]
1878-1895	*Saugerties Post* [4 #0930817 item 2]

WARREN COUNTY

Glens Falls

1829	*Glens Falls Messenger*, marriage and deaths, (from *The Patents*, the newsletter of the Northeastern NY Genealogical Society) Vol. 9, #1. [1,2,4]

1859   *Glens Falls Messenger* (Jan.-May 1859) [**1,5**, D-Bible 98:83-89]
1859   *Glens Falls Messenger* (Jan.-May 1859), marriage and deaths. (from *THE PAT-ENTS*, the newsletter of the Northeastern NY Genealogical Society) Vol. 6. [**1,2,4**]
1916   *Post Star*, births, marriages and deaths. [**4** #0851126 item 3]

WASHINGTON COUNTY
Greenwich
1835-1850   *Washington County Journal*, surnames A-Cr. [**1,2,3,4,5**, *NYG&B RECORD* 118:135-142]
1835-1850   *Washington County Journal*, surnames Cr-Hen. [**1,2,3,4,5**, *NYG&B RECORD* 118:203-209]
1835-1850   *Washington County Journal*, surnames Her-Pit. [**1,2,3,4,5**, *NYG&B RECORD* 119:35-43]
1835-1850   *Washington County Journal*, surnames Po-T. [**1,2,3,4,5**, *NYG&B RECORD* 119:91-98]
1835-1850   *Washington County Journal*, surnames V-Y. [**1,2,3,4,5**, *NYG&B RECORD* 119:166-170]
1850   *Union Village Journal*, surnames A-Cr. [**1,2,3,4,5**, *NYG&B RECORD* 118:135-142]
1850   *Union Village Journal*, surnames Cr-Hen. [**1,2,3,4,5**, *NYG&B RECORD* 118:203-209]
1850   *Union Village Journal*, surnames Her-Pit. [**1,2,3,4,5**, *NYG&B RECORD* 119:35-43]
1850   *Union Village Journal*, surnames Po-T. [**1,2,3,4,5**, *NYG&B RECORD* 119:91-98]
1850   *Union Village Journal*, surnames V-Y. [**1,2,3,4,5**, *NYG&B RECORD* 119:166-170]
Salem
1818-1820   *Northern Post* [**1,5**, D-Cem 289:88-103]

WAYNE COUNTY
1810-1854   Misc. newspapers [**4** # 0018016]
Newark
1869-1873   *Newark Weekly Courier* [**3,4**]
1907-1942   Misc. newspapers, deaths. [**3**]
Palmyra
????-????   *Wayne Sentinel* [**4** #0896628 item 4]
1817-1821   *Palmyra Register* [**4** #0017863]
1817-1821   *Palmyra Register*; *10,000 Vital Records of Western New York, 1809-1850*, Fred Q. Bowman. Genealogical Publishing Co., Baltimore, MD, 1985. (book) [**1,2,3,4,5**]
1821-1844   *Wayne Sentinel*; *10,000 Vital Records of Western New York, 1809-1850*, Fred Q. Bowman. Genealogical Publishing Co., Baltimore, MD, 1985. (book) [**1,2,3,4,5**]
1823-1840   *Wayne Sentinel* [**4** #0813656 item 1]
1823-1840   *Wayne Sentinel* [**4** #0982173 item 2]
1823-1828   *Wayne Sentinel* (Oct. 1, 1823-Sept. 19, 1828) [**4** #0017865]
1823-1859   *Wayne Sentinel*, Harriet M. Wiles, 1933. [**3**]
1828-1834   *Wayne Sentinel* (Sept. 26, 1828-Sept. 19, 1834) [**4** #0017866]
1834-1840   *Wayne Sentinel* (Sept. 26, 1834-Sept. 30, 1840) [**4** #0017867]
1840-1844   *Wayne Sentinel* (Oct. 7, 1840-Sept. 25, 1844) [**4** #0017868]
1861-1866   *Palmyra Courier*, marriages. [**3**]
1861-1867   *Palmyra Courier*, deaths. [**3**]

WESTCHESTER COUNTY
Ossining
1838-1839   *Hudson River Chronicle* [**1,5**, D-Cem 104:171-172]

Sing Sing
1839-1850	*Hudson River Chronicle* [4 #0982409 item 7]
1888-1889	*Sing Sing Republican* [**1,5**, D-Cem 237:24-34]

WYOMING COUNTY
1824-1847	Wyoming Co. marriages reported in various Livingston County newspapers [**1,2,4,5**, *Tree Talks* 10:286-12:120; Wyoming Co. pp. 28-32]
1824-1847	Wyoming Co. deaths reported in various Livingston County newspapers [**1,2,4,5**, *Tree Talks* 12:120-236; Wyoming Co. pp. 32-34]

Warsaw
1842-1843	*Western New Yorker*, marriages [**1,2,4,5** *Tree Talks* 3:138-4:52, 8:173-233; Wyoming Co. pp. 1-2, 19-20]
1842-1843	*Western New Yorker*, deaths [**1,2,4,5**, *Tree Talks* 8:233-9:187; Wyoming Co. pp. 20-22]

YATES COUNTY
????-????	Misc. newspapers [4 #0532973 item 2]
1823-1833	*Genealogical Gleanings Abstracted from Newspapers of Penn Yann, Yates County, NY, 1823-1833 and 1841-1855*, Diane Stenzel. Heritage Books, Inc., Bowie, MD, 1991. (book) [**2**]
1841-1855	*Genealogical Gleanings Abstracted from Newspapers of Penn Yann, Yates County, NY, 1823-1833 and 1841-1855*, Diane Stenzel. Heritage Books, Inc., Bowie, MD, 1991. (book) [**2**]
1849-1858	Misc. newspapers, clippings of deaths [**1,2,4,5**, *Tree Talks* 6:194; Yates Co. p. 14]
1856-1867	*Genealogical Gleanings Abstracted from "The Yates County Chronicle" May 1856-October 1867*, Diane Stenzel. Heritage Books, Inc., Bowie, MD, 1992. (book) [**2**]

Penn Yan
1855-1856	*Pen Yann Democrat/Yates County Chronicle*, marriages and deaths. [**1,2,4,5**, *Tree Talks* 23:127; Yates Co. p. 43]
1857	*Yates County Chronicle*, marriages. [**1,2,4,5**, *Tree Talks* 4:53-164; Yates Co. pp. 6-8]
1857	*Yates County Chronicle*, deaths. [**1,2,4,5**, *Tree Talks* 4:164-5:202; Yates Co. pp. 8-13]
1859-1860	*Yates County Chronicle*, deaths. [**1,2,4,5** *Tree Talks* 4:164-5:202; Yates Co. pp. 8-13]
1860	*Yates County Chronicle*, marriages. [**1,2,4,5** *Tree Talks* 4:164-5:202; Yates Co. pp. 8-13]
1873	*Yates County Chronicle*, deaths. [**1,2,4,5**, *Tree Talks* 15:167-168; Yates Co. pp. 37-38]

In the introductory section of this book the following two unsubstantiated claims were made. Towns of residence of persons identified in newspaper marriage and death columns are by no means confined to the counties within which the newspapers of reference were published. Frequently these newspaper postings contain specific detail not found in the more commonly sought cemetery, church, and town record books. Several samplings in support of these two claims follow.

Persons pursuing their Axtell ancestries, for example, will find within the starred segments of the five sets of record postings below towns of residence of individuals in that surname spread across New York, New Jersey, Ohio and Indiana. In most of the entries (entry 273 for example) towns of residence of individuals are clearly stated. In others (entry 276 for example) this information is not directly posted. In this latter example underline probably both bride and groom lived in Geneva, the village where the newspaper of reference was published. However, one or both of these persons could have been living at wedding time in the next county to that wherein the newspaper was published or on the other hand, for all that is shown, either one could have their permanent home in such a remote place as "West Florida", Argentina, Gibralter, or Greece, each of these latter being residence places defined in my book, *10,000 Vital Records of Western New York, 1809-1850.*

271. Avery, Sylvanus, 17, d 6/15/17 in Phelps ("drowned in Dickinson's mill pond") (3-7/9)

272. Avery, Thomas., 15, d in Groton "from eating wild cherries which had been in rum and cider" (3-11/22/15)

* 273. Axtell, Daniel m Sally Axtell, both of Friendship, Alleg, Co., in F (3-10/29/28)

* 274. Axtell, Henry (Maj.), 80, d 4/6/18 in Mendham, NJ (3-4/22)

* 275. Axtell, Henry, 55, D.D., d 2/11/29 in Geneva. His oldest dau., Rebecca, age, 30, d 2/14. Both were buried in the same grave. (He b. in Mendham, NJ in 1773; grad from Princeton in 1796; settled in Geneva, NY by 1804. Co-pastor of Presby. Ch. with Jedidiah Chapman in 1812. On death of latter in 1813, Dr. Axtell became sole pastor) (3-2/18 and 5-2/20)

* 276. Axtell, John m. Sally Bennet in Geneva; Rev. Orin Clark (3-9/8/19)

* 277. Axtell, Martha, 36, wf of Hiram, d in Canandaigua (3-11/12/28)

* 278. Axtell, Phebe, 89, relict of late Maj. Henry and mother of late Rev. Henry, d 7/6/29 "near Seneca" ("She was a subject of the religious revival in Morris Town (N.J.) in . . . 1764") (3-7/22)

* 279. Axtell, Phoebe Ann C., 16, second dau. of Rev. Henry, d 4/6/22 in Geneva (3-4/10). She d 4/5 (5-4/17)

* 280. Axtell, Silas (Col.), 54, of Mendham, NJ, bro of Henry of Geneva, NY, d 9/29/23 in Zanesville, Ohio (3-11/12)

281. Ayers, John m 2/16/15 Polly Cowing in Seneca; Rev. Axtell (3-2/22)

282. Aylsworth, John R., 17, s of Levi D., d in Phelps (3-11/28/27)

283. Ayrault, Lyman m Eunice M. Mills, formerly of Canandaigua, in Pike, Alleg. Co. (3-4/2/23)

284. Ayres, John m 7/4/29 Kazia Clark in Palmyra; Rev. Gear (3-7/15 and 5-7/10)

285. Ayres, Lewis of Ithaca m 11/2/24 Rebecca Osborn of Geneva in G; Rev. Dr. Axtell (3-11/10).

286. Ayres, Peter m Harriet Capell, both of Milo, in Benton (3-4/8/29)

287. Ayres, Samuel, Esq., 59, d at his home in Mason Co., VA (lived many years in Chaut, Co., NY; surv. by wf and ch) (4-10/28/29)

The postings above are drawn from the book identified in the previous paragraph and the index to this same book leads to the following starred entry #209:

204. Applegate, John, Esq., 48, d "in Enfield near Ithaca" (3-12/28/25)

205. Applegate, William F. m 12/20/31 Elizabeth Gardner, both of Macedon, in Palmyra; F. Smith, Esq. (5-12/27)
206. Archer, Thomas L. of Rochester m. Laura Lacy of Chili, NY in C (3-1/14/29)
207. Arden, Mary (Mrs.), 91, d in NYC (3-2/26/17)
208. Armington, Emily, inf dau of Henry and Aurelia, d 8/23/40 in Palmyra (5-8/26)
* 209. Arms, Israel m 5/15/20 Sally Axtell in Sodus (3-5/24)
210. Armstrong, _____, ch of Mr. Armstrong, d "in Canandaigua Lake" (3-8/23/15)
211. Armstrong, ____, 3 yrs, dau of Francis, d in Geneseo (3-5/2/27)
212. Armstrong, Ackerson of Pulteney m 11/18/41 Eliza Wheeler, dau of the Hon. Grattan H. Wheeler, in Wheeler; Rev. Gaylord (2-12/1)
213. Armstrong, Alida, wf of Gen John A., late Secretary of War, d 12/24/22 in Red Hook (5-1/29/23)
213a. Armstrong, James A. m 1/23/23 Nancy PcPherson in Seneca; Rev. Axtell (3-1/29)

In the two sets of postings above (pertaining to #273-280 and #209) the **3** and the **5** found in the end parentheses identify the sources respectively as the *Geneva Gazette* and the *Wayne Sentinel*, the latter published in Palmyra.

From my book *10,000 Vital Records of Central New York, 1813-1850* comes this starred information:

221. Avery, John S. m 2/22/44 Caroline Hollenbeck, both of Greene, in G; Rev. J.T. Goodrich (Oxford Republican, 2/29)
222. Avery, Oren S., 41, d 8/3/35 in Perryville (surv by wf, 2 sons, and an aged widowed mother) (3-8/10)
223. Avery, T.H., attorney, m 4/14/47 Margaret E. Morris, dau of Late Harvey, in Cazenovia; Rev. Daniel Putnam (9-4/16)
224. Avery, William m 12/19/19 Hannah Dixon in Sherburne; Rev. Joshua Knight (7-1/26/20)
225. Avery, William (Deacon) m 10/17/43 Juliett Brown; Rev. Brown (of Sherburne?) (9-10/27)
226. Axon, Robert m 5/9/48 Jane Dutcher, both of Upper New York Mills, in U.N.Y.M.; Rev. Dr. Paddock (9-5/18)
* 227. Axtell, Daniel C. (Rev.), pastor-elect of 2nd Presby. Ch. in Auburn, m 10/28/30 Maria L. Dey, dau. of A. Dey, Esq., of NYC in NYC (**6**-11/10)
* 228. Axtell, Daniel Cook (Rev.), 37, oldest s of Rev. Dr. Axtell of Geneva and formerly pastor of 2nd Presby. Ch. in Auburn, d 7/12/37 in Patterson, NJ (**6**-7/19)
* 229. Axtell, Henry (Rev.) of Lawrenceville, NJ m 9/7/30 Juliet Lay, dau of John, Esq. of Clinton, Oneida Co., NY, in Clinton; Rev. D.C. Axtell (**6**-9/15)
* 230. Axtell, Stephen, 28, d 10/21/31 at the home of his father in Sodus (**6**-11/9)
231. Ayer, James C. (Dr.) m 11/14/50 Josephine M. Southwick, dau of Hon. Royal, in Lowell, MA (9-12/7)
232. Ayer, William B. of Utica m 4/23/48 Cornelia M. Hills of Oneida in Syracuse; Rev. S.J. May (9-5/2)
233. Aylsworth, Mary De Forest (Miss), 22, d 9/28/47 at the home of her father in Utica (funeral at 62 Fayette St.) (9-9/30)
234. Aylsworth, William, formerly of Canaan, Col. Co., d 8/23/26 in Clarence, NY (surv by wife "and a numerous family") (9-10/3)

The index to the above book leads to the starred entry #4096 below:

4094. Haws, Sylvanus S. m 5/22/31 Louisa Hunt, both of Chittenango, in Woodstock (3-5/24)
4095. Hay, George (Hon.), district judge of the U.S. for the district of Virginia, d 9/18/30 in Richmond, VA (6-10/13)
* 4096. Hay, George D., Esq. of Vincennes, IN m 5/10/46 Harriet H. Axtell, youngest dau. of late Rev. Axtell of Geneva, in Indianapolis, IN (**6**-6/26)

The **6** in the end parentheses found in the two starred sets above (entries #227-230 and #4096) identifies the source as the *Geneva Gazette*.

From my book *10,000 Vital Records of Eastern New York, 1777-1834* comes this:

319. Averill, Joseph, about 14, s of Wyman Averill of Peru, NY d 9/5/12 (fell under the wagon on which he was drawing rails) (7-9/11)
320. Averill, Rosannah, wf of Nathan, Sr., d "some days since" in Plattsburgh (7-1/8)
321. Averill, Stephen m 4/4/12 Susannah Moor, dau. of Joel F., in Plattsburgh; Noah Broadwell, Esq. All of Plattsburgh (7-4/17)
322. Avery, Albert of Eaton, (Mad. Co.) m 3/6 Orpah Ransom of Middlefield in M; Rev. Hazelius (3-3/10)
323. Avery, Humphrey J., 23, s of John H. of Owego, NY, d 7/21/31 in Petersburg, VA (1-8/13)
324. Avery, John, m 12/23/23 Caroline Osborn; Rev. Tiffany (3-12/29)
325. Avery, Lewis m 3/4/24 Sally Black in Ballston; Rev. Reuben Smith (2-3/9)
326. Avery, Solomon, 25, d 6/20/08 in Hudson (6-6/28)
* 327. Axtell, _____, age 5, and Axtell, _____, age 3, d 1/26/21 "in the evening in the flames (when) the house of their father, a Mr. Axtell" in Pierpont (St. Law. Co.) burned (copied from the *Potsdam Gazette*) (7-2/3)
* 328. Axtell, Henry of Lawrenceville, NJ m Juliet Lay, dau of John, Esq. of Clinton (Oneida Co.), NY, in Clinton; Rev. D.C. Axtell (**1**-9/18/30)
* 329. Axtell, Phebe, 89, relict of late Maj Henry and mother of Rev. Henry of Geneva, NY, d 7/6/29 near Morristown, NJ (**1**-7/21)
330. Aylsworth, Asahel m Sylvia Olmstead in Canaan (6-2/9/13)
331. Aylsworth, Sylvia, 21, wf of Asahel and dau of Nathaniel Olmstead of Canaan, d 4/13/14 in De Ruyter (Mad. Co.) (6-5/10)
332. Aylsworth, William D., 52, d 3/18/13 in Canaan (6-4/6)
333. Aylwin, John Cushing (Lt.) of U.S. Navy d 1/28/13 at sea on board the frigate *Constitution* (mortally wounded in the battle with the *Java*) (3-3/13)

The **1** and the **7** found within the end parentheses of starred entries #327 through #329 above identify the sources as the *Albany Daily Argus* and the *Plattsburgh Republican* respectively.

The five sets of inserts above reflect cumulatively a total of 60 vital records. These records in turn reflect 117 persons whose towns of residence are clearly defined. When each such person's town of residence is compared to the county of publication of the newspaper within which the applicable record is posted the geographical distributions displayed on the next page are found.

GEOGRAPHICAL DISTRIBUTIONS

residence places	number of persons	percent of total
county of newspaper's publication	54	46.1
counties to the north	3	2.6
counties to the east	14	12.0
counties to the south	12	10.3
counties to the west	15	12.8
New England	3	2.6
states to the south	12	10.3
states to the west	3	2.6
"at sea"	1	0.8

In an attempt to gain a broader perspective in the above regard a total of six newspapers' towns of publication spread across New York were selected with results summarized in Table 1 (the number postings per column reflect percentages of the totals). For each columnar posting 100 sequential vital record postings (wherein residence towns were clearly stated) were reviewed within the central pages of each of my four "vital records" books (the three of previous mention plus *8,000 More Vital Records of Eastern New York, 1804-1850*).

Table 1 is designed solely to illustrate the fact that vital records in newspapers are by no means confined solely to the counties within which these newspapers are published. If larger samplings had been taken the percentage distributions per column might have been appreciably different. For personal convenience only 100 records were reviewed in the formation of each column's distributions. The books from which the records were drawn contain the following numbers of records per town of concern: Batavia 729 (1822-1850), Utica 3722 (1824-1850), Albany 1985 (1829-1831), Ogdensburgh 960 (1826-1843), Poughkeepsie 3380 (1785-1834), and Huntington 1912 (1826-1827 and 1839-1850).

Table 1

GEOGRAPHICAL DISTRIBUTION OF SIX NEWSPAPERS' VITAL RECORD POSTINGS
(numbers reflect percentage of the total per entry per column)

residence places	Western NY Bativia Genesee Co. 495 sq mi	Central NY Utica Oneida Co. 1219 sq mi	Eastern NY Albany Albany Co. 524 sq mi	Northern NY Ogdensburgh St. Law. Co. 2728 sq mi	Southern NY Poughkeepsie Dutchess Co. 804 sq mi	Long Island Huntington Suffolk Co. 912 sq mi
county of newspaper's public.	66.7	63.0	21.7	71.9	67.6	33.3
counties to the north	2.4	3.4	0.9	- -*	11.2	1.3
counties to the east	10.5	8.0	5.5	3.5	- -**	- -**
counties to the south	6.7	5.5	32.2***	9.9	5.3	- -****
counties to the west	4.3	8.4	30.0	0.6	8.5	64.1*****
New England	1.9	2.5	3.7	2.3	3.2	1.3
states to the south	1.9	0.4	2.3	0.6	2.7	0.0
states to the west	4.8	5.9	0.4	2.9	0.0	0.0
other countries	1.8	2.9	3.2	8.2	1.6	0.0

* St. Lawrence County lies on the northern border of New York.

** Dutchess and Suffolk counties lie on the eastern border of New York.

*** One half of the number of persons then reported as living in New York south of Albany County were then living in New York County.

**** Suffolk County lies on the southern border of New York.

***** Distribution of this 64.1%: 24.7% in present-day Nassau County formed from Queens County, January 1, 1899, 28.7% in Kings and Queens Counties and 10.7% in New York and Richmond counties.

APPENDIX B

The locations of cities, towns, and villages across New York state are a direct result of the topography of the state. Towns and villages evolved along the banks of lakes, rivers, and natural harbors in the colonial period of settlement, as these were the nation's first highways. Water was the primary means of transportation with sailing vessels or canoes, the first vehicles.

In the post colonial - pre industrial period, paths and trails spread out from early towns forming a primitive road network into the hinterlands. Often these roads followed early Indian pathways or trappers trails. Horses, oxen, wagons, and the settlers' own two feet were the means of transportation into those newly settled areas of New York where water navigation was impossible.

During the Industrial Revolution, New York's transportation system blossomed. Settlers no longer were dependent on horses, wagons, or sailing vessels. They now had railroads and a new means of water transportation, canals. These latter day transportation systems were capable of distributing more and heavier manufactured goods over a larger area in a shorter period of time. They not only provided transportation but were an early communication link between villages and towns of northern, central, and western New York. The post-colonial US mail service became dependent on these new transportation systems.

New York's newspapers used all these transportation systems extensively. In fact, early newspapers were often mailed to remote towns and posted at town halls so all could read the news of the day.

When seeking vital records in newspapers, the reader should be acutely aware of the transportation systems available for the time and location of the period being researched.

Early-day newspapers of Albany, Kingston, and New York were widely distributed along the Hudson river and often vital records of individuals in towns some distance from the publication source were regularly reported. Thus someone living in Claverack in 1822 might have vital records reported in Albany's or Kingston's newspapers.

Schenectady newspapers were distributed west and Auburn newspapers both east and west in towns situated on the Great Western Turnpike. Buffalo, Rochester, Syracuse, Albany, and Mohawk Valley newspapers were distributed extensively along the Erie canal. Binghamton and Utica papers were distributed along the Chenango canal; Elmira newspapers along the Chemung canal and Utica and Watertown newspapers along the Black River canal.

Railroads also were a major distribution network. Saratoga Springs newspapers were distributed along the Adirondack-North Creek railroad towns of Greenfield, Hadley, Corinth, Luzerne and Warrensburgh. Utica newspapers were distributed along the Adirondack-Lake Placid railroad towns of Forestport, Thendara (Old Forge), Big Moose, Long Lake, Tupper Lake, and Lake Placid.

Early maps are available in many libraries. A glance at a good map of New York state will reveal a wealth of possibilities and new ideas for research.

Thomas J. Lynch

APPENDIX C

Genealogical writings by Fred Q. Bowman

Books

Landholders of Northeastern New York, 1739-1802. 228 pp. Baltimore: Genealogical Publishing Co., 1983

10,000 Vital Records of Western New York, 1809-1850. 318 pp. Baltimore: Genealogical Publishing Co., 1985.

10,000 Vital Records of Central New York, 1813-1850. 338 pp. Baltimore: Genealogical Publishing Co., 1986.

10,000 Vital Records of Eastern New York, 1777-1834. 356 pp. Baltimore: Genealogical Publishing Co., 1987.

New York's Detailed Census of 1855 - Greene County. 277 pp. Rhinebeck, NY: Kinship Publishing, 1988.

8,000 More Records of Eastern New York State, 1804-1850. 287 pp. Rhinebeck, NY: Kinship Publishing, 1991.

Journal Articles

"Redding Grandsons of Thomas[1] Redding," (New England-based) *The Genealogist* 3 (1982): 161.

"Vital Records Listing of an Indian Missionary in Western New York, 1832-1879," *New York Genealogical and Biographical Record* 117 (1986): 20.

"John[1] Horsington of New England," *New England Historical and Genealogical Register* 141 (1987): 38.

Lynch, Thomas J., co-author. "1,100 Vital Records of Northeastern New York, 1835-1850," *New York Genealogical and Biographical Record* 118 (1987): 135.

"Towns and Families of Ontario County, New York - 1790," *Heritage Quest* 46 (July-August, 1993): 54.

Part <u>Two</u>

Alphabetical List of Cities, Villages and Hamlets
Showing Location by County and Town

(6710 communities, many obsolete, here identified)

[Adapted, with approval, from the *Gazetteer - New York State*,
State Department of Health, Albany, 1980 (out of print)]

NAME	COUNTY	TOWN
ABBOTT CORNERS	ERIE	HAMBURG
ABBOTT RD. STA.	ERIE	HAMBURG
ABBYVILLE	LEWIS	GREIG
ACADEMY	ONTARIO	CANANDAIGUA
ACCORD	ULSTER	ROCHESTER
ACIDALIA	SULLIVAN	FREMONT
ACRA	GREENE	CAIRO
ADAMS BASIN	MONROE	OGDEN
ADAMS CORNERS	PUTNAM	PUTNAM VALLEY
ADAMS CROSSING	COLUMBIA	NEW LEBANON
ADAMS CTR.	JEFFERSON	ADAMS
ADAMS V.	JEFFERSON	ADAMS
ADAMSVILLE	WASHINGTON	KINGSBURY
ADAMSVILLE	WASHINGTON	HARTFORD
ADAMSVILLE	ALBANY	BETHLEHEM
ADDISON HILL	STEUBEN	TUSCARORA
ADDISON V.	STEUBEN	ADDISON
ADEN	SULLIVAN	NEVERSINK
ADIRONDACK	WARREN	HORICON
ADIRONDACK CLUB	ESSEX	NEWCOMB
ADIRONDACK SAN.	ESSEX	ST. ARMAND
ADIRONDACK STATE HATCHERY	FRANKLIN	SANTA CLARA
ADRIAN	STEUBEN	CANISTEO
AFTON CENTER	CHENANGO	AFTON
AFTON V.	CHENANGO	AFTON
AGAYAGO	YATES	JERUSALEM
AIDEN LAIR	ESSEX	MINERVA
AIRMONT	ROCKLAND	RAMAPO
AKRON V.	ERIE	NEWSTEAD
ALABAMA	GENESEE	ALABAMA
ALABAMA CTR.	GENESEE	ALABAMA
ALABAMA STA.	GENESEE	ALABAMA
ALBANY C.	ALBANY	ALBANY C.
ALBANY BUSH	MONTGOMERY	MOHAWK
ALBERTSON	NASSAU	NO. HEMPSTEAD
ALBIA	RENSSELAER	TROY C.
ALBION RICHES CTR.	ORLEANS	ALBION
ALBION ST.TR.SCH.	ORLEANS	ALBION
ALBION V.	ORLEANS	GAINES
ALEURG	FRANKLIN	DICKINSON
ALCOVE	ALBANY	COEYMANS
ALDEN CTR.	ERIE	ALDEN
ALDEN V.	ERIE	ALDEN
ALDER BEND	CLINTON	ALTONA
ALDER BROOK	FRANKLIN	FRANKLIN
ALDER BROOK FARMS	FRANKLIN	FRANKLIN
ALDER CREEK	ONEIDA	BOONVILLE
ALDER CREEK STA.	ONEIDA	BOONVILLE
ALDRICH	ST.LAWRENCE	FINE
ALDRICH SETTLEMENT	LEWIS	DIANA
ALENE	MADISON	LINCOLN
ALEXANDER STA.	GENESEE	ALEXANDER
ALEXANDER V.	GENESEE	ALEXANDER
ALEXANDRIA BAY V.	JEFFERSON	ALEXANDRIA
ALEXANDRIA STA.	JEFFERSON	ALEXANDRIA
ALFRED STA.	ALLEGANY	ALFRED
ALFRED V.	ALLEGANY	ALFRED
ALGONA	JEFFERSON	RODMAN
ALGONQUIN	FRANKLIN	HARRIETSTOWN
ALLARD CORNERS	ORANGE	MONTGOMERY
ALLEGANY ST. PARK	CATTARAUGUS	ELKO
ALLEGANY V.	CATTARAUGUS	ALLEGANY
ALLEN	ALLEGANY	ALLEN
ALLEN CREEK	ALLEGANY	ALLEN
ALLEN DISTRICT	JEFFERSON	LORRAINE
ALLENDALE	JEFFERSON	LORRAINE
ALLENS	ESSEX	WESTPORT
ALLENS FALLS	ST.LAWRENCE	PARISHVILLE
ALLENS HILL	ONTARIO	RICHMOND
ALLENTOWN	ALLEGANY	ALMA
ALLIGERVILLE	ULSTER	ROCHESTER
ALLOWAY	WAYNE	LYONS
ALMA	ALLEGANY	ALMA
ALMOND V.	ALLEGANY	ALMOND
ALMOND V.	STEUBEN	HORNELLSVILLE
ALOQUIN	ONTARIO	HOPEWELL
ALPINA	LEWIS	DIANA
ALPINE	SCHUYLER	CATHARINE
ALPINE STATION	SCHUYLER	CATHARINE
ALPLAUS	SCHENECTADY	GLENVILLE
ALPS	RENSSELAER	NASSAU
ALSEN	GREENE	CATSKILL
ALTAMONT V.	ALBANY	GUILDERLAND
ALTAY	SCHUYLER	TYRONE
ALTMAR V.	OSWEGO	ALBION
ALTON	WAYNE	SODUS
ALTONA	CLINTON	ALTONA
ALVERSONS	JEFFERSON	HOUNSFIELD
AMAGANSETT	SUFFOLK	E. HAMPTON
AMAWALK	WESTCHESTER	SOMERS
AMBER	ONONDAGA	OTISCO
AMBLUCO	WYOMING	GENESEE FALLS
AMBOY	ONONDAGA	CAMILLUS
AMBOY CTR.	OSWEGO	AMBOY
AMCHIR V.	ORANGE	MIDDLETOWN C.
AMENIA	DUTCHESS	AMENIA
AMENIA UNION	DUTCHESS	AMENIA
AMES V.	MONTGOMERY	CANAJOHARIE
AMITY	ORANGE	WARWICK
AMITY HARBOR	SUFFOLK	BABYLON
AMITYVILLE V.	SUFFOLK	BABYLON
AMPERSAND	FRANKLIN	HARRIETSTOWN
AMSTERDAM C.	MONTGOMERY;	AMSTERDAM C.
ANAQUASSCOOK	WASHINGTON	JACKSON
ANCRAM	COLUMBIA	ANCRAM
ANCRAM LEAD MINES	COLUMBIA	ANCRAM
ANCRAMDALE	COLUMBIA	ANCRAM
ANDES V.	DELAWARE	ANDES
ANDOVER V.	ALLEGANY	ANDOVER
ANGEL CORNERS	WAYNE	GALEN
ANGELICA V.	ALLEGANY	ANGELICA
ANGLE SEA(OUTSIDE E. ROCKAWAY)	NASSAU	HEMPSTEAD
ANGOLA V.	ERIE	EVANS
ANGOLA-ON-LAKE	ERIE	EVANS
ANGUS	YATES	BENTON
ANNADALE	RICHMOND	NYC
ANNADALE-ON-HUDSON	DUTCHESS	RED HOOK
ANNSVILLE	WESTCHESTER	CORTLANDT
ANOS SIDING	ONEIDA	FORESTPORT
ANSONS CROSSING	DUTCHESS	STANFORD
ANTLERS	HAMILTON	LONG LAKE
ANTWERP	JEFFERSON	ANTWERP
APALACHIN	TIOGA	OWEGO
APAQUOGA	SUFFOLK	E. HAMPTON
APEX	DELAWARE	TOMPKINS
APPELGATE	TOMPKINS	ENFIELD
APPLETON	NIAGARA	NEWFANE
APULIA	ONONDAGA	FABIUS
APULIA STA.	ONONDAGA	FABIUS
AQUEBOGUE	SUFFOLK	RIVERHEAD
AQUEDUCT	QUEENS	NYC
AQUETUCK	ALBANY	COEYMANS
ARBUTUS	BROOME	MAINE
ARCADE V.	WYOMING	ARCADE
ARCADIA	WAYNE	ARCADIA
ARCHDALE	WASHINGTON	EASTON
ARCHVILLE	WESTCHESTER	MT. PLEASANT
ARDEN	ORANGE	TUXEDO
ARDEN HOUSE	ORANGE	TUXEDO
ARDONIA	ULSTER	PLATTEKILL
AROSLEY V.	WESTCHESTER	GREENBURGH
ARENA	DELAWARE	MIDDLETOWN
ARGUSVILLE	SCHOHARIE	SHARON
ARGUSVILLE	SCHOHARIE	CARLISLE
ARGYLE V.	WASHINGTON	ARGYLE
ARIETTA	HAMILTON	ARIETTA
ARISTOTLE	ALLEGANY	ANGELICA
ARKPORT V.	STEUBEN	HORNELLSV'L
ARKVILLE	DELAWARE	MIDDLETOWN
ARKWRIGHT	CHAUTAUQUA	ARKWRIGHT
ARKWRIGHT SUM.	CHAUTAUQUA	ARKWRIGHT
ARLINGTON	DUTCHESS	POUGHKEEPSIE
ARLINGTON	RICHMOND	NYC
ARMONK	WESTCHESTER	NO. CASTLE
ARMOR	ERIE	ORCHARD PARK
ARMOR	ERIE	HAMBURG
ARNOLD HILL	CLINTON	AUSABLE
ARNOT	CHEMUNG	CHEMUNG
ARROCHAR	RICHMOND	NYC
ARTHUR	OSWEGO	MEXICO
ARTHURSBURG	DUTCHESS	LAGRANGE
ARTIC	DELAWARE	MASONVILLE
ARVERNE	QUEENS	NYC
ASBURY	TOMPKINS	LANSING
ASBURY	ULSTER	SAUGERTIES
ASHANTEE	LIVINGSTON	AVON
ASHAROKEN V.	SUFFOLK	HUNTINGTON
ASHFORD	CATTARAUGUS	ASHFORD
ASHFORD HOLL.	CATTARAUGUS	ASHFORD
ASHFORD JCT.	CATTARAUGUS	ELLICOTTVILLE
ASHFORD STA.	CATTARAUGUS	ASHFORD
ASHGROVE	WASHINGTON	WHITE CREEK
ASHLAND	GREENE	ASHLAND
ASHOKAN	ULSTER	OLIVE
ASHVILLE	CHAUTAUQUA	NO. HARMONY
ASHWOOD	ORLEANS	CARLTON
ASHWOOD	ORLEANS	YATES
ASTORIA	QUEENS	NYC
ATHENS JCT.	SCHENECTADY	ROTTERDAM
ATHENS V.	GREENE	ATHENS
ATHOL	WARREN	THURMAN
ATHOL SPRGS.	ERIE	HAMBURG
ATLANTA	STEUBEN	COHOCTON
ATLANTIC BEACH V.	NASSAU	HEMPSTEAD
ATLANTICVILLE	SUFFOLK	SOUTHAMPTON
ATTICA CORRECTIONAL FACILITY	WYOMING	ATTICA T.
ATTICA CTR.	WYOMING	ATTICA
ATTICA V.	WYOMING	ATTICA
ATTLEBURY	DUTCHESS	STANFORD
ATWATER	CAYUGA	GENOA
ATWELL	HERKIMER	OHIO

C=City V=Village

The source citation is found on the previous page.

NAME	COUNTY	TOWN
ATWOOD	ULSTER	MARBLETOWN
AUBURN C.	CAYUGA	AUBURN C.
AUBURN CORRECTIONAL FACILITY	CAYUGA	AUBURN C.
AUBURN JCT.	TOMPKINS	ITHACA
AUBURNDALE	QUEENS	NYC
AUGUSTA	ORANGE	TUXEDO
AUGUSTA	ONEIDA	AUGUSTA
AURELIUS	CAYUGA	AURELIUS
AURELIUS STA.	CAYUGA	AURELIUS
AURIESVILLE	MONTGOMERY	GLEN
AURORA V.	CAYUGA	LEDYARD
AUSABLE CHASM	CLINTON	AUSABLE
AUSABLE FORKS	CLINTON	BLACK BROOK
AUSABLE FORKS	ESSEX	JAY
AUSABLE FORKS P.O.	ESSEX	JAY
AUSABLE FORKS STA.	ESSEX	JAY
AUSKERADA	FULTON	CAROGA
AUSTERLITZ	COLUMBIA	AUSTERLITZ
AUSTIN	CAYUGA	NILES
AVA	ONEIDA	AVA
AVERILL PARK	RENSSELAER	SAND LAKE
AVERY PLACE	HAMILTON	ARIETTA
AVERYVILLE	ESSEX	NO. ELBA
AVOCA V.	STEUBEN	AVOCA
AVON SPRGS.	LIVINGSTON	AVON
AVON V.	LIVINGSTON	AVON
AWOSTING	ULSTER	SHAWANGUNK
AXTON	FRANKLIN	HARRIETSTOWN
AXVILLE	CATTARAUGUS	CONEWANGO

-B-

NAME	COUNTY	TOWN
BABCOCK HILL	ONEIDA	BRIDGEWATER
BABCOCK LAKE	RENSSELAER	GRAFTON
BABYLON V.	SUFFOLK	BABYLON
BACKUS	ST.LAWRENCE	PITCAIRN
BACON	ST.LAWRENCE	PITCAIRN
BACON HILL	SARATOGA	NORTHUMBERLAND
BACON STA.	ST.LAWRENCE	PITCAIRN
BAGDAD	ERIE	COLLINS
BAGGS	CLINTON	PERU
BAILEYTOWN	ORANGE	WOODBURY
BAINBRIDGE V.	CHENANGO	BAINBRIDGE
BAIRD CORNERS	SCHOHARIE	JEFFERSON
BAITING HOLLOW	SUFFOLK	RIVERHEAD
BAKER	WARREN	STONY CREEK
BAKER CORNERS	HERKIMER	SCHUYLER
BAKERS FALLS	SARATOGA	MOREAU
BAKERS MILLS	WARREN	JOHNSBURG
BALCOM	CHAUTAUQUA	VILLENOVA
BALCOM CORNERS	CHAUTAUQUA	VILLENOVA
BALD MT.	WASHINGTON	GREENWICH
BALDWIN	NASSAU	HEMPSTEAD
BALDWIN CORNER	WASHINGTON	KINGSBURY
BALDWIN HARBOR	NASSAU	HEMPSTEAD
BALDWIN PLACE	WESTCHESTER	SOMERS
BALDWINSVILLE V.	ONONDAGA	VAN BUREN
BALDWINSVILLE V.	ONONDAGA	LYSANDER
BALFOUR	ESSEX	MINERVA
BALLINA	MADISON	CAZENOVIA
BALLSTON JCT.	SARATOGA	MALTA
BALLSTON LAKE	SARATOGA	BALLSTON
BALLSTON LAKE	SARATOGA	CLIFTON PARK
BALLSTON SPA V.	SARATOGA	BALLSTON
BALLSTON SPA V.	SARATOGA	MILTON
BALLSTON STA.	SARATOGA	MILTON
BALMAT	ST.LAWRENCE	FOWLER
BALMVILLE	ORANGE	NEWBURGH
BANGALL	DUTCHESS	STANFORD
BANGOR	FRANKLIN	BANGOR
BANGOR STA.	FRANKLIN	BANGOR
BANKSVILLE	WESTCHESTER	NO. CASTLE
BANNERHOUSE	FRANKLIN	BELLMONT
BAPTIST HILL	ONTARIO	BRISTOL
BAPTIST 4 CORS.	CAYUGA	OWASCO
BARBER CORS.	CAYUGA	LEDYARD
BARBERS	CHENANGO	NORWICH
BARBERVILLE	RENSSELAER	POESTENKILL
BARBOURVILLE	DELAWARE	DEPOSIT
BARBURS STA.	CHENANGO	NORWICH
BARCELONA	CHAUTAUQUA	WESTFIELD
BARDONIA	ROCKLAND	CLARKSTOWN
BARDWELL MILLS	ONEIDA	TRENTON
BARETOWN	ONEIDA	WESTERN
BARKER CHURCH	YATES	ITALY
BARKER V.	NIAGARA	SOMERSET
BARKERSVILLE	SARATOGA	PROVIDENCE
BARKERTOWN	LIVINGSTON	NUNDA
BARNARD	MONROE	GREECE
BARNARD CROSS.	MONROE	GREECE
BARNERVILLE	SCHOHARIE	COBLESKILL
BARNES	ONEIDA	BOONVILLE
BARNES CORS.	LEWIS	PINCKNEY
BARNES HOLE	SUFFOLK	E. HAMPTON
BARNEVELD	ONEIDA	TRENTON
BARNEY	TOMPKINS	DRYDEN

NAME	COUNTY	TOWN
BARNEY MILLS	STEUBEN	W. UNION
BARNHARTS	ST.LAWRENCE	MASSENA
BARNUM ISLAND	NASSAU	HEMPSTEAD
BARNVELD V.	ONEIDA	TRENTON
BARRE CTR.	ORLEANS	BARRE
BARREN ISLAND	KINGS	NYC
BARRETT HOLL.	DELAWARE	SIDNEY
BARRINGTON	YATES	BARRINGTON
BARRYTOWN	DUTCHESS	RED HOOK
BARRYTOWN CRS.	DUTCHESS	RED HOOK
BARRYVILLE	SULLIVAN	HIGHLAND
BARTLETT	ONEIDA	WESTMORELAND
BARTLETT CARRY	FRANKLIN	HARRIETSTOWN
BARTO HILL	HERKIMER	FAIRFIELD
BARTON	TIOGA	BARTON
BARTON CTR.	TIOGA	BARTON
BARTON-ON-SD.	WESTCHESTER	PELHAM
BARTONVILLE	CLINTON	PERU
BARTOW	BRONX	NYC
BASKET	SULLIVAN	FREMONT
BASOM	GENESEE	ALABAMA
BATAVIA C.	GENESEE	BATAVIA C.
BATCHELLERV'L	SARATOGA	EDINBURG
BATCHFORD	LEWIS	GREIG
BATES	SCHOHARIE	BROOME
BATH BEACH	KINGS	NYC
BATH V.	STEUBEN	BATH
BATH-ON-HUDSON	RENSSELAER	RENSSELAER
BATTENVILLE	WASHINGTON	GREENWICH
BAXTER ESTATES V.	NASSAU	N. HEMPSTEAD
BAY CHESTER	BRONX	NYC
BAY HEAD STA.	SUFFOLK	SOUTHAMPTON
BAY PARK	NASSAU	HEMPSTEAD
BAY POND	FRANKLIN	SANTA CLARA
BAY POND STA.	FRANKLIN	SANTA CLARA
BAY RIDGE	KINGS	NYC
BAY SHORE	SUFFOLK	ISLIP
BAY SHORE MANOR	QUEENS	NYC
BAY SIDE	QUEENS	NYC
BAY VIEW	CHAUTAUQUA	ELLERY
BAY VIEW	ERIE	HAMBURG
BAY VIEW STA.	ERIE	HAMBURG
BAYPORT	SUFFOLK	ISLIP
BAYVILLE V.	NASSAU	OYSTER BAY
BEACH CHANNEL STA.	QUEENS	NYC
BEACH RIDGE	NIAGARA	PENDLETON
BEACHER	HAMILTON	INLET
BEACHERTOWN	ST.LAWRENCE	STOCKHOLM
BEACHES COR.	GREENE	JEWETT
BEACHVIEW	GREENE	CATSKILL
BEACHWOOD PARK	MONROE	HAMLIN
BEACON C.	DUTCHESS	BEACON C.
BEAN HILL	JEFFERSON	ALEXANDRIA
BEANS	STEUBEN	PRATTSBURG
BEANTOWN	CHEMUNG	CHEMUNG
BEAR MARKET	DUTCHESS	STANFORD
BEAR MOUNTAIN	ROCKLAND	STONY POINT
BEAR TOWN	LEWIS	CROGHAN
BEARD HOLLOW	SCHOHARIE	RICHMONDVILLE
BEARSVILLE	ULSTER	WOODSTOCK
BEATIE	MONROE	GREECE
BEAVER	CATTARAUGUS	ASHFORD
BEAVER BROOK	SULLIVAN	TUSTEN
BEAVER DAM	ORANGE	MONTGOMERY
BEAVER DAMS	SCHUYLER	DIX
BEAVER DAMS STA.	ORANGE	MONTGOMERY
BEAVER FALLS	LEWIS	NEW BREMEN
BEAVER FALLS	LEWIS	CROGHAN
BEAVER KILL	SULLIVAN	ROCKLAND
BEAVER LAKE	CATTARAUGUS	FREEDOM
BEAVER MEADOW	CHENANGO	OTSELIC
BEAVER RIVER	HERKIMER	WEBB
BECKERS CORS.	ALBANY	BETHLEHEM
BEDELL	DELAWARE	ROXBURY
BEDFORD	WESTCHESTER	BEDFORD
BEDFORD	KINGS	NYC
BEDFORD HILLS	WESTCHESTER	BEDFORD
BEDFORD HILLS CORRECTIONAL FAC	WESTCHESTER	BEDFORD
BEDFORD PARK STA.	BRONX	NYC
BEDFORD STA.	KINGS	NYC
BEDFORD VILLAGE	WESTCHESTER	BEDFORD
BEDLOE ISLAND	NEW YORK	NYC
BEECHER CAMP	HAMILTON	INLET
BEECHER HOLLOW	SARATOGA	EDINBURG
BEECHERTOWN	ST.LAWRENCE	STOCKHOLM
BEECHERVILLE	OSWEGO	ORWELL
BEECHHURST	QUEENS	NYC
BEECHVILLE	STEUBEN	DANSVILLE
BEECHWOOD	MONROE	ROCHESTER C.
BEEKMAN	DUTCHESS	BEEKMAN
BEEKMAN CORS.	SCHOHARIE	SHARON
BEEKMANTOWN	CLINTON	BEEKMANTOWN
BEERS	TIOGA	OWEGO
BEERSTON	DELAWARE	WALTON
BELCHER	WASHINGTON	HEBRON
BELCODA	MONROE	WHEATLAND

NAME	COUNTY	TOWN	NAME	COUNTY	TOWN
BELDEN	BROOME	COLESVILLE	BINGHAMTON C.	BROOME	BINGHAMTON C.
BELFAST	ALLEGANY	BELFAST	BINGHAMTON PSYCHIATRIC CTR.	BROOME	BINGHAMTON C.
BELFAST MILLS	GREENE	CATSKILL	BINGLEY	MADISON	FENNER
BELFORT	LEWIS	CROGHAN	BINGLEY MILLS	MADISON	CAZENOVIA
BELFREY HILL	ESSEX	MORIAH	BINGLEY STA.	MADISON	FENNER
BELL	OSWEGO	VOLNEY			
BELL TOWN	CAYUGA	GENOA	BINNEWATER	ULSTER	ROSENDALE
BELLAIRE	QUEENS	NYC	BIRD	CATTARAUGUS	MACHIAS
BELLE TERRE V.	SUFFOLK	BROOKHAVEN	BIRDSALL	ALLEGANY	BIRDSALL
BELLEAYRE	ULSTER	HARDENBURGH	BIRMINGHAM F'LS	ESSEX	CHESTERFIELD
BELLEROSE MANOR	QUEENS	NYC	BISHOP COPS.	WYOMING	CASTILE
BELLEROSE TERRACE	NASSAU	HEMPSTEAD	BISHOP STREET	JEFFERSON	HENDERSON
BELLEROSE V.	NASSAU	HEMPSTEAD	BISHOPVILLE	ALLEGANY	ALMOND
BELLEVIEW	CHAUTAUQUA	ELLERY	BLACK BRIDGE	HAMILTON	WELLS
BELLEVILLE	JEFFERSON	ELLISBURG	BLACK BROOK	CLINTON	BLACK BROOK
BELLEVUE	ERIE	CHEEKTOWAGA	BLACK CREEK	ALLEGANY	NEW HUDSON
BELLINGERTOWN	ONEIDA	FORESTPORT	BLACK GROCERY	COLUMBIA	COPAKE
BELLMONT	FRANKLIN	BELLMONT	BLACK LAKE	SULLIVAN	BETHEL
BELLMONT CTR.	FRANKLIN	BELLMONT	BLACK LAKE	ST.LAWRENCE	MORRISTOWN
BELLMORE	NASSAU	HEMPSTEAD	BLACK RIVER V.	JEFFERSON	RUTLAND
BELLONA	YATES	BENTON	BLACK RIVER V.	JEFFERSON	LERAY
BELLONA STA.	YATES	BENTON	BLACK ROCK	ERIE	BUFFALO C.
BELLPORT V.	SUFFOLK	BROOKHAVEN	BLACK ROCK	CAYUGA	LEDYARD
BELLVALE	ORANGE	WARWICK	BLACK ROCK STA.	ERIE	BUFFALO C.
BELLWOOD	LEWIS	HARRISBURG	BLAINE	MONTGOMERY	CANAJOHARIE
BELMONT	BRONX	NYC	BLAKE	ST.LAWRENCE	PAPISHVILLE
BELMONT CTR.	BRONX	NYC	BLAKESLEE STA.	MADISON	SULLIVAN
BELMONT V.	ALLEGANY	AMITY	BLASDELL V.	ERIE	HAMBURG
BELVIDERE	ALLEGANY	AMITY	BLATCHLEY	BROOME	WINDSOR
BEMIS HGTS.	SARATOGA	STILLWATER	BLAUVELT	ROCKLAND	ORANGETOWN
BEMUS POINT V.	CHAUTAUQUA	ELLERY	BLEECKER	FULTON	BLEECKER
BENEDICT	FULTON	BROADALBIN	BLEECKER CENTER	FULTON	BLEECKER
BENNETT	ONTARIO	PHELPS	BLISS	WYOMING	EAGLE
BENNETT BRIDGE	OSWEGO	ORWELL	BLISS SUMMIT	WYOMING	EAGLE
BENNETT CREEK	STEUBEN	CANISTEO	BLISSVILLE	QUEENS	NYC
BENNETTS	ALLEGANY	W. ALMOND	BLIVINVILLE	GREENE	CATSKILL
BENNETTS	STEUBEN	CANISTEO	BLOCKVILLE	CHAUTAUQUA	HARMONY
BENNETTS STA.	STEUBEN	CANISTEO	BLODGETT MILLS	CORTLAND	CORTLANDVILLE
BENNETTSBURG	SCHUYLER	HECTOR	BLOODVILLE	SARATOGA	MILTON
BENNETTSVILLE	CHENANGO	BAINBRIDGE	BLOODY CORS.	GENESEE	ALEXANDER
BENNINGTON	WYOMING	BENNINGTON	BLOOMERVILLE	STEUBEN	AVOCA
BENNINGTON COR.	WYOMING	BENNINGTON	BLOOMFIELD	RICHMOND	NYC
BENNINGTON CTR.	WYOMING	BENNINGTON	BLOOMING GROVE	ORANGE	BLOOMING GR.
BENSON	HAMILTON	BENSON	BLOOMING GROVE STA.	ORANGE	BLOOMING GR.
BENSON COR.	ROCKLAND	STONY POINT	BLOOMINGBURG V.	SULLIVAN	MAMAKATING
BENSON MINES	ST.LAWRENCE	CLIFTON	BLOOMINGDALE P.O.	FRANKLIN	FRANKLIN
BENSONHURST	KINGS	NYC	BLOOMINGDALE STA.	FRANKLIN	FRANKLIN
BENT STLT.	LEWIS	CROGHAN	BLOOMINGDALE V.	ESSEX	ST. ARMAND
BENTLEY CORS.	JEFFERSON	ANTWERP	BLOOMINGTON	ULSTER	ROSENDALE
BENTON CTR.	YATES	BENTON	BLOOMVILLE	DELAWARE	KORTRIGHT
BENTON STA.	YATES	BENTON	BLOSSOM	ERIE	ELMA
BERATOWN	CLINTON	BEEKMANTOWN	BLOSSVALE	ONEIDA	ANNSVILLE
BERBANK	DUTCHESS	LAGRANGE	BLUE MOUNTAIN	ULSTER	SAUGERTIES
BEREA	ORANGE	MONTGOMERY	BLUE MT. LAKE	HAMILTON	INDIAN LAKE
BERGEN BEACH	KINGS	NYC	BLUE POINT	SUFFOLK	BROOKHAVEN
BERGEN STA.	GENESEE	BERGEN	BLUE STORES	COLUMBIA	LIVINGSTON
BERGEN V.	GENESEE	BERGEN	BLUESTONE	WYOMING	GENESEE FALLS
BERGHOLTZ	NIAGARA	WHEATFIELD	BLUFF POINT	CLINTON	PLATTSBURG
BERKSHIRE	TIOGA	BERKSHIRE	BLUFF POINT	STEUBEN	DANSVILLE
BERKSHIRE	FULTON	JOHNSTOWN	BLUFF POINT	YATES.	JERUSALEM
BERLIN	RENSSELAER	BERLIN	BLYTHEBURNE	KINGS	NYC
BERNE	ALBANY	BERNE	BOG LAKE STA.	HAMILTON	LONG LAKE
BERNHARDS BAY	OSWEGO	CONSTANTIA	BOGHT CORS.	ALBANY	COLONIE
BERRY BROOK	DELAWARE	COLCHESTER	BOHEMIA	SUFFOLK	ISLIP
BERRYVILLE	MONTGOMERY	MOHAWK	BOICE	ST.LAWRENCE	LISBON
BESEMER STA.	TOMPKINS	CAROLINE	BOICEVILLE	ULSTER	OLIVE
BESEMERS	TOMPKINS	DRYDEN	BOLIVAR	MADISON	SULLIVAN
BEST	RENSSELAER	E. GREENBUSH	BOLIVAR V.	ALLEGANY	BOLIVAR
BETHANY	GENESEE	BETHANY	BOLT CORS.	CAYUGA	SCIPIO
BETHANY CTR.	GENESEE	BETHANY	BOLTON	WARREN	BOLTON
BETHEL	SULLIVAN	BETHEL	BOLTON LDG.	WARREN	BOLTON
BETHEL	HERKIMER	LITTLE FALLS	BOMBAY	FRANKLIN	BOMBAY
BETHEL	CAYUGA	IRA	BONAPARTE	LEWIS	DIANA
BETHLEHEM	ALBANY	BETHLEHEM	BONITA	CHAUTAUQUA	ELLICOTT
BETHLEHEM	ORANGE	CORNWALL	BONNICASTLE	WAYNE	HURON
BETHLEHEM	MONROE	ROCHESTER C.	BONNY	CHENANGO	SMYRNA
BETHLEHEM CTR.	ALBANY	BETHLEHEM	BONNY HILL	STEUBEN	THURSTON
BETHPAGE	NASSAU	OYSTER BAY	BOOMERTOWN	CHAUTAUQUA	BUSTI
BETHPAGE	NASSAU	HEMPSTEAD	BOONVILLE V.	ONEIDA	BOONVILLE
BETTSBURG	CHENANGO	AFTON	BORDEN	STEUBEN	WOODHULL
BEULAH	MONROE	WHEATLAND	BOREAS RIVER	ESSEX	MINERVA
BIBLE SCH. PK.	BROOME	JOHNSON C., V.	BORNT HILL	TIOGA	OWEGO
BICKNELLVILLE	ST.LAWRENCE	STOCKHOLM	BORODINO	ONONDAGA	SPAFFORD
BIG BROOK	ONEIDA	WESTERN	BOSTON	ERIE	BOSTON
BIG CREEK	STEUBEN	FREMONT	BOSTON CORS.	COLUMBIA	ANCRAM
BIG FLATS	CHEMUNG	BIG FLATS	BOSTON CTR.	ERIE	BOSTON
BIG HOLLOW	GREENE	WINDHAM	BOSWELL CORS.	COLUMBIA	ANCRAM
BIG INDIAN	ULSTER	SHANDAKEN	BOUCKVILLE	MADISON	MADISON
BIG ISLAND	ORANGE	WARWICK	BOUQUET	ESSEX	ESSEX
BIG MOOSE	HERKIMER	WEBB	BOUQUET	ESSEX	WILLSBORO
BIG TREE	ERIE	HAMBURG	BOURNE	OTSEGO	OTSEGO
BIG TUPPER	FRANKLIN	ALTAMONT	BOVINA	DELAWARE	BOVINA
BIG WOLFE LAKE	FRANKLIN	ALTAMONT	BOVINA CTR.	DELAWARE	BOVINA
BIGELOW	ST.LAWRENCE	DE KALB	BOVINA VALLEY	DELAWARE	BOVINA
BIGELOW CORS.	WYOMING	GENESEE FALLS	BOWEN	CATTARAUGUS	RANDOLPH
BILLINGS	DUTCHESS	LAGRANGE	BOWEN CORS.	OSWEGO	GRANBY
BINGHAM MILLS	COLUMBIA	LIVINGSTON	BOWERTON	OTSEGO	MIDDLEFIELD

NAME	COUNTY	TOWN
BOWLER	ALLEGANY	GENESEE
BOWMAN CREEK	MONTGOMERY	CANAJOHARIE
BOWMANSVILLE	ERIE	LANCASTER
BOYD	LEWIS	MONTAGUE
BOYD CORS.	PUTNAM	KENT
BOYLSTON	OSWEGO	BOYLSTON
BOYLSTON CTR.	OSWEGO	BOYLSTON
BOYNTONVILLE	RENSSELAER	PITTSTOWN
BRADFORD	STEUBEN	BRADFORD
BRADFORD JCT.	CATTARAUGUS	GREAT VALLEY
BRADLEY	SULLIVAN	FALLSBURG
BRADLEY POND	CLINTON	DANNEMORA
BRADLEY PT. KLN.	CLINTON	DANNEMORA
BRADTVILLE	FULTON	EPHRATAH
BRAINARD	RENSSELAER	NASSAU
BRAINARD CORS.	OTSEGO	EXETER
BRAINARD STA.	RENSSELAER	NASSAU
BRAINARDSVILLE	FRANKLIN	BELLMONT
BRAMAN CORS.	SCHENECTADY	DUANESBURG
BRAMANVILLE	SCHOHARIE	COBLESKILL
BRANCH	ULSTER	DENNING
BRANCHPORT	YATES	JERUSALEM
BRANDON	FRANKLIN	SANTA CLARA
BRANDRETH LAKE	HAMILTON	LONG LAKE
BRANDY BROOK	CLINTON	ELLENBURG
BRANT	ERIE	BRANT
BRANT LAKE	WARREN	HORICON
BRANTINGHAM	LEWIS	GREIG
BRASHER CTR.	ST.LAWRENCE	BRASHER
BRASHER FALLS	ST.LAWRENCE	BRASHER
BRASHER IRON WKS.	ST.LAWRENCE	BRASHER
BRASHER STA.	ST.LAWRENCE	STOCKHOLM
BRAYTON	WARREN	QUEENSBURY
BRAYTON CORS.	HERKIMER	NEWPORT
BREAKABEEN	SCHOHARIE	FULTON
BREARLEY	TOMPKINS	CAROLINE
BREED	ESSEX	CROWN POINT
BREESPORT	CHEMUNG	HORSEHEADS
BREEZE HILL	ORANGE	WAWAYANDA
BRENTWOOD	SUFFOLK	ISLIP
BRENTWOOD PK.	SUFFOLK	ISLIP
BREWER CORS.	ALLEGANY	GROVE
BREWERTON	ONONDAGA	CICERO
BREWSTER V.	PUTNAM	SOUTHEAST
BRIARCLIFF MANOR V.	WESTCHESTER	OSSINING
BRIARCLIFF MANOR V.	WESTCHESTER	MT.PLEASANT
BRICE	ORLEANS	CARLTON
BRICE STA.	ORLEANS	CARLTON
BRICK CHURCH	CAYUGA	CATO
BRIDGEHAMPTON	SUFFOLK	SOUTHAMPTON
BRIDGEPORT	SENECA	SENECA FALLS
BRIDGEPORT	MADISON	SULLIVAN
BRIDGEPORT	ONONDAGA	CICERO
BRIDGEVILLE	SULLIVAN	THOMPSON
BRIDGEWATER V.	ONEIDA	BRIDGEWATER
BRIER HILL	ST.LAWRENCE	MORRISTOWN
BRIGGS	ST.LAWRENCE	FINE
BRIGGS CRS.	WASHINGTON	WHITE CREEK
BRIGGS STA.	DUTCHESS	LAGRANGE
BRIGGSTREET	ULSTER	WAWARSING
BRIGHTON	MONROE	BRIGHTON
BRIGHTON BEACH	KINGS	NYC
BRIGHTON CORS.	WASHINGTON	WHITE CREEK
BRIGHTON CORS.	OTSEGO	RICHFIELD
BRIGHTSIDE	HAMILTON	LONG LAKE
BRIGHTWATERS V.	SUFFOLK	ISLIP
BRINCKERHOFF	DUTCHESS	FISHKILL
BRISBEN	CHENANGO	GREENE
BRISCOE	SULLIVAN	BETHEL
BRISTOL	ONTARIO	BRISTOL
BRISTOL CTR.	ONTARIO	BRISTOL
BRISTOL SPRGS.	ONTARIO	SO. BRISTOL
BROAD CHANNEL STA.	QUEENS	NYC
BROAD ST. HOLL.	GREENE	LEXINGTON
BROADALBIN JCT.	FULTON	MAYFIELD
BROADALBIN V.	FULTON	BROADALBIN
BROADWAY	QUEENS	NYC
BROCKPORT V.	MONROE	SWEDEN
BROCKVILLE	ORLEANS	MURRAY
BROCKWAY CORS.	ONEIDA	CAMDEN
BROCKWAY CORS.	DUTCHESS	FISHKILL
BROCTON V.	CHAUTAUQUA	PORTLAND
BROKENSTRAW	CHAUTAUQUA	HARMONY
BRONXVILLE MANOR	WESTCHESTER	EASTCHESTER
BROOKDALE	ST.LAWRENCE	STOCKHOLM
BROOKDALE STA.	MONROE	CHILI
BROOKFIELD	MADISON	BROOKFIELD
BROOKHAVEN	SUFFOLK	BROOKHAVEN
BROOKLYN	KINGS	NYC
BROOKMAN COR.	MONTGOMERY	MINDEN
BROOKS GROVE	LIVINGSTON	MT. MORRIS
BROOKSBURG	GREENE	WINDHAM
BROOKTON	TOMPKINS	CAROLINE
BROOKTONDALE	TOMPKINS	CAROLINE
BROOKVALE	BROOME	KIRKWOOD
BROOKVIEW	RENSSELAER	SCHODACK
BROOKVILLE	GENESEE	ALEXANDER
BROOKVILLE V.	NASSAU	OYSTER BAY
BROOKWOOD	SARATOGA	HALFMOON
BROOME CTR.	SCHOHARIE	GILBOA
BROOME DEVELOPMENT CTR.	BROOME	DICKINSON
BROTHERTON	ONEIDA	MARSHALL
BROWN STA.	ULSTER	OLIVE
BROWN'S CORS.	JEFFERSON	ALEXANDRIA
BROWN'S HOLL.	MONTGOMERY	ROOT
BROWNTOWN	STEUBEN	CATON
BROWNVILLE	ONTARIO	FARMINGTON
BROWNVILLE V.	JEFFERSON	BROWNVILLE
BRONXVILLE V.	WESTCHESTER	EASTCHESTER
BRUCEVILLE	ULSTER	ROSENDALE
BRUNER FALLS	ST.LAWRENCE	HOPKINTON
BRUNSWICK	RENSSELAER	BRUNSWICK
BRUNSWICK CTR.	RENSSELAER	BRUNSWICK
BRUSHLAND	DELAWARE	BOVINA
BRUSHTON V.	FRANKLIN	MOIRA
BRUYNSWICK	ULSTER	SHAWANGUNK
BRYN MAWR PK.	WESTCHESTER	YONKERS C.
BUCHANAN V.	WESTCHESTER	CORTLANDT
BUCK BROOK	SULLIVAN	FREMONT
BUCK'S CORS.	ONEIDA	BOONVILLE
BUCKBEES CORS.	MONROE	CHILI
BUCKBROOK	SULLIVAN	CALLICOON
BUCKS BRIDGE	ST.LAWRENCE	POTSDAM
BUCKTON	ST.LAWRENCE	STOCKHOLM
BUCKTOOTH	CATTARAUGUS	SALAMANCA
BUCKTOOTH RUN	CATTARAUGUS	SALAMANCA
BUEL	MONTGOMERY	CANAJOHARIE
BUENA VISTA	STEUBEN	HOWARD
BUFFALO C	ERIE	BUFFALO C.
BUFFALO PSYCHIATRIC CENTER	ERIE	BUFFALO C.
BULL HEAD	DUTCHESS	CLINTON
BULL RUN	ULSTER	DENNING
BULL'S HEAD	RICHMOND	NYC
BULLVILLE	ORANGE	CRAWFORD
BUNDY	OSWEGO	VOLNEY
BUNGTOWN	HERKIMER	SALISBURY
BUNKER	CAYUGA	LEDYARD
BURDEN	COLUMBIA	LIVINGSTON
BURDETT V.	SCHUYLER	HECTOR
BURDICK CRSG.	ESSEX	CROWN POINT
BURDICKS	ESSEX	CROWN POINT
BURHAM PT. PK.	JEFFERSON	CAPE VINCENT
BURK HILL	WYOMING	PERRY
BURKE CTR.	FRANKLIN	BURKE
BURKE V.	FRANKLIN	BURKE
BURLINGHAM	SULLIVAN	MAMAKATING
BURLINGTON	OTSEGO	BURLINGTON
BURLINGTON FLATS	OTSEGO	BURLINGTON
BURNETT	LEWIS	DIANA
BURNHAMS	CHAUTAUQUA	STOCKTON
BURNS	STEUBEN	DANSVILLE
BURNS VILLAGE	ALLEGANY	BURNS
BURNSIDE	ORANGE	HAMPTONBURG
BURNSIDE STA.	ORANGE	HAMPTONBURG
BURNT HILLS	SARATOGA	BALLSTON
BURNWOOD	DELAWARE	HANCOCK
BURRELL CORS.	HERKIMER	SALISBURY
BURRS MILLS	JEFFERSON	WATERTOWN
BURRVILLE	JEFFERSON	WATERTOWN
BURT	NIAGARA	NEWFANE
BURT COOMER	NIAGARA	NEWFANE
BURTONVILLE	MONTGOMERY	CHARLESTON
BUSHES BRIDGE	ERIE	TONAWANDA C.
BUSHES LANDING	LEWIS	WATSON
BUSHNELL BASIN	MONROE	PERINTON
BUSHNELLVILLE	GREENE	LEXINGTON
BUSHVILLE	SULLIVAN	BETHEL
BUSHVILLE	SULLIVAN	THOMPSON
BUSHVILLE	ORANGE	GREENVILLE
BUSHWICK	KINGS	NYC
BUSHWICK JCT.	KINGS	NYC
BUSKIRK	RENSSELAER	HOOSICK
BUSKIRK BRIDGE	WASHINGTON	CAMBRIDGE
BUSTI	CHAUTAUQUA	BUSTI
BUTCHER HILL	SENECA	LODI
BUTLER CORS.	OTSEGO	ROSEBOOM
BUTLER CTR.	WAYNE	BUTLER
BUTLER SETT.	WAYNE	BUTLER
BUTTERFIELD MILLS	ST.LAWRENCE	CANTON
BUTTERFLY	OSWEGO	NEW HAVEN
BUTTERMILK	TOMPKINS	ITHACA
BUTTERMILK FALLS	COLUMBIA	CLAVERACK
BUTTERNUT GROVE	DELAWARE	COLCHESTER
BUTTERNUTS	OTSEGO	BUTTERNUTS
BUTTS CORS.	DELAWARE	DAVENPORT
BYERSVILLE	LIVINGSTON	W. SPARTA
BYRON	GENESEE	BYRON
BYRON CTR. STA.	GENESEE	BYRON

NAME	COUNTY	TOWN
	-C-	
CAANAN LAKE	SUFFOLK	BROOKHAVEN
CABIN HILL	DELAWARE	ANDES
CADIZ	CATTARAUGUS	FRANKLINVILLE
CADOSIA	DELAWARE	HANCOCK
CADY STA.	GENESEE	ALEXANDER
CADYVILLE	CLINTON	SCHUYLER FALLS
CADYVILLE	CLINTON	PLATTSBURG
CAIRO	GREENE	CAIRO
CAIRO FORGE	GREENE	CAIRO
CAIRO JCT.	GREENE	CATSKILL
CALCIUM	JEFFERSON	LE RAY
CALDWELL	ROCKLAND	STONY POINT
CALEDONIA V.	LIVINGSTON	CALEDONIA
CALIFORNIA	TOMPKINS	DRYDEN
CALIFORNIA	HERKIMER	SALISBURY
CALLANAN COR.	ALBANY	NEW SCOTLAND
CALLICOON CTR.	SULLIVAN	CALLICOON
CALVERTON	SUFFOLK	RIVERHEAD
CAMBRIA	NIAGARA	CAMBRIA
CAMBRIA CTR.	NIAGARA	CAMBRIA
CAMBRIA STA.	NIAGARA	CAMBRIA
CAMBRIDGE V.	WASHINGTON	WHITE C
CAMBRIDGE V.	WASHINGTON	CAMBRIDGE
CAMBY	DUTCHESS	UNION VALE
CAMDEN V.	ONEIDA	CAMDEN
CAMELOT	DUTCHESS	POUGHKEEPSIE
CAMERON	STEUBEN	CAMERON
CAMERON MILLS	STEUBEN	RATHBONE
CAMILLUS V.	ONONDAGA	CAMILLUS
CAMP DEER TRAIL PK.	ROCKLAND	STONY POINT
CAMP DRUM	JEFFERSON	LE RAY
CAMP DRUM	JEFFERSON	WILNA
CAMP LAGUARDIA	ORANGE	CHESTER
CAMP MAPLE	ORANGE	CRAWFORD
CAMP MILLS	JEFFERSON	HOUNSFIELD
CAMP RECRO	ORANGE	TUXEDO
CAMP SANTANOI	ESSEX	NEWCOMB
CAMP SMITH	WESTCHESTER	CORTLANDT
CAMPBELL	STEUBEN	CAMPBELL
CAMPBELL HALL	ORANGE	HAMPTONBURG
CAMPBELL HALL JCT.	ORANGE	HAMPTONBURG
CAMPBELLTOWN	STEUBEN	CAMPBELL
CAMPBELLWOOD	LEWIS	OSCEOLA
CAMPTON	DUTCHESS	HYDE PARK
CAMPVILLE	TIOGA	OWEGO
CANAAN	CLINTON	MOOERS
CANAAN	COLUMBIA	CANAAN
CANAAN CTR.	COLUMBIA	CANAAN
CANAAN FOUR CORS.	COLUMBIA	CANAAN
CANAAN SHAKERS	COLUMBIA	CANAAN
CANAAN STA.	COLUMBIA	CANAAN
CANADA	GENESEE	BETHANY
CANADA LAKE	FULTON	CAROGA
CANADICE	ONTARIO	CANADICE
CANAJOHARIE V.	MONTGOMERY	CANAJOHARIE
CANANDAIGUA C.	ONTARIO	CANANDAIGUA C.
CANARSIE	KINGS	NYC
CANARSIE LDG.	KINGS	NYC
CANASERAGA STA.	MADISON	SULLIVAN
CANASERAGA V.	ALLEGANY	BURNS
CANASTOTA V.	MADISON	LENOX
CANDOR V.	TIOGA	CANDOR
CANEADEA	ALLEGANY	CANEADEA
CANFIELD CORS.	TIOGA	NICHOLS
CANISTEO V.	STEUBEN	CANISTEO
CANNON CORS.	CLINTON	MOOERS
CANOE PLACE	SUFFOLK	SOUTHAMPTON
CANOGA	SENECA	FAYETTE
CANTERBURY	ORANGE	CORNWALL
CANTERSKILL	GREENE	CATSKILL
CANTON CENTER	STEUBEN	CATON
CANTON V.	ST. LAWRENCE	CANTON
CAPE VINCENT V.	JEFFERSON	CAPE VINCENT
CAPRON	ONEIDA	NEW HARTFORD
CARDIFF	ONONDAGA	LAFAYETTE
CARGIL MT.	PUTNAM	PHILIPSTOWN
CARGO LAKE	HAMILTON	ARIETTA
CARLE PLACE	NASSAU	NO. HEMPSTEAD
CARLETON ISL.	JEFFERSON	CAPE VINCENT
CARLEY MILLS	OSWEGO	HASTINGS
CARLISLE	SCHOHARIE	CARLISLE
CARLISLE CTR.	SCHOHARIE	CARLISLE
CARLTON	ORLEANS	CARLTON
CARLTON STA.	ORLEANS	CARLTON
CARLYOU	ORLEANS	CARLTON
CARMAN	SCHENECTADY	ROTTERDAM
CARMEL	PUTNAM	CARMEL
CAROGA LAKE	FULTON	CAROGA
CAROLINE	TOMPKINS	CAROLINE
CAROLINE CTR.	TOMPKINS	CAROLINE
CAROLINE DEPOT	TOMPKINS	CAROLINE
CAROLINE JCT.	TOMPKINS	CAROLINE
CARR CORS.	CHEMUNG	ELMIRA C.
CARPOLL	CATTARAUGUS	PORTVILLE
CARROLLTON	CATTARAUGUS	CARROLLTON
CARTERVILLE	OSWEGO	AMBOY

NAME	COUNTY	TOWN
CARTHAGE LDG.	DUTCHESS	WAPPINGER
CARTHAGE V.	JEFFERSON	WILNA
CARYL	WESTCHESTER	YONKERS C.
CARYTOWN	MONTGOMERY	CHARLESTON
CASCADE	ESSEX	NO. ELBA
CASCADE	CAYUGA	VENICE
CASCADE MILLS STA.	YATES	MILO
CASCADE PARK	ERIE	CONCORD
CASCADE VALLEY	BROOME	WINDSOR
CASCHASCO	CAYUGA	SCIPIO
CASSADAGA V.	CHAUTAUQUA	STOCKTON
CASSVILLE	ONEIDA	PARIS
CASTILE CTR.	WYOMING	CASTILE
CASTILE STA.	WYOMING	CASTILE
CASTILE V.	WYOMING	CASTILE
CASTLE CREEK	BROOME	CHENANGO
CASTLE POINT	DUTCHESS	WAPPINGER
CASTLETON CORS.	RICHMOND	NYC
CASTLETON-ON-HUDSON V.	RENSSELAER	SCHODACK
CASTOR CORS.	OSWEGO	ORWELL
CASTORLAND V.	LEWIS	DENMARK
CATAMOUNT	FRANKLIN	FRANKLIN
CATATONK	TIOGA	CANDOR
CATAWBA	STEUBEN	PULTENEY
CATFISH	OSWEGO	PALERMO
CATHARINE	SCHUYLER	CATHARINE
CATLIN	HAMILTON	LONG LAKE
CATLIN HILL	TIOGA	TIOGA
CATO V.	CAYUGA	IRA
CATO V.	CAYUGA	CATO
CATON	STEUBEN	CATON
CATSKILL LDG.	GREENE	CATSKILL
CATSKILL MT. STA.	GREENE	HUNTER
CATSKILL V.	GREENE	CATSKILL
CATTARAUGUS V.	CATTARAUGUS	NEW ALBION
CAUGHDENOY	OSWEGO	HASTINGS
CAUTERSKILL	GREENE	CATSKILL
CAYUGA HEIGHTS V.	TOMPKINS	ITHACA
CAYUGA JCT.	CAYUGA	SPRINGPORT
CAYUGA LAKE PK.	SENECA	SENECA FALLS
CAYUGA V.	CAYUGA	AURELIUS
CAYUTA	SCHUYLER	CAYUTA
CAYUTAVILLE	SCHUYLER	HECTOR
CAYUTAVILLE	SCHUYLER	CATHARINE
CAYWOOD	SENECA	LODI
CAZENOVIA STA.	MADISON	CAZENOVIA
CAZENOVIA V.	MADISON	CAZENOVIA
CEDAR BLUFF	SARATOGA	SARATOGA
CEDAR CLIFF	ORANGE	NEWBURGH
CEDAR GROVE	ULSTER	SAUGERTIES
CEDAR HILL	ALBANY	BETHLEHEM
CEDAR HILL	ORANGE	NEWBURGH
CEDAR LAKE	HERKIMER	LITCHFIELD
CEDAR PT. PK.	JEFFERSON	CAPE VINCENT
CEDAR RIVER	HAMILTON	INDIAN LAKE
CEDAR SWAMP	MONROE	HENRIETTA
CEDARHURST V.	NASSAU	HEMPSTEAD
CEDARS	ST. LAWRENCE	MORRISTOWN
CEDARVALE	ONONDAGA	ONONDAGA
CEDARVILLE	HERKIMER	COLUMBIA
CEDARVILLE P.O.	HERKIMER	LITCHFIELD
CELORON V.	CHAUTAUQUA	ELLICOTT
CEMENTON	GREENE	CATSKILL
CENTER	HERKIMER	FRANKFORT
CENTER	MADISON	EATON
CENTER BERLIN	RENSSELAER	BERLIN
CENTER BRUNSWICK	RENSSELAER	BRUNSWICK
CENTER CAMBRIDGE	WASHINGTON	CAMBRIDGE
CENTER CANISTEO	STEUBEN	CANISTEO
CENTER FALLS	WASHINGTON	GREENWICH
CENTER LISLE	BROOME	LISLE
CENTER MORICHES	SUFFOLK	BROOKHAVEN
CENTER VALLEY	OTSEGO	ROSEBOOM
CENTER VILLAGE	BROOME	COLESVILLE
CENTER WHITE CREEK	WASHINGTON	WHITE CREEK
CENTEREACH	SUFFOLK	BROOKHAVEN
CENTERFIELD	ONTARIO	CANANDAIGUA
CENTERPORT	SUFFOLK	HUNTINGTON
CENTERVILLE	SUFFOLK	RIVERHEAD
CENTERVILLE	ULSTER	LLOYD
CENTERVILLE	WESTCHESTER	CORTLANDT
CENTERVILLE	ALLEGANY	CENTERVILLE
CENTERVILLE	OSWEGO	ALBION
CENTERVILLE STA.	SULLIVAN	FALLSBURG
CENTRAL BRIDGE	SCHOHARIE	ESPERANCE
CENTRAL BRIDGE	SCHOHARIE	SCHOHARIE
CENTRAL ISLIP	SUFFOLK	ISLIP
CENTRAL ISLIP PSYCHIATRIC CTR.	SUFFOLK	ISLIP
CENTRAL NASSAU	RENSSELAER	NASSAU
CENTRAL NYACK	ROCKLAND	CLARKSTOWN
CENTRAL SQUARE V.	OSWEGO	HASTINGS
CENTRAL VALLEY	ORANGE	WOODBURY
CENTRALIA	CHAUTAUQUA	STOCKTON
CENTRE ISLAND V.	NASSAU	OYSTER BAY
CERES	ALLEGANY	GENESEE

NAME	COUNTY	TOWN
CHACE	WYOMING	CASTILE
CHADWICKS	ONEIDA	NEW HARTFORD
CHAFEE	ERIE	SARDINIA
CHAMBERLAIN CORS.	ST.LAWRENCE	WADDINGTON
CHAMBERLAIN MILLS	WASHINGTON	HEBRON
CHAMBERLINS	JEFFERSON	HOUNSFIELD
CHAMBERS	CHEMUNG	CATLIN
CHAMPION	JEFFERSON	CHAMPION
CHAMPION HUDDLE	JEFFERSON	CHAMPION
CHAMPLAIN V.	CLINTON	CHAMPLAIN
CHAPEL CORS.	CAYUGA	LEDYARD
CHAPIN	ONTARIO	HOPEWELL
CHAPPAQUA	WESTCHESTER	NEW CASTLE
CHAPPAQUA SPRGS.	WESTCHESTER	NEW CASTLE
CHARLESTON	MONTGOMERY	CHARLESTON
CHARLESTON FOUR CORS	MONTGOMERY	CHARLESTON
CHARLIE HILL	ESSEX	SCHROON
CHARLOTTE	NIAGARA	NEWFANE
CHARLOTTE CTR.	CHAUTAUQUA	CHARLOTTE
CHARLOTTEVILLE	SCHOHARIE	SUMMIT
CHARLOTTEVILLE	QUEENS	NYC
CHARLTON	SARATOGA	CHARLTON
CHASE	WYOMING	CASTILE
CHASE	FRANKLIN	FRANKLIN
CHASE	OTSEGO	HARTWICK
CHASE LAKE	LEWIS	WATSON
CHASE MILLS	ST.LAWRENCE	WADDINGTON
CHASE MILLS	ST.LAWRENCE	LOUISVILLE
CHASE STA.	WYOMING	CASTILE
CHASEVILLE	OTSEGO	MARYLAND
CHASM FALLS	FRANKLIN	MALONE
CHASM FALLS STA.	FRANKLIN	MALONE
CHATEAUGAY	OSWEGO	ORWELL
CHATEAUGAY LAKE	FRANKLIN	BELLMONT
CHATEAUGAY V.	FRANKLIN	CHATEAUGAY
CHATHAM CTR.	COLUMBIA	CHATHAM
CHATHAM V.	COLUMBIA	CHATHAM
CHATHAM V.	COLUMBIA	GHENT
CHAUFTY CORS.	JEFFERSON	THERESA
CHAUMONT V.	JEFFERSON	LYME
CHAUTAUQUA	CHAUTAUQUA	CHAUTAUQUA
CHAUTAUQUA INST.	CHAUTAUQUA	CHAUTAUQUA
CHAUTAUQUA UTILITY DIST.	CHAUTAUQUA	CHAUTAUQUA
CHAZY	CLINTON	CHAZY
CHAZY JCT.	CLINTON	CHAZY
CHAZY LANDING	CLINTON	CHAZY
CHAZY LK. HOUSE	CLINTON	DANNEMORA
CHAZY LK. STA.	CLINTON	DANNEMORA
CHEEKTOWAGA	ERIE	CHEEKTOWAGA
CHELSEA	RICHMOND	NYC
CHELSEA	DUTCHESS	WAPPINGER
CHEMUNG	CHEMUNG	CHEMUNG
CHEMUNG CTR.	CHEMUNG	CHEMUNG
CHENANGO BRIDGE	BROOME	CHENANGO
CHENANGO FORKS	BROOME	CHENANGO
CHENANGO LAKE	CHENANGO	NEW BERLIN
CHENANGO SHORES	BROOME	DICKINSON
CHENANGO VALLEY ST. PK.	BROOME	FENTON
CHENEY COBBLE	ESSEX	NEWCOMB
CHENEYS POINT	CHAUTAUQUA	NO. HARMONY
CHENINGO	CORTLAND	TRUXTON
CHERRY CREEK V.	CHAUTAUQUA	CHERRY CR.
CHERRY GROVE	SUFFOLK	BROOKHAVEN
CHERRY ISLAND	JEFFERSON	LYME
CHERRY PLAIN	RENSSELAER	BERLIN
CHERRY VALLEY V.	OTSEGO	CHERRY VALLEY
CHESHIRE	ONTARIO	CANANDAIGUA
CHESTER V.	ORANGE	CHESTER
CHESTERTOWN	WARREN	CHESTER
CHESTNUT RIDGE	NIAGARA	LOCKPORT
CHESTNUT ST.	SARATOGA	SARATOGA
CHEVIOT	COLUMBIA	GERMANTOWN
CHICHESTER	ULSTER	SHANDAKEN
CHILDS	ORLEANS	GAINES
CHILDWOLD	ST.LAWRENCE	PIERCEFIELD
CHILDWOLD STA.	FRANKLIN	ALTAMONT
CHILDWOLD STA.	ST.LAWRENCE	HOPKINTON
CHILI	MONROE	CHILI
CHILI CENTER	MONROE	CHILI
CHILOWAY	DELAWARE	HANCOCK
CHINA	DELAWARE	DEPOSIT
CHINA	DELAWARE	MASONVILLE
CHIPMAN	ST.LAWRENCE	WADDINGTON
CHIPMONK	CATTARAUGUS	CARROLLTON
CHIPMONK	CATTARAUGUS	ALLEGANY
CHIPPEWA BAY	ST.LAWRENCE	HAMMOND
CHITTENANGO FLS.	MADISON	FENNER
CHITTENANGO FLS. ST. PK.	MADISON	CAZENOVIA
CHITTENANGO SPG.	MADISON	SULLIVAN
CHITTENANGO STA.	MADISON	SULLIVAN
CHITTENANGO V.	MADISON	SULLIVAN
CHITTENDEN FLS.	COLUMBIA	STOCKPORT
CHUBB DOCK STA.	WASHINGTON	DRESDEN

NAME	COUNTY	TOWN
CHURCH MILLS	ST.LAWRENCE	ROSSIE
CHURCHTOWN	COLUMBIA	CLAVERACK
CHURCHVILLE	ONEIDA	VERONA
CHURCHVILLE V.	MONROE	RIGA
CHURUBUSCO	CLINTON	CLINTON
CICERO	ONONDAGA	CICERO
CINCINNATUS	CORTLAND	CINCINNATUS
CINCONIA	YATES	JERUSALEM
CIRCLEVILLE	ORANGE	WALLKILL
CLARE	ST.LAWRENCE	CLARE
CLAREMONT PK. STA.	NEW YORK	NYC
CLARENCE	ERIE	CLARENCE
CLARENCE CTR.	ERIE	CLARENCE
CLARENCEVILLE	QUEENS	NYC
CLARENDON	ORLEANS	CLARENDON
CLARK	CHAUTAUQUA	POLAND
CLARK CORS.	SARATOGA	MOREAU
CLARK CORS.	CHAUTAUQUA	POLAND
CLARK MILLS	ONEIDA	WESTMORELAND
CLARK MILLS	ONEIDA	WHITESTOWN
CLARK MILLS	ONEIDA	KIRKLAND
CLARK'S MILLS	WASHINGTON	GREENWICH
CLARKBURG	ERIE	EDEN
CLARKSON	MONROE	CLARKSON
CLARKSVILLE	ALBANY	NEW SCOTLAND
CLARKSVILLE	ALLEGANY	CLARKSVILLE
CLARKVILLE	OTSEGO	MIDDLEFIELD
CLARYVILLE	SULLIVAN	NEVERSINK
CLAVERACK	COLUMBIA	CLAVERACK
CLAY	ONONDAGA	CLAY
CLAYBURG	CLINTON	BLACK BROOK
CLAYBURG	CLINTON	SARANAC
CLAYTON CTR.	JEFFERSON	CLAYTON
CLAYTON V.	JEFFERSON	CLAYTON
CLAYTONVILLE	LIVINGSTON	SPRINGWATER
CLAYVILLE V.	ONEIDA	PARIS
CLEAR CREEK	CHAUTAUQUA	ELLINGTON
CLEAR POND	FRANKLIN	HARRIETSTOWN
CLEAR VIEW	CAYUGA	GENOA
CLEAVER	DELAWARE	TOMPKINS
CLEMONS	WASHINGTON	DRESDEN
CLERMONT	COLUMBIA	CLERMONT
CLEVELAND HILL	ERIE	CHEEKTOWAGA
CLEVELAND V.	OSWEGO	CONSTANTIA
CLEVERDALE	WARREN	QUEENSBURY
CLIFF HAVEN	CLINTON	PLATTSBURG
CLIFFORD	OSWEGO	PALERMO
CLIFTON	MONROE	CHILI
CLIFTON	RICHMOND	NYC
CLIFTON PARK	SARATOGA	CLIFTON PARK
CLIFTON PARK	SARATOGA	HALFMOON
CLIFTON SPRINGS V.	ONTARIO	PHELPS
CLIFTON SPRINGS V.	ONTARIO	MANCHESTER
CLIMAX	GREENE	COXSACKIE
CLINTON CORRECTIONAL FACILITY	CLINTON	DANNEMORA V.
CLINTON CORS.	DUTCHESS	CLINTON
CLINTON HEIGHTS	RENSSELAER	E. GREENBUSH
CLINTON HOLLOW	DUTCHESS	CLINTON
CLINTON MILLS	CLINTON	CLINTON
CLINTON V.	ONEIDA	KIRKLAND
CLINTONDALE	ULSTER	LLOYD
CLINTONDALE	ULSTER	PLATTEKILL
CLINTONVILLE	CLINTON	AUSABLE
CLINTONVILLE	OTSEGO	HARTWICK
CLINTONVILLE	ESSEX	CHESTERFIELD
CLINTONVILLE	ONONDAGA	MARCELLUS
CLOCKVILLE	MADISON	LINCOLN
CLOSEVILLE	FULTON	MAYFIELD
CLOVE	DUTCHESS	UNION VALE
CLOVE BRANCH JCT.	DUTCHESS	E. FISHKILL
CLOVE VALLEY	DUTCHESS	BEEKMAN
CLOVERBANK	ERIE	HAMBURG
CLOVESVILLE	DELAWARE	MIDDLETOWN
CLUM CORS.	RENSSELAER	BRUNSWICK
CLYDE V.	WAYNE	GALEN
CLYMER	CHAUTAUQUA	CLYMER
CLYMER CTR.	CHAUTAUQUA	CLYMER
CLYMER HILL	CHAUTAUQUA	CLYMER
CLYMER STA.	CHAUTAUQUA	CLYMER
COBB	SUFFOLK	SOUTHAMPTON
COBBLEHILL	WYOMING	ORANGEVILLE
COBINE	DELAWARE	FRANKLIN
COBLESKILL V.	SCHOHARIE	COBLESKILL
COBURNS	CHENANGO	GUILFORD
COCHECTON	SULLIVAN	COCHECTON
COCHECTON CTR.	SULLIVAN	COCHECTON
COCONUT CTR.	BROOME	UNION
COEYMAN'S HOLLOW	ALBANY	COEYMANS
COEYMANS	ALBANY	COEYMANS
COFFIN MILLS	ST.LAWRENCE	FINE
COHOCTON V.	STEUBEN	COHOCTON
COHOES C.	ALBANY	COHOES C.
COILA	WASHINGTON	CAMBRIDGE
COLBURNS	CHAUTAUQUA	ELLERY
COLCHESTER	DELAWARE	COLCHESTER
COLCHESTER STA.	DELAWARE	WALTON

NAME	COUNTY	TOWN	NAME	COUNTY	TOWN
COLD BROOK	CLINTON	BLACK BROOK	CORNELL HOLLOW	TIOGA	OWEGO
COLD BROOK V.	HERKIMER	RUSSIA	CORNERS	ORLEANS	ALBION
COLD SPR. HARBOR	SUFFOLK	HUNTINGTON	CORNING C.	STEUBEN	CORNING C.
COLD SPRING	ESSEX	CROWN POINT	CORNWALL DAM	WESTCHESTER	CORTLANDT
COLD SPRING PARK	ESSEX	CROWN POINT	CORNWALL LDG.	ORANGE	CORNWALL
COLD SPRING STA.	STEUBEN	URBANA	CORNWALL STA.	ORANGE	CORNWALL
COLD SPRING V.	PUTNAM	PHILLIPSTOWN	CORNWALL T.	ORANGE	CORNWALL
COLD WATER	MONROE	GATES	CORNWALL-ON-HUDSON V.	ORANGE	CORNWALL
COLDEN	ERIE	COLDEN	CORNWALLVILLE	GREENE	DURHAM
COLDENHAM	ORANGE	NEWBURGH	CORONA	QUEENS	NYC
COLDENHAM	ORANGE	MONTGOMERY	CORTLAND C.	CORTLAND	CORTLAND C.
COLE SETTLEMENT	MADISON	STOCKBRIDGE	CORTLAND JCT.	CORTLAND	CORTLANDVILLE
COLEMAN MILLS	ONEIDA	WHITESTOWN	CORTLANDVILLE	WESTCHESTER	CORTLANDT
COLEMAN STA.	DUTCHESS	NORTHEAST	COPWINS	NIAGARA	NEWFANE
COLES CLOVE	DELAWARE	COLCHESTER	COSAD	SENECA	JUNIUS
COLES MILLS	PUTNAM	KENT	COSSAYUNA	WASHINGTON	GREENWICH
COLLABAR	ORANGE	CRAWFORD	COTTAGE	CATTARAUGUS	DAYTON
COLLAMER	MONROE	PARMA			
COLLEGE HILL	ONEIDA	KIRKLAND	COTTAGE CITY	ONTARIO	GORHAM
COLLEGE POINT	QUEENS	NYC	COTTEKILL	ULSTER	ROSENDALE
COLLIER STA.	OTSEGO	MILFORD	COUNTRYMAN	HERKIMER	FAIRFIELD
COLLIERS	OTSEGO	MILFORD	COUNTRYMAN STA.	HERKIMER	FAIRFIELD
COLLIERSVILLE	OTSEGO	MILFORD	COUNTY HOUSE	ALLEGANY	ANGELICA
COLLINS	ERIE	COLLINS	COUNTY HOUSE STA.	HERKIMER	HERKIMER
COLLINS	ST.LAWRENCE	FINE	COUNTY LINE	ORLEANS	YATES
COLLINS CTR.	ERIE	COLLINS	COURTRIGHT CORS.	CAYUGA	MORAVIA
COLLINSVILLE	LEWIS	W. TURIN	COUSE	RENSSELAER	E. GREENBUSH
COLONIAL SPRGS.	SUFFOLK	BABYLON	COVE NECK V.	NASSAU	OYSTER BAY
COLONIE V.	ALBANY	COLONIE	COVENTRY	CHENANGO	COVENTRY
COLOSSE	OSWEGO	MEXICO	COVENTRY STA.	CHENANGO	OXFORD
COLUMBIA CENTER	HERKIMER	COLUMBIA	COVENTRYVILLE	CHENANGO	COVENTRY
COLUMBIA SPRGS.	HERKIMER	LITCHFIELD	COVERT	SENECA	COVERT
COLUMBIAVILLE	COLUMBIA	STOCKPORT	COVEVILLE	SARATOGA	SARATOGA
COLUMBUS CENTER	CHENANGO	COLUMBUS	COVINGTON	WYOMING	COVINGTON
COLUMBUS QUARTER	CHENANGO	COLUMBUS	COWLES SETTLEMENT	CORTLAND	CUYLER
COLUMBUSVILLE	QUEENS	NYC	COWLES STA.	CORTLAND	CUYLER
COMMACK	SUFFOLK	SMITHTOWN	COWLESVILLE	WYOMING	BENNINGTON
COMMACK	SUFFOLK	HUNTINGTON	COXSACKIE V.	GREENE	COXSACKIE
COMSTOCK	WASHINGTON	FORT ANN	CRAFTS	PUTNAM	CARMEL
CONCORD	RICHMOND	NYC	CRAGIE CLAIR	SULLIVAN	ROCKLAND
CONCORD	ERIE	CONCORD	CRAGSMOOR	ULSTER	WAWARSING
CONESUS	LIVINGSTON	CONESUS	CRAIG	SCHENECTADY	GLENVILLE
CONESUS CTR.	LIVINGSTON	CONESUS	CRAIG DEVELOPMENTAL CTR.	LIVINGSTON	GROVELAND
CONESUS STA.	LIVINGSTON	CONESUS	CRAIGS	LIVINGSTON	YORK
CONESVILLE	SCHOHARIE	CONESVILLE	CRAIGSVILLE	ORANGE	BLOOMING GR.
CONEWANGO	CATTARAUGUS	CONEWANGO	CRAIN MILLS	CORTLANDT	TRUXTON
CONEWANGO VALLEY	CHAUTAUQUA	ELLINGTON	CRAMER CORS.	HERKIMER	STARK
CONEY ISLAND	KINGS	NYC			
CONGERS	ROCKLAND	CLARKSTOWN	CRANBERRY CREEK	FULTON	MAYFIELD
CONIFER	ST.LAWRENCE	PIERCEFIELD	CRANBERRY LAKE	ST.LAWRENCE	CLIFTON
CONKLIN	BROOME	CONKLIN	CRANDELL CORS.	WASHINGTON	EASTON
CONKLIN BRIDGE	HERKIMER	OHIO	CRANE VIL.STA.	MONTGOMERY	AMSTERDAM
CONKLIN CTR.	BROOME	CONKLIN	CRANE VILLAGE	SARATOGA	MILTON
CONKLIN FORKS	BROOME	CONKLIN	CRANES CORS.	HERKIMER	LITCHFIELD
CONKLINGVILLE	SARATOGA	HADLEY	CRANES CORS.	HERKIMER	WARREN
CONNELLY	ULSTER	ESOPUS	CRANEVILLE	MONTGOMERY	AMSTERDAM
CONOVER	TOMPKINS	ITHACA	CRANSTON STA.	ORANGE	HIGHLANDS
CONQUEST	CAYUGA	CONQUEST	CRARY MILLS	ST.LAWRENCE	CANTON
CONSTABLE	FRANKLIN	CONSTABLE	CRARYVILLE	COLUMBIA	COPAKE
CONSTABLEVILLE V.	LEWIS	WEST TURIN	CRATERCLUB	ESSEX	ESSEX
CONSTANTIA	OSWEGO	CONSTANTIA	CRAWFORD	ULSTER	SHAWANGUNK
CONSTANTIA CTR.	OSWEGO	CONSTANTIA	CRAWFORD JCT.	ORANGE	WALLKILL
CONSTINE BRIDGE	MADISON	CAZENOVIA	CREAM HILL	STEUBEN	DANSVILLE
CONTINENTAL VILLAGE	PUTNAM	PUTNAM VALLEY	CREAM STREET	DUTCHESS	HYDE PARK
CONVERSE	ST.LAWRENCE	STOCKHOLM	CREEDMOOR	QUEENS	NYC
COOK CORS.	FRANKLIN	FORT COVINGTON	CREEDMOOR ST. HOSP.	QUENNS	NYC
COOK CORS.	ST.LAWRENCE	PIERREPONT	CREEK CTR.	WARREN	STONY CREEK
COOK FALLS	DELAWARE	COLCHESTER	CREEK LOCKS	ULSTER	ROSENDALE
COOK FALLS STA.	DELAWARE	COLCHESTER	CRESCENT	SARATOGA	CLIFTON PARK
COOKSBURG	ALBANY	RENSSELAERVILLE	CRESCENT P.O.	SARATOGA	HALFMOON
COOKSBURY	SCHOHARIE	BROOME	CRESCENT STA.	ALBANY	COLONIE
COOLEY	SULLIVAN	LIBERTY	CRESTWOOD	WESTCHESTER	YONKERS C.
COOMER	NIAGARA	NEWFANE	CRICKETOWN	ROCKLAND	STONY POINT
COOMER STA.	NIAGARA	NEWFANE	CRITTENDEN	ERIE	ALDEN
COON HOLLOW	ALLEGANY	GENESEE	CROCKETT	CAYUGA	STERLING
COONEY CORS.	CAYUGA	LEDYARD	CROFT CORS.	PUTNAM	PUTNAM VALLEY
COONROD	ONEIDA	ROME C.	CROGHAN	LEWIS	NEW BREMEN
COONS	SARATOGA	HALFMOON	CROGHAN V.	LEWIS	CROGHAN
COOPER FALLS	ST.LAWRENCE	DE KALB	CROGHAN V.	LEWIS	NEW BREMEN
COOPERSTOWN JCT.	OTSEGO	MILFORD	CROMPOND	WESTCHESTER	CORTLANDT
COOPERSTOWN V.	OTSEGO	MIDDLEFIELD	CRONK CORS.	LEWIS	PINCKNEY
COOPERSTOWN V.	OTSEGO	OTSEGO	CRONOMER VAL.	ORANGE	NEWBURGH
COOPERSVILLE	CLINTON	CHAMPLAIN	CROOKED BROOK	ONEIDA	UTICA C.
COOPERVILLE	LIVINGSTON	NUNDA	CROOKERVILLE	DELAWARE	SIDNEY
COPAKE	COLUMBIA	COPAKE	CROPSEYVILLE	RENSSELAER	BRUNSWICK
COPAKE FALLS	COLUMBIA	COPAKE	CROSBY	YATES	BARRINGTON
COPAKE IRON WKS.	COLUMBIA	COPAKE	CROSBYSIDE	WARREN	QUEENSBURY
COPENHAGEN V.	LEWIS	DENMARK	CROSS	ESSEX	LEWIS
COPIAGUE	SUFFOLK	BABYLON	CROSS RDS. STA.	CAYUGA	SPRINGPORT
CORAM	SUFFOLK	BROOKHAVEN	CROSS RIVER	WESTCHESTER	LEWISBORO
CORBETT	DELAWARE	COLCHESTER	CROTON	DELAWARE	FRANKLIN
CORBETTSVILLE	BROOME	CONKLIN	CROTON DAM	WESTCHESTER	CORTLANDT
CORBIN CORS.	JEFFERSON	CLAYTON	CROTON FALLS	WESTCHESTER	NO. SALEM
CORDOVA	CHAUTAUQUA	POMFRET	CROTON HEIGHTS	WESTCHESTER	YORKTOWN
COREYS	FRANKLIN	HARRIETSTOWN	CROTON LDG. STA.	WESTCHESTER	CORTLANDT
CORFU V.	GENESEE	PEMBROKE	CROTON LK.	WESTCHESTER	YORKTOWN
CORINTH V.	SARATOGA	CORINTH	CROTON STA.	HERKIMER	SCHUYLER

NAME	COUNTY	TOWN
CROTON-ON-HUDSON V.	WESTCHESTER	CORTLANDT
CROUS STORE	DUTCHESS	UNION VALE
CROWN POINT	ESSEX	CROWN POINT
CROWN POINT CTR.	ESSEX	CROWN POINT
CRUGERS	WESTCHESTER	CORTLANDT
CRUM CREEK	FULTON	OPPENHEIM
CRUM ELBOW	DUTCHESS	HYDE PARK
CRUM HILL	MADISON	DERUYTER
CRUSOE	WAYNE	SAVANNAH
CRYSTAL DALE	LEWIS	NEW BREMEN
CRYSTAL LAKE	ALBANY	RENSSELAERVILL
CRYSTAL LAKE	CATTARAUGUS	FREEDOM
CRYSTAL RUN	ORANGE	WALLKILL
CRYSTAL SPR.	YATES	BARRINGTON
CUBA V.	ALLEGANY	CUBA
CUDDEBACK	ONTARIO	PHELPS
CULLEN	HERKIMER	WARREN
CUMBERLAND HEAD	CLINTON	PLATTSBURG
CUMMINGSVILLE	LIVINGSTON	NO. DANSVILLE
CURRIER CORS.	WYOMING	JAVA
CURRIERS	WYOMING	JAVA
CURRIERS STA.	WYOMING	JAVA
CURRY	SULLIVAN	NEVERSINK
CURRYTOWN	MONTGOMERY	ROOT
CURTIS	STEUBEN	CAMPBELL
CURTIS CORS.	HERKIMER	SALISBURY
CUTCHOGUE	SUFFOLK	SOUTHOLD
CUTTING	CHAUTAUQUA	FRENCH CR.
CUYLER	CORTLAND	CUYLER
CUYLER HILL	CORTLAND	CUYLER
CUYLERVILLE	LIVINGSTON	LEICESTER
CYPRESS HILLS	KINGS	NYC

-D-

NAME	COUNTY	TOWN
DAHLIA	SULLIVAN	LIBERTY
DAIRYLAND	ULSTER	WAWARSING
DAKINS CORS.	ONEIDA	PARIS
DALE	WYOMING	MIDDLEBURY
DALTON	LIVINGSTON	NUNDA
DAMASCUS	BROOME	WINDSOR
DANBY	TOMPKINS	DANBY
DANLEY	WYOMING	BENNINGTON
DANNEMORA V.	CLINTON	DANNEMORA
DANNEMORA V.	CLINTON	SARANAC
DANSVILLE STA.	LIVINGSTON	NO. DANSVILLE
DANSVILLE V.	LIVINGSTON	N. DANSVILLE
DANUBE	HEPKIMER	DANUBE
DANVILLE	BROOME	SANFORD
DARIEN	GENESEE	DARIEN
DARIEN CTR.	GENESEE	DARIEN
DARIEN STA.	GENESEE	DARIEN
DARLINGTON	SUFFOLK	SMITHTOWN
DARROWSVILLE	WARREN	CHESTER
DAVENPORT	DELAWARE	DAVENPORT
DAVENPORT CTR.	DELAWARE	DAVENPORT
DAVIS CORS.	ULSTER	MARBLETOWN
DAVIS CROSS.	CHENANGO	NEW BERLIN
DAVY'S CORS.	HERKIMER	DANUBE
DAY	SARATOGA	DAY
DAYS MILL	ST.LAWRENCE	HOPKINTON
DAYSVILLE	OSWEGO	RICHLAND
DAYTON	CATTARAUGUS	DAYTON
DEAN CHASE STL.	CLINTON	BLACK BROOK
DEAN CORS.	SARATOGA	SARATOGA
DEANS TANNERY	TIOGA	OWEGO
DEANSBORO	ONEIDA	MARSHALL
DEANVILLE	ONEIDA	MARSHALL
DEBRUCE	SULLIVAN	ROCKLAND
DECATUR	OTSEGO	DECATUR
DECK	HERKIMER	STARK
DECK	HERKIMER	LITTLE FALLS
DEER CREEK	ALLEGANY	GENESEE
DEER PARK	SUFFOLK	BABYLON
DEER RIVER	LEWIS	DENMARK
DEERFIELD	ONEIDA	UTICA C.
DEERFIELD	SUFFOLK	SOUTHAMPTON
DEERHEAD	ESSEX	LEWIS
DEERLAND	HAMILTON	LONG LAKE
DEERLAND LODGE	HAMILTON	LONG LAKE
DEFERIET V.	JEFFERSON	WILNA
DEFOREST CORS.	PUTNAM	SOUTHEAST
DEFREESTVILLE	RENSSELAER	NO. GREENBUSH
DEGRASSE	ST.LAWRENCE	RUSSELL
DEGROFF	CAYUGA	OWASCO
DE KALB	ST.LAWRENCE	DE KALB
DE KALB JCT.	ST.LAWRENCE	DE KALB
DELANCEY	DELAWARE	HAMDEN
DELANSON V.	SCHENECTADY	DUANESBURG
D.L. & W. JCT.	LIVINGSTON	LEICESTER
D.L. & W.R.R. & P. JCT.	GENESEE	PAVILION
DELEVAN	ERIE	BUFFALO C.
DELEVAN V.	CATTARAUGUS	YORKSHIRE
DELHI V.	DELAWARE	DELHI
DELMAR	ALBANY	BETHLEHEM
DELPHI	ONONDAGA	POMPEY

NAME	COUNTY	TOWN
DELPHI FALLS	ONONDAGA	POMPEY
DELPHI STA.	MADISON	CAZENOVIA
DELTA	ONEIDA	LEE
DEMPSTER CORS.	FULTON	EPHRATAH
DEMSTER	OSWEGO	NEW HAVEN
DENLEY STA.	LEWIS	LEYDEN
DENMARK	LEWIS	DENMARK
DENNING	PUTNAM	PHILIPSTOWN
DENNING	ULSTER	DENNING
DENNISON CORS.	HERKIMER	COLUMBIA
DENNYTOWN	PUTNAM	PUTNAM VALLEY
DENTON	CHAUTAUQUA	STOCKTON
DENTON	ORANGE	WAWAYANDA
DENVER	DELAWARE	MIDDLETOWN
DEPAUVILLE	JEFFERSON	CLAYTON
DEPEW V.	ERIE	CHEEKTOWAGA
DEPEW V.	ERIE	LANCASTER
DEPEYSTER	ST.LAWRENCE	DEPEYSTER
DEPOSIT V.	DELAWARE	DEPOSIT
DEFOSIT V.	BROOME	SANFORD
DERBY	ERIE	EVANS
DERING HARBOR	SUFFOLK	SHELTER ISLAND
DERING HARBOR V.	SUFFOLK	SHELTER ISLAND
DERRICK	FRANKLIN	ALTAMONT
DERUYSTER V.	MADISON	DERUYTER
DESBROUGH PARK	WAYNE	WOLCOTT
DEVEREAUX	HERKIMER	SALISBURY
DEVEREAUX STA.	CATTARAUGUS	ELLICOTTVILLE
DEVILS HOLE	NIAGARA	LEWISTON
DEVON	SUFFOLK	E. HAMPTON
DEWELLS CORS.	ERIE	HAMBURG
DEWEY BRIDGE	WASHINGTON	FORT ANN
DEWITT	ONONDAGA	DEWITT
DEWITTVILLE	ULSTER	DENNING
DEWITTVILLE	CHAUTAUQUA	CHAUTAUQUA
DEXTER JCT.	JEFFERSON	BROWNVILLE
DEXTER V.	JEFFERSON	BROWNVILLE
DEXTERVILLE	OSWEGO	GRANBY
DIAMOND	JEFFERSON	WORTH
DIAMOND HILL	HERKIMER	SALISBURY
DIAMOND PT.	WARREN	LAKE GEORGE
DIANA	LEWIS	DIANA
DIANA CTR.	LEWIS	DIANA
DIANA STA.	LEWIS	DIANA
DIBBLETOWN	ONEIDA	VIENNA
DICKERSONVILLE	NIAGARA	LEWISTON
DICKINSON	FRANKLIN	DICKINSON
DICKINSON CTR.	FRANKLIN	DICKINSON
DIDELL	DUTCHESS	WAPPINGER
DILLIN	JEFFERSON	RODMAN
DINEHARTS	STEUBEN	WHEELER
DISCO	CLINTON	BLACK BROOK
DISHAWS	ST.LAWRENCE	NORFOLK
DIVINE CORS.	SULLIVAN	FALLSBURG
DIVINITY HILL	SUFFOLK	E. HAMPTON
DIX	ONEIDA	WESTMORELAND
DIX HILLS	SUFFOLK	HUNTINGTON
DIXIE	WESTCHESTER	CORTLANDT
DOANSBURG	PUTNAM	SOUTHEAST
DOBBS FERRY V.	WESTCHESTER	GREENBURGH
DODGE	CHAUTAUQUA	CARROLL
DOLGEVILLE V.	FULTON	OPPENHEIM
DOLGEVILLE V.	HERKIMER	MANHEIM
DONNATTSBURG	LEWIS	GREIG
DONGAN MILLS	RICHMOND	NYC
DOODLETOWN	ROCKLAND	STONY POINT
DORAVILLE	BROOME	COLESVILLE
DORLOO	SCHOHARIE	SEWARD
DORMANSVILLE	ALBANY	WESTERLO
DOTYS CORS.	STEUBEN	DANSVILLE
DOUGLASS	ESSEX	CHESTERFIELD
DOUGLASS CROSS.	JEFFERSON	THERESA
DOUGLASTON	QUEENS	NYC
DOUWSBURGH	ALBANY	GUILDERLAND
DOVER PLAINS	DUTCHESS	DOVER
DOWNING STA.	MONTGOMERY	ROOT
DOWNSVILLE	DELAWARE	COLCHESTER
DOYLE	ERIE	CHEEKTOWAGA
DRESDEN CTR.	WASHINGTON	DRESDEN
DRESDEN STA.	WASHINGTON	DRESDEN
DRESDEN V.	YATES	TORREY
DRESSERVILLE	CAYUGA	SEMPRONIUS
DRIFTWOOD	CHAUTAUQUA	ELLERY
DRY BROOK	ULSTER	HARDENBURGH
DRYDEN V.	TOMPKINS	DRYDEN
DUANE	FRANKLIN	DUANE
DUANE CTR.	FRANKLIN	DUANE
DUANESBURG	SCHENECTADY	DUANESBURG
DUBLIN	SENECA	JUNIUS
DUCHARM	CLINTON	DANNEMORA
DUGWAY	OSWEGO	ALBION
DULCHTOWN	HERKIMER	SALISBURY
DUNBAR	BROOME	WINDSOR
DUNBARTON	ONEIDA	VERONA
DUNHAM BASIN	WASHINGTON	KINGSBURY
DUNHAM HOLLOW	RENSSELAER	NASSAU
DUNKIRK C.	CHAUTAUQUA	DUNKIRK C.

NAME	COUNTY	TOWN	NAME	COUNTY	TOWN
DUNN BROOK	ONEIDA	WESTERN	E. FREETOWN	CORTLAND	FREETOWN
DUNNINGS	YATES	JERUSALEM	E. GAINES	ORLEANS	GAINES
DUNNSBACK FERRY	ALBANY	COLONIE	E. GAINESVILLE	WYOMING	GAINESVILLE
DUNNSVILLE	ALBANY	GUILDERLAND	E. GALWAY	SARATOGA	GALWAY
DUNRAVEN	DELAWARE	MIDDLETOWN	E. GARDEN CITY	NASSAU	HEMPSTEAD
DUNSBACH FERRY	SARATOGA	HALFMOON	E. GENOA	CAYUGA	GENOA
DUNSBACH FY. STA.	ALBANY	COLONIE	E. GERMAN	CHENANGO	GERMAN
DUNTON	QUEENS	NYC	E. GLENVILLE	SCHENECTADY	GLENVILLE
DUNWOODIE	WESTCHESTER	YONKERS C.	E. GRAFTON	RENSSELAER	PETERSBURG
DURAND-EASTMAN PK.	MONROE	IRONDEQUOIT	E. GRANGER	ALLEGANY	GRANGER
DURHAM	GREENE	DURHAM	E. GREENBUSH	RENSSELAER	E. GREENBUSH
DURHAMVILLE	ONEIDA	VERONA	E. GREENVILLE	GREENE	GREENVILLE
DURKEETOWN	WASHINGTON	FORT EDWARD	E. GREENWICH	WASHINGTON	GREENWICH
DURLANDVILLE	ORANGE	GOSHEN	E. GROVE	CHEMUNG	VETERAN
DUTCH HOLLOW	WYOMING	SHELDON	E. GUILFORD	CHENANGO	GUILFORD
DUTCH HOLLOW	ORANGE	WARWICK	E. HAMBURG	ERIE	ORCHARD PARK
DUTCH KILLS	QUEENS	NYC	E. HAMILTON	MADISON	HAMILTON
DUTCH SETTLEMENT	ULSTER	ULSTER	E. HAMLIN	MONROE	HAMLIN
DUTCH SETTLEMENT	HERKIMER	SCHUYLER	E. HAMPTON V.	SUFFOLK	E. HAMPTON
DUTCHESS JCT.	DUTCHESS	FISHKILL	E. HARTFORD	WASHINGTON	HARTFORD
DWAAR KILL	ULSTER	SHAWANGUNK	E. HARVEY	ONTARIO	PHELPS
DYKE	STEUBEN	HORNBY	E. HAUPPAUGE	SUFFOLK	SMITHTOWN
DYKEMAN	PUTNAM	SOUTHEAST	E. HEMPSTEAD	NASSAU	HEMPSTEAD
DYSINGER	NIAGARA	ROYALTON	E. HERKIMER	HERKIMER	HERKIMER
			E. HILLS V.	NASSAU	N. HEMPSTEAD
-E-			E. HOLLAND	ERIE	HOLLAND
			E. HOMER	CORTLAND	HOMER
EAGLE	WYOMING	EAGLE	E. HOOSICK	RENSSELAER	HOOSICK
EAGLE BAY	HERKIMER	WEBB	E. HOUNSFIELD	JEFFERSON	HOUNSFIELD
EAGLE BRIDGE	WASHINGTON	WHITE CREEK	E. HOUNSFIELD STA.	JEFFERSON	HOUNSFIELD
EAGLE BRIDGE	RENSSELAER	HOOSICK	E. IRVINGTON	WESTCHESTER	GREENBURGH
EAGLE HARBOR	ORLEANS	GAINES	E. ISLIP	SUFFOLK	ISLIP
EAGLE HARBOR	ORLEANS	ALBION	E. ITHACA	TOMPKINS	ITHACA
EAGLE HARBOR STA.	ORLEANS	ALBION	E. ITHACA STA.	TOMPKINS	ITHACA
EAGLE MILLS	RENSSELAER	BRUNSWICK	E. JAVA	WYOMING	JAVA
EAGLE NEST	HAMILTON	INDIAN LAKE	E. JEFFERSON	SCHOHARIE	JEFFERSON
EAGLE STA.	WYOMING	EAGLE	E. JEWETT	GREENE	JEWETT
EAGLE VALLEY	ORANGE	TUXEDO	E. KILNS	CLINTON	BLACK BROOK
EAGLEVILLE	MADISON	EATON	E. KINGSTON	ULSTER	ULSTER
EARL	YATES	BENTON	E. KOY	WYOMING	PIKE
EARLS	WYOMING	BENNINGTON	E. LANCASTER	ERIE	LANCASTER
EARLTON	GREENE	COXSACKIE	E. LANSING	TOMPKINS	LANSING
EARLVILLE STA.	MADISON	HAMILTON	E. LINE	SARATOGA	MALTA
EARLVILLE V.	MADISON	HAMILTON	E. MAINE	BROOME	MAINE
EARLVILLE V.	CHENANGO	SHERBURNE	E. MARION	SUFFOLK	SOUTHOLD
E. ALEXANDER	GENESEE	ALEXANDER	E. MARTINSBURG	LEWIS	MARTINSBURG
E. AMHERST	ERIE	CLARENCE	E. MASONVILLE	DELAWARE	MASONVILLE
E. AMHERST	ERIE	AMHERST	E. MCDONOUGH	CHENANGO	MCDONOUGH
E. ANTWERP	JEFFERSON	ANTWERP	E. MEADOWS	NASSAU	HEMPSTEAD
E. ASHFORD	CATTARAUGUS	ASHFORD	E. MEREDITH	DELAWARE	MEREDITH
E. ASHLAND	GREENE	ASHLAND	E. MIDDLE PATENT	WESTCHESTER	NO. CASTLE
E. ATLANTIC BEACH	NASSAU	HEMPSTEAD	E. MORICHES	SUFFOLK	BROOKHAVEN
E. AURORA V.	ERIE	AURORA	E. NASSAU	RENSSELAER	NASSAU
E. AVON	LIVINGSTON	AVON	E. NEW YORK STA.	KINGS	NYC
E. BACON	ST. LAWRENCE	PITCAIRN	E. NICHOLS	TIOGA	NICHOLS
E. BAY	WAYNE	HURON	E. NORFOLK	ST. LAWRENCE	NORFOLK
E. BEEKMANTOWN	CLINTON	BEEKMANTOWN	E. NORTHPORT	SUFFOLK	HUNTINGTON
E. BENNINGTON	WYOMING	BENNINGTON	E. NORWICH	NASSAU	OYSTER BAY
E. BERGEN	GENESEE	BERGEN	E. NORWICH	CHENANGO	NORWICH
E. BERKSHIRE	TIOGA	BERKSHIRE	E. OAK HILL	CHAUTAUQUA	ELLICOTT
E. BERNE	ALBANY	BERNE	E. ORANGE	SCHUYLER	ORANGE
E. BETHANY	GENESEE	BETHANY	E. OTTO	CATTARAUGUS	E. OTTO
E. BLOOMFIELD V.	ONTARIO	E. BLOOMFIELD	E. PALERMO	OSWEGO	PALERMO
E. BOSTON	MADISON	SULLIVAN	E. PALMYRA	WAYNE	PALMYRA
E. BOYLSTON	OSWEGO	BOYLSTON	E. PARK	DUTCHESS	HYDE PARK
E. BRACH	DELAWARE	HANCOCK	E. PEMBROKE	GENESEE	PEMBROKE
E. BRANCH STA.	DELAWARE	HANCOCK	E. PENFIELD	MONROE	PENFIELD
E. BROOK	DELAWARE	WALTON	E. PHARSALIA	CHENANGO	PHARSALIA
E. BUFFALO	ERIE	BUFFALO C.	E. PIERREPONT	ST. LAWRENCE	PIERREPONT
E. BUSKIRK	RENSSELAER	HOOSICK	E. PITCAIRN	ST. LAWRENCE	PITCAIRN
E. BUSKIRK STA.	RENSSELAER	HOOSICK	E. POESTENKILL	RENSSELAER	POESTENKILL
E. CAMP	COLUMBIA	GERMANTOWN	E. QUOGUE	SUFFOLK	SOUTHAMPTON
E. CAMPBELL	STEUBEN	CAMPBELL	E. RANDOLPH V.	CATTARAUGUS	RANDOLPH
E. CANDOR	TIOGA	CANDOR	E. RANDOLPH V.	CATTARAUGUS	CONEWANGO
E. CARLTON STA.	ORLEANS	CARLTON	E. RICHFORD	TIOGA	RICHFORD
E. CHATHAM	COLUMBIA	CHATHAM	E. RIVER	CORTLAND	HOMER
E. CHESTER	BRONX	NYC	E. ROAD	ST. LAWRENCE	RUSSELL
E. CLARKSON	MONROE	CLARKSON	E. ROCHESTER V.	MONROE	PERINTON
E. COBLESKILL	SCHOHARIE	COBLESKILL	E. ROCHESTER V.	MONROE	PITTSFORD
E. CONCORD	ERIE	CONCORD	E. ROCKAWAY V.	NASSAU	HEMPSTEAD
E. CONSTABLE	FRANKLIN	CONSTABLE	E. RODMAN	JEFFERSON	RODMAN
E. CORNING	STEUBEN	CORNING	E. RUSH	MONROE	RUSH
E. CREEK	MONTGOMERY	ST. JOHNSVILLE	E. RUSHFORD	ALLEGANY	RUSHFORD
E. CREEK	HERKIMER	MANHEIM	E. SALEM	WASHINGTON	SALEM
E. CROSSING	ONTARIO	PHELPS	E. SARATOGA JCT.	SARATOGA	STILLWATER
E. DE KALB	ST. LAWRENCE	DE KALB	E. SCHAGHTICOKE	RENSSELAER	SCHAGHTICOKE
E. DELHI	DELAWARE	DELHI	E. SCHODACK	RENSSELAER	SCHODACK
E. DICKINSON	FRANKLIN	DICKINSON	E. SCHUYLER	HERKIMER	SCHUYLER
E. DURHAM	GREENE	DURHAM	E. SETAUKET	SUFFOLK	BROOKHAVEN
E. EDEN	ERIE	EDEN	E. SHELBY	ORLEANS	SHELBY
E. ELMA	ERIE	ELMA	E. SIDNEY	DELAWARE	SIDNEY
E. ELMIRA	CHEMUNG	ELMIRA	E. SPENCER	TIOGA	SPENCER
E. END STA.	BROOME	COLESVILLE	E. SPRINGFIELD	OTSEGO	SPRINGFIELD
E. FARMINGDALE	SUFFOLK	BABYLON	E. SPRINGWATER	LIVINGSTON	SPRINGWATER
E. FISHKILL	DUTCHESS	E. FISHKILL	E. STEAMBURG	SCHUYLER	HECTOR
E. FLORENCE	ONEIDA	FLORENCE	E. STEUBEN	ONEIDA	STEUBEN
E. FRANKFORT	HERKIMER	FRANKFORT	E. STOCKHOLM	ST. LAWRENCE	STOCKHOLM

NAME	COUNTY	TOWN
E. SYRACUSE V.	ONONDAGA	DEWITT
E. TOWNSHIP	ALBANY	KNOX
E. TROUPSBURG	STEUBEN	TROUPSBURG
E. UTICA STA.	ONEIDA	UTICA C.
E. VARICK	SENECA	VARICK
E. VENICE	CAYUGA	VENICE
E. VERONA	ONEIDA	VERONA
E. VICTOR	ONTARIO	VICTOR
E. VIEW	WESTCHESTER	MT. PLEASANT
E. VIRGIL	CORTLAND	VIRGIL
E. WALDEN	ORANGE	MONTGOMERY
E. WALDEN STA.	ORANGE	MONTGOMERY
E. WATERTOWN	JEFFERSON	WATERTOWN
E. WAVERLY	TIOGA	BARTON
E. WAVERLY STA.	TIOGA	BARTON
E. WILLIAMSON	WAYNE	WILLIAMSON
E. WILLISTON V.	NASSAU	N. HEMPSTEAD
E. WILSON	NIAGARA	WILSON
E. WINDHAM	GREENE	WINDHAM
E. WINDSOR	BROOME	WINDSOR
E. WOODHULL	STEUBEN	WOODHULL
E. WORCESTER	OTSEGO	WORCESTER
EASTERN NY CORRECTIONAL FAC.	ULSTER	WAWARSING
EASTON	WASHINGTON	EASTON
EASTON STA.	WASHINGTON	EASTON
EASTPORT	SUFFOLK	BROOKHAVEN
EASTPORT	SUFFOLK	SOUTHAMPTON
EASTSIDE	SUFFOLK	E. HAMPTON
EATON	MADISON	EATON
EATON CORS.	SCHENECTADY	DUANESBURG
EATON NECK	SUFFOLK	HUNTINGTON
EATON STA.	MADISON	EATON
EATONVILLE	HERKIMER	LITTLE FALLS
EBEN	ST.LAWRENCE	POTSDAM
EDDY	ST.LAWRENCE	CANTON
EDDYVILLE	CATTARAUGUS	MANSFIELD
EDDYVILLE	ULSTER	ULSTER
EDEN	ERIE	EDEN
EDEN VALLEY	ERIE	EDEN
EDENVILLE	ORANGE	WARWICK
EDGEBERT	LEWIS	CROGHAN
EDGEMER	QUEENS	NYC
EDGEWATER	CAYUGA	SCIPIO
EDGEWATER PK.	ST.LAWRENCE	MORRISTOWN
EDGEWOOD	GREENE	HUNTER
EDGEWOOD STA.	SUFFOLK	ISLIP
EDGEWOOD STA.	MONROE	HENRIETTA
EDINBURG	SARATOGA	EDINBURG
EDMESTON	OTSEGO	EDMESTON
EDSON	BROOME	WINDSOR
EDSON CORS.	OTSEGO	MILFORD
EDWARDS PARK	COLUMBIA	CANAAN
EDWARDS STA.	COLUMBIA	CANAAN
EDWARDS V.	ST.LAWRENCE	EDWARDS
EDWARDSVILLE	ST.LAWRENCE	MORRISTOWN
EGBERTVILLE	RICHMOND	NYC
EGGERTSVILLE	ERIE	AMHERST
EGYPT	ONTARIO	BRISTOL
EGYPT	MONROE	PERINTON
EIGHMYVILLE	DUTCHESS	RHINEBECK
ELBA V.	GENESEE	ELBA
ELBRIDGE V.	ONONDAGA	ELBRIDGE
ELDRED	SULLIVAN	HIGHLAND
ELGIN	CATTARAUGUS	LYNDON
ELIZABETH CHURCH MANOR	BROOME	DICKINSON
ELIZABETH TOWN	HERKIMER	COLUMBIA
ELIZABETHTOWN V.	ESSEX	ELIZABETHTOWN
ELIZAVILLE	COLUMBIA	GALLATIN
ELIZAVILLE	COLUMBIA	LIVINGSTON
ELK CREEK	OTSEGO	MARYLAND
ELKA PARK	GREENE	HUNTER
ELKBROOK	DELAWARE	HANCOCK
ELKDALE	CATTARAUGUS	LITTLE VALLEY
ELLENBURG	CLINTON	ELLENBURG
ELLENBURG CORS.	CLINTON	ELLENBURG
ELLENBURG CTR.	CLINTON	ELLENBURG
ELLENBURG DEPOT	CLINTON	ALTONA
ELLENBURG DEPOT	CLINTON	ELLENBURG
ELLENVILLE V.	ULSTER	WAWARSING
ELLERY CENTER	CHAUTAUQUA	ELLERY
ELLICOTT	ERIE	ORCHARD PARK
ELLICOTTVILLE V.	CATTARAUGUS	ELLICOTTVILLE
ELLINGTON	CHAUTAUQUA	ELLINGTON
ELLIS	TOMPKINS	DRYDEN
ELLIS ISLAND	NEW YORK	NYC
ELLISBURG V.	JEFFERSON	ELLISBURG
ELLSWORTH	CAYUGA	LEDYARD
ELM GROVE	OTSEGO	MORRIS
ELM PARK	RICHMOND	NYC
ELM VALLEY	ALLEGANY	ANDOVER
ELMA	ERIE	ELMA
ELMA CTR.	ERIE	ELMA
ELMBOYS	STEUBEN	PULTENEY
ELMDALE	ST.LAWRENCE	GOUVERNEUR
ELMGROVE	MONROE	GATES

NAME	COUNTY	TOWN
ELMGROVE	MONROE	GREECE
ELMHURST	QUEENS	NYC
ELMHURST	CHAUTAUQUA	ELLICOTT
ELMHURST	CAYUGA	AURELIUS
ELMIRA C.	CHEMUNG	ELMIRA C.
ELMIRA HEIGHTS V.	CHEMUNG	HORSEHEADS
ELMIRA HEIGHTS V.	CHEMUNG	ELMIRA
ELMIRA REFORMATORY	CHEMUNG	ELMIRA
ELMONT	NASSAU	HEMPSTEAD
ELMSFORD V.	WESTCHESTER	GREENBURGH
ELMWOOD	ALLEGANY	WILLING
ELNORA	SARATOGA	CLIFTON PARK
ELPIS	ONEIDA	VIENNA
ELSMERE	ALBANY	BETHLEHEM
ELTINGVILLE	RICHMOND	NYC
ELTON	CATTARAUGUS	FREEDOM
ELWOOD	SUFFOLK	HUNTINGTON
EMERALD GREEN	SULLIVAN	THOMPSON
EMERICK	ALBANY	COLONIE
EMERSON CORS.	SARATOGA	WILTON
EMERYVILLE	ST.LAWRENCE	FOWLER
EMINENCE	SCHOHARIE	SUMMIT
EMMONSBURG	HERKIMER	SALISBURY
EMMONSBURG	FULTON	STRATFORD
EMPEYVILLE	ONEIDA	FLORENCE
ENDICOTT V.	BROOME	UNION
ENDORLIN	ORANGE	CORNWALL
ENDWELL	BROOME	UNION
ENFIELD CTR.	TOMPKINS	ENFIELD
ENFIELD FALLS	TOMPKINS	ENFIELD
ENGELVILLE	SCHOHARIE	SHARON
ENGELWOOD	QUEENS	NYC
ENNERDALE STA.	ONTARIO	HOPEWELL
ENOS	ONEIDA	FORESTPORT
ENSENORE	CAYUGA	SCIPIO
ENTERPRISE	DUTCHESS	MILAN
EPHRATAH	FULTON	EPHRATAH
EPWORTH INN	WYOMING	CASTILE
ERIE	WYOMING	WARSAW
ERIEVILLE	MADISON	NELSON
ERIN	CHEMUNG	ERIN
ERVINE MILLS	CATTARAUGUS	CARROLLTON
ERWIN	STEUBEN	ERWIN
ESOPUS	ULSTER	ESOPUS
ESPERANCE STA.	SCHENECTADY	DUANESBURG
ESPERANCE V.	SCHOHARIE	ESPERANCE
ESSEX	ESSEX	ESSEX
ESSEX STA.	ESSEX	ESSEX
ETNA	TOMPKINS	DRYDEN
EUBA MILLS	ESSEX	ELIZABETHTOWN
EUREKA	ONEIDA	WESTMORELAND
EUREKA	SULLIVAN	NEVERSINK
EVANS	ERIE	EVANS
EVANS CTR.	ERIE	EVANS
EVANS MILLS V.	JEFFERSON	LERAY
EVANS STA.	JEFFERSON	LE RAY
EVANSVILLE	WASHINGTON	ARGYLE
EVERGREEN	QUEENS	NYC
EVERTON	FRANKLIN	SANTA CLARA
EVESPORT	ULSTER	SAUGERTIES
EXETER	OTSEGO	EXETER

-F-

NAME	COUNTY	TOWN
FABIUS V.	ONONDAGA	FABIUS
FACTORY VILLAGE	SARATOGA	MILTON
FACTORYVILLE	ESSEX	CROWN POINT
FACTORYVILLE	TIOGA	BARTON
FAIR HARBOR	SUFFOLK	ISLIP
FAIR HAVEN V.	CAYUGA	STERLING
FAIR OAKS	ORANGE	WALLKILL
FAIRDALE	OSWEGO	HANNIBAL
FAIRFIELD	HERKIMER	FAIRFIELD
FAIRGROUND	SUFFOLK	HUNTINGTON
FAIRHAVEN	ORLEANS	GAINES
FAIRLAND	SCHOHARIE	FULTON
FAIRMOUNT	ONONDAGA	CAMILLUS
FAIRMOUNT PK.	BROOME	UNION
FAIRPORT V.	MONROE	PERINTON
FAIRVIEW	ALLEGANY	CENTERVILLE
FAIRVIEW	CATTARAUGUS	FREEDOM
FAIRVIEW	DUTCHESS	POUGHKEEPSIE
FAIRVIEW	OSWEGO	VOLNEY
FAIRVIEW	ALLEGANY	RUSHFORD
FAIRVIEW	WYOMING	CASTILE
FAIRVIEW	CATTARAUGUS	FARMERSVILLE
FAIRVILLE	WAYNE	ARCADIA
FAIRVILLE STA.	WAYNE	ARCADIA
FALCONER JCT.	CHAUTAUQUA	ELLICOTT
FALCONER V.	CHAUTAUQUA	ELLICOTT
FALL BRIDGE	OTSEGO	NEW LISBON
FALL ST. PK.	TOMPKINS	ITHACA
FALLSBURG	SULLIVAN	FALLSBURG
FALLSBURG STA.	SULLIVAN	FALLSBURG
FANCHER	ORLEANS	MURRAY
FAR ROCKAWAY	QUEENS	NYC
FARGO STA.	GENESEE	DARIEN

NAME	COUNTY	TOWN
FARLEY	CAYUGA	SPRINGPORT
FARMER	SENECA	COVERT
FARMERS MILLS	PUTNAM	KENT
FARMERSVILLE	CATTARAUGUS	FARMERSVILLE
FARMERSVILLE STA.	CATTARAUGUS	FARMERSVILLE
FARMINGDALE STA.	ORANGE	BLOOMING GR.
FARMINGDALE V.	NASSAU	OYSTER BAY
FARMINGTON	ONTARIO	FARMINGTON
FARMINGTON STA.	ONTARIO	FARMINGTON
FARMINGVILLE	SUFFOLK	BROOKHAVEN
FARNHAM V.	ERIE	BRANT
FAUST	FRANKLIN	ALTAMONT
FAYETTE	SENECA	FAYETTE
FAYETTE SIDING	SENECA	VARICK
FAYETTEVILLE V.	ONONDAGA	MANLIUS
FAYVILLE	SARATOGA	PROVIDENCE
FECOE CORS.	FULTON	EPHRATAH
FEEDER DAM	SARATOGA	MOREAU
FELTS MILLS	JEFFERSON	RUTLAND
FENNER	MADISON	FENNER
FENNER GRV. STA.	HERKIMER	NEWPORT
FENTONVILLE	CHAUTAUQUA	CARROLL
FERENBAUGH	STEUBEN	HORNBY
FERGUSON CORS.	YATES	BENTON
FERGUSONVILLE	DELAWARE	DAVENPORT
FERNDALE	SULLIVAN	LIBERTY
FERNWOOD	SULLIVAN	FREMONT
FERNWOOD	OSWEGO	RICHLAND
FERNWOOD HALL	ST. LAWRENCE	HOPKINTON
FERO	CHEMUNG	CATLIN
FERRONA	CLINTON	AUSABLE
FEURA BUSH	ALBANY	BETHLEHEM
FEURA BUSH	ALBANY	NEW SCOTLAND
FICAL CORS.	FULTON	EPHRATAH
FIELDHOME	WESTCHESTER	YORKTOWN
FILLMORE V.	ALLEGANY	HUME
FILTS CORS.	TOMPKINS	GROTON
FINCH HOLLOW	BROOME	MAINE
FINCHVILLE	ORANGE	MT. HOPE
FINDLEY LAKE	CHAUTAUQUA	MINA
FINE	ST. LAWRENCE	FINE
FINE VIEW	JEFFERSON	ORLEANS
FINKS BASIN	HERKIMER	DANUBE
FIRE ISLAND	SUFFOLK	ISLIP
FIRE PLACE	SUFFOLK	E. HAMPTON
FIRTHCLIFFE	ORANGE	CORNWALL
FISH CREEK	LEWIS	LEWIS
FISH CREEK	ONEIDA	VERONA
FISH CREEK LDG.	ULSTER	SAUGERTIES
FISH CREEK LDG.	ONEIDA	ROME C.
FISH CREEK LDG.	ONEIDA	VIENNA
FISH EDDY	DELAWARE	HANCOCK
FISH LAKE	CATTARAUGUS	FREEDOM
FISHERS	ONTARIO	VICTOR
FISHERS ISL.	SUFFOLK	SOUTHOLD
FISHERS LDG.	JEFFERSON	ORLEANS
FISHERVILLE STA.	ONTARIO	VICTOR
FISHKILL FURNACE	DUTCHESS	E. FISHKILL
FISHKILL HOOK	DUTCHESS	E. FISHKILL
FISHKILL LDG.	DUTCHESS	BEACON C.
FISHKILL PLAINS	DUTCHESS	E. FISHKILL
FISHKILL V.	DUTCHESS	FISHKILL
FISHKILL-ON-HUDSON	DUTCHESS	FISHKILL
FITCH	CATTARAUGUS	FRANKLINVILLE
FITCH BRIDGE	CHEMUNG	BIG FLATS
FITCH POINT	WASHINGTON	SALEM
FITTS CORS.	TOMPKINS	GROTON
FITZGERALD	LEWIS	DIANA
FIVE CORS.	WYOMING	CASTILE
FIVE CORS.	ORLEANS	GAINES
FIVE CORS.	CAYUGA	GENOA
FIVE MILE	CATTARAUGUS	HUMPHREY
FIVE MILE POINT	BROOME	KIRKWOOD
FLACKVILLE	ST. LAWRENCE	LISBON
FLAGG	ESSEX	JAY
FLANDERS	SUFFOLK	SOUTHAMPTON
FLAT CREEK	MONTGOMERY	ROOT
FLAT CREEK	SCHOHARIE	GILBOA
FLATBROOK	COLUMBIA	CANAAN
FLATBUSH	ULSTER	SAUGERTIES
FLATBUSH	KINGS	NYC
FLATBUSH AVE. STA.	KINGS	NYC
FLATLANDS	KINGS	NYC
FLATLANDS STA.	KINGS	NYC
FLEETWOOD	WESTCHESTER	MT. VERNON
FLEISCHMANNS V.	DELAWARE	MIDDLETOWN
FLEMING	CAYUGA	FLEMING
FLEMINGVILLE	TIOGA	OWEGO
FLINT	ULSTER	PLATTEKILL
FLINT	ONTARIO	SENECA
FLOODWOOD STA.	FRANKLIN	SANTA CLARA
FLORAL PARK	QUEENS	NYC
FLORAL PARK CREST	NASSAU	HEMPSTEAD
FLORAL PARK CTR.	NASSAU	NO. HEMPSTEAD
FLORAL PARK V.	NASSAU	N. HEMPSTEAD
FLORAL PARK V.	NASSAU	HEMPSTEAD
FLORENCE	ONEIDA	FLORENCE

NAME	COUNTY	TOWN
FLORENCE HILL	ONEIDA	FLORENCE
FLORIDA V.	ORANGE	WARWICK
FLOWER HILL V.	NASSAU	N. HEMPSTEAD
FLOWERFIELD	SUFFOLK	SMITHTOWN
FLOWERS	BROOME	WINDSOR
FLOYD	ONEIDA	FLOYD
FLUSHING	QUEENS	NYC
FLUVANNA	CHAUTAUQUA	ELLICOTT
FLY CREEK	OTSEGO	OTSEGO
FLY MOUNTAIN	ULSTER	ULSTER
FLY POINT	SUFFOLK	SOUTHAMPTON
FLY SUMMIT	WASHINGTON	CAMBRIDGE
FOGGINTOWN	PUTNAM	SOUTHEAST
FOLSOMDALE	WYOMING	BENNINGTON
FOLTS CORS.	CAYUGA	MORAVIA
FONDA JOHNSTOWN	MONTGOMERY	MOHAWK
FONDA V.	MONTGOMERY	MOHAWK
FONT GROVE	ALBANY	BETHLEHEM
FOOTS CORS.	LIVINGSTON	CONESUS
FORD CLEARING	LEWIS	DIANA
FORD'S CLEARING	LEWIS	DIANA
FORDHAM	BRONX	NYC
FORDHAM HEIGHTS	BRONX	NYC
FORDS BROOK	ALLEGANY	WILLING
FORDS BROOK	ALLEGANY	ALMA
FOREST	CLINTON	ALTONA
FOREST CITY	LEWIS	CROGHAN
FOREST GLEN	ULSTER	GARDINER
FOREST HILLS	QUEENS	NYC
FOREST HOME	TOMPKINS	ITHACA
FOREST HOME	WYOMING	PERRY
FOREST LAWN	MONROE	WEBSTER
FOREST LAWN	STEUBEN	DANSVILLE
FOREST OF DEAN	ORANGE	HIGHLANDS
FOREST PARK	QUEENS	NYC
FOREST VALLEY	GREENE	LEXINGTON
FORESTBURGH	SULLIVAN	FORESTBURGH
FORESTDALE	FRANKLIN	FRANKLIN
FORESTINE	SULLIVAN	BETHEL
FORESTPORT	ONEIDA	FORESTPORT
FORESTVILLE V.	CHAUTAUQUA	HANOVER
FORGE HOLLOW	ONEIDA	MARSHALL
FORKS	ERIE	CHEEKTOWAGA
FORT ANN V.	WASHINGTON	FT. ANN
FORT BULL	ONEIDA	ROME C.
FORT EDWARD CTR.	WASHINGTON	FORT EDWARD
FORT EDWARD V.	WASHINGTON	FT. EDWARD
FORT GEORGE	NEW YORK	NYC
FORT HAMILTON	KINGS	NYC
FORT HUNTER	MONTGOMERY	FLORIDA
FORT JACKSON	ST. LAWRENCE	HOPKINTON
FORT JOHNSON V.	MONTGOMERY	AMSTERDAM
FORT MILLER	WASHINGTON	FORT EDWARD
FORT MILLER	WASHINGTON	GREENWICH
FORT MILLER BRDG.	WASHINGTON	GREENWICH
FORT MONTGOMERY	CLINTON	CHAMPLAIN
FORT MONTGOMERY	ORANGE	HIGHLANDS
FORT NIAGARA	NIAGARA	PORTER
FORT PLAIN STA.	MONTGOMERY	PALATINE
FORT PLAIN V.	MONTGOMERY	MINDEN
FORT PLAIN V.	MONTGOMERY	CANAJOHARIE
FORT POPTER	ERIE	BUFFALO C.
FORT SALONGA	SUFFOLK	SMITHTOWN
FORT SALONGA	SUFFOLK	HUNTINGTON
FORT SCHUYLER	BRONX	NYC
FORT TILDEN	QUEENS	NYC
FORT WADSWORTH	RICHMOND	NYC
FORT WASHINGTON	NEW YORK	NYC
FORTSVILLE	SARATOGA	MOREAU
FOSTER	TIOGA	OWEGO
FOSTER HOLLOW	TIOGA	OWEGO
FOSTERDALE	SULLIVAN	COCHECTON
FOSTERTOWN	ORANGE	NEWBURGH
FOSTERVILLE	CAYUGA	AURELIUS
FOUR MILE	CATTARAUGUS	ALLEGANY
FOUR MILE GROC.	HERKIMER	FRANKFORT
FOWLER	ST. LAWRENCE	FOWLER
FOWLERSVILLE	LEWIS	LYONSDALE
FOWLERVILLE	ERIE	CONCORD
FOWLERVILLE	LIVINGSTON	YORK
FOX HILLS	SARATOGA	EDINBURG
FOX ISLAND	JEFFERSON	CAPE VINCENT
FOX RIDGE	CAYUGA	MONTEZUMA
FRANK CORS.	CORTLAND	CORTLANDVILLE
FRANK'S CORNERS	CORTLAND	VIRGIL
FRANKFORT HILL	HERKIMER	FRANKFORT
FRANKFORT STA.	HERKIMER	SCHUYLER
FRANKFORT V.	HERKIMER	FRANKFORT
FRANKLIN DEPOT	DELAWARE	SIDNEY
FRANKLIN FALLS	FRANKLIN	FRANKLIN
FRANKLIN SPRGS.	ONEIDA	KIRKLAND
FRANKLIN SQ.	NASSAU	HEMPSTEAD
FRANKLIN V.	DELAWARE	FRANKLIN
FRANKLINTON	SCHOHARIE	BROOME
FRANKLINVILLE V.	CATTARAUGUS	FRANKLINVILLE
FRASER	LIVINGSTON	YORK
FRECK	CATTARAUGUS	RED HOUSE

NAME	COUNTY	TOWN
FREDERICK CORS.	JEFFERSON	WORTH
FREDONIA V.	CHAUTAUQUA	POMFRET
FREEDOM	CATTARAUGUS	FREEDOM
FREEDOM PLAINS	DUTCHESS	LAGRANGE
FREEHOLD	GREENE	GREENVILLE
FREEMAN	STEUBEN	TUSCARORA
FREEMANSBURG	ST. LAWRENCE	EDWARDS
FREEPORT V.	NASSAU	HEMPSTEAD
FREETOWN	SUFFOLK	E. HAMPTON
FREETOWN CORS.	CORTLAND	FREETOWN
FREEVILLE V.	TOMPKINS	DRYDEN
FREMONT CTR.	SULLIVAN	FREMONT
FRENCH CREEK	CHAUTAUQUA	FRENCH CR.
FRENCH MILLS	ALBANY	GUILDERLAND
FRENCH MOUNTAIN	WARREN	QUEENSBURY
FRENCH WOODS	DELAWARE	HANCOCK
FRENCHVILLE	ONEIDA	WESTERN
FRESH POND	SUFFOLK	SHITHTOWN
FRESH POND	QUEENS	NYC
FRESH POND LDG.	SUFFOLK	RIVERHEAD
FRESHKILLS	RICHMOND	NYC
FREWSBURG	CHAUTAUQUA	CARROLL
FREYBUSH	MONTGOMERY	MINDEN
FREYDENBURGH FALLS	CLINTON	PLATTSBURG
FRIAR HEAD LDG.	SUFFOLK	RIVERHEAD
FRIEND	YATES	JERUSALEM
FRIENDSHIP	ALLEGANY	FRIENDSHIP
FRISBEE ST.	COLUMBIA	CANAAN
FRONTENAC	JEFFERSON	CLAYTON
FRONTIER	DUTCHESS	CLINTON
FROST HILL	ONTARIO	SO. BRISTOL
FROST VALLEY	ULSTER	DENNING
FRUITLAND	WAYNE	ONTARIO
FT. BREWERTON	OSWEGO	HASTINGS
FULLER STA.	ALBANY	GUILDERLAND
FULLERVILLE	ST. LAWRENCE	FOWLER
FULMER VALLEY	ALLEGANY	INDEPENDENCE
FULTON C.	OSWEGO	FULTON C.
FULTONHAM	SCHOHARIE	FULTON
FULTONVILLE V.	MONTGOMERY	GLEN
FURNACE	WAYNE	WOLCOTT
FURNACE WOODS	WESTCHESTER	CORTLANDT
FURNACEVILLE	WAYNE	ONTARIO
FYLER SETT.	MADISON	SULLIVAN

-G-

NAME	COUNTY	TOWN
GABRIELS	FRANKLIN	BRIGHTON
GAGE	YATES	BENTON
GAINES	ORLEANS	GAINES
GAINES BASIN	ORLEANS	GAINES
GAINESVILLE	WYOMING	GAINESVILLE
GAINESVILLE CTR.	WYOMING	GAINESVILLE
GAINESVILLE V.	WYOMING	GAINESVILLE
GALE	ST. LAWRENCE	HOPKINTON
GALENA	CHENANGO	NO. NORWICH
GALENA STA.	CHENANGO	NO. NORWICH
GALEVILLE	ULSTER	SHAWANGUNK
GALEVILLE	WASHINGTON	GREENWICH
GALEVILLE	ONONDAGA	SALINA
GALILEE	ST. LAWRENCE	OSWEGATCHIE
GALLATINVILLE	COLUMBIA	GALLATIN
GALLUPVILLE	SCHOHARIE	WRIGHT
GALOP ISLAND	ST. LAWRENCE	LISBON
GALWAY V.	SARATOGA	GALWAY
GANAGHOTE	ULSTER	GARDINER
GANG MILLS	HERKIMER	RUSSIA
GANSEVOORT	SARATOGA	NORTHUMBERLAND
GARBUTT	MONROE	WHEATLAND
GARDEN CITY PK.	NASSAU	NO. HEMPSTEAD
GARDEN CITY SOUTH	NASSAU	HEMPSTEAD
GARDEN CITY V.	NASSAU	HEMPSTEAD
GARDENERS ISLAND	SUFFOLK	E. HAMPTON
GARDINER	ULSTER	GARDINER
GARDINERS CORS.	OSWEGO	HASTINGS
GARDNER CORS.	LEWIS	MONTAGUE
GARDNERTOWN	ORANGE	NEWBURGH
GARDNERVILLE	SCHOHARIE	SEWARD
GARDNERVILLE	ORANGE	WAWAYANDA
GARFIELD	RENSSELAER	STEPHENTOWN
GARLAND	MONROE	CLARKSON
GARLEY	WARREN	LAKE LUZERNE
GARLINGHOUSE	ONTARIO	NAPLES
GARNERVILLE	ROCKLAND	HAVERSTRAW
GAPNET LAKE	WARREN	JOHNSBURG
GAROGA	FULTON	EPHRATAH
GAPRATTSVILLE	OTSEGO	NEW LISBON
GAPPETSONS	RICHMOND	NYC
GARRISON	PUTNAM	PHILIPSTOWN
GARWOOD	ALLEGANY	BURNS
GARWOODS STA.	ALLEGANY	BURNS
GAS SPRING	ALLEGANY	BURNS
GASKILL	TIOGA	OWEGO
GASPORT	NIAGARA	ROYALTON
GATES	MONROE	GATES
GATES CTR.	MONROE	GATES
GAY HEAD	DUTCHESS	E. FISHKILL

NAME	COUNTY	TOWN
GAYHEAD	GREENE	GREENVILLE
GAYVILLE	OSWEGO	CONSTANTIA
GEDNEY WAY	WESTCHESTER	WHITE PLAINS C
GEE BROOK	CORTLAND	CINCINNATUS
GEEDS CORS.	ST. LAWRENCE	PITCAIRN
GENEGANTSLET	CHENANGO	GREENE
GENESEE RAPIDS	MONROE	ROCHESTER C.
GENESEO V.	LIVINGSTON	GENESEO
GENEVA C.	ONTARIO	GENEVA C.
GENOA	CAYUGA	GENOA
GEORGETOWN	MADISON	GEORGETOWN
GEORGETOWN	CORTLAND	WILLET
GEORGETOWN HEIGHTS	CORTLAND	WILLET
GEORGETOWN STA.	MADISON	GEORGETOWN
GEORGICA	SUFFOLK	E. HAMPTON
GERMAN	CHENANGO	GERMAN
GERMANTOWN	COLUMBIA	GERMANTOWN
GERMANTOWN STA.	COLUMBIA	GERMANTOWN
GERRY	CHAUTAUQUA	GERRY
GETMAN CORS.	HERKIMER	COLUMBIA
GETZVILLE	ERIE	AMHERST
GHENT	COLUMBIA	GHENT
GIBSON	STEUBEN	CORNING
GIBSON CORS.	TIOGA	OWEGO
GIBSON LDG.	STEUBEN	PULTENEY
GIFFORDS	RICHMOND	NYC
GIFFORDS	CHAUTAUQUA	ELLERY
GILBERT	SENECA	OVID
GILBERT L. STATE PARK	OTSEGO	LAURENS
GILBERT MILLS	OSWEGO	SCHROEPPEL
GILBERTSVILLE V.	OTSEGO	BUTTERNUTS
GILBOA	SCHOHARIE	GILBOA
GILMANTOWN	HAMILTON	WELLS
GLADE	SARATOGA	CORINTH
GLASCO	ULSTER	SAUGERTIES
GLASCO MILLS	FULTON	CAPOGA
GLASS HOUSE	RENSSELAER	SAND LAKE
GLASS HOUSE	ALBANY	GUILDERLAND
GLASS LAKE	RENSSELAER	SAND LAKE
GLEN	MONTGOMERY	GLEN
GLEN AUBREY	BROOME	NANTICOKE
GLEN BROOK	STEUBEN	URBANA
GLEN CASTLE	BROOME	CHENANGO
GLEN COVE C.	NASSAU	GLEN COVE C.
GLEN EDITH	MONROE	WEBSTER
GLEN HAVEN	CAYUGA	SEMPRONIUS
GLEN HAVEN VALLEY	MONROE	IRONDEQUOIT
GLEN HEAD	NASSAU	OYSTER BAY
GLEN ISLAND	WARREN	BOLTON
GLEN LAKE	WARREN	QUEENSBURY
GLEN PAPK V.	JEFFERSON	BROWNVILLE
GLEN PARK V.	JEFFERSON	PAMELIA
GLEN SPEY	SULLIVAN	LUMBERLAND
GLEN STATE PARK	TOMPKINS	ENFIELD
GLEN WILD	SULLIVAN	FALLSBURG
GLEN WILD	SULLIVAN	THOMPSON
GLENBURNIE ON L. GEORGE	WASHINGTON	PUTNAM
GLENCAIRN	TIOGA	BARTON
GLENCO MILLS	COLUMBIA	LIVINGSTON
GLENDALE	LEWIS	MARTINSBURG
GLENDALE STA.	QUEENS	NYC
GLENERIE	ULSTER	ULSTER
GLENFIELD	LEWIS	MARTINSBURG
GLENFORD	ULSTER	HURLEY
GLENHAM	DUTCHESS	FISHKILL
GLENMARK	WAYNE	ROSE
GLENMONT	ALBANY	BETHLEHEM
GLENMORE	ONEIDA	ANNSVILLE
GLENORA	YATES	STARKEY
GLENS FALLS C.	WARREN	GLENS FALLS C.
GLENVILLE	SCHENECTADY	GLENVILLE
GLENVILLE	WESTCHESTER	GREENBURGH
GLENVILLE STA.	SCHENECTADY	GLENVILLE
GLENWILD	SARATOGA	PROVIDENCE
GLENWOOD	TOMPKINS	ULYSSES
GLENWOOD	ERIE	COLDEN
GLENWOOD LDG.	NASSAU	OYSTER BAY
GLENWOOD LDG.	NASSAU	NO. HEMPSTEAD
GLOVERSVILLE C.	FULTON	GLOVERSVILLE C
GODEFFROY	ORANGE	DEER PARK
GOLAH	MONROE	RUSH
GOLDEN GLOW HEIGHTS	CHEMUNG	BIG FLATS
GOLDENS BRIDGE	WESTCHESTER	LEWISBORO
GOLDIN PARK	ORANGE	CRAWFORD
GOLDRICKS LDG.	ULSTER	ULSTER
GOLDSMITH	FRANKLIN	FRANKLIN
GOOD GROUND	SUFFOLK	SOUTHAMPTON
GOODHUE LAKE	STEUBEN	ADDISON
GOODIER CORS.	HERKIMER	LITCHFIELD
GOODING LDG.	ONTARIO	GORHAM
GOODRICH MILLS	CLINTON	BLACK BROOK
GOODRICH SETT.	TIOGA	TIOGA
GOODWILL	ORANGE	MONTGOMERY
GOODYEAR	CAYUGA	GENOA
GOOLEY	ESSEX	MINERVA

Alphabetical List of Cities, Villages and Hamlets
Showing Location by County and Town
PART TWO

NAME	COUNTY	TOWN	NAME	COUNTY	TOWN
GOOSE BAY	JEFFERSON	ALEXANDRIA	GREENVILLE	ORANGE	GREENVILLE
GOOSE CREEK STA.	QUEENS	NYC	GREENVILLE	WESTCHESTER	GREENBURGH
GOOSETREE	CAYUGA	GENOA	GREENVILLE	GREENE	GREENVILLE
GORDON STA.	CATTARAUGUS	PORTVILLE	GREENVILLE CTR.	GREENE	GREENVILLE
GORHAM	ONTARIO	GORHAM	GREENWAY	ONEIDA	ROME C.
GOSHEN	CLINTON	PERU	GREENWICH JCT.	WASHINGTON	SALEM
GOSHEN V.	ORANGE	GOSHEN	GREENWICH V.	WASHINGTON	GREENWICH
GOSLEY	ESSEX	MINERVA	GREENWICH V.	WASHINGTON	EASTON
GOULD	COLUMBIA	STOCKPORT	GREENWOOD	STEUBEN	GREENWOOD
GOULDS	DELAWARE	HANCOCK	GREENWOOD IRON WORK	ORANGE	TUXEDO
GOULDS MILLS	LEWIS	LYONSDALE	GREENWOOD LAKE V.	ORANGE	WARWICK
GOUVERNEUR V.	ST. LAWRENCE	GOUVERNEUR	GREENWOOD STA.	STEUBEN	GREENWOOD
GOVERNOR'S ISLAND	NEW YORK	NYC	GREGORYTOWN	DELAWARE	COLCHESTER
GOWANDA PSYCHIATRIC CENTER	ERIE	COLLINS T.	GREIG	LEWIS	GREIG
			GREIGSVILLE	LIVINGSTON	YORK
GOWANDA V.	CATTARAUGUS	PERSIA	GRENADIER ISLAND	JEFFERSON	CAPE VINCENT
GOWANDA V.	ERIE	COLLINS	GRENELL	JEFFERSON	CLAYTON
GRACIE	CORTLAND	CORTLANDVILLE	GRENELL ISLAND	JEFFERSON	CLAYTON
GRAFTON	RENSSELAER	GRAFTON	GRETNA	DUTCHESS	PLEASANT VALLEY
GRAHAM'S CHURCH	ORANGE	CRAWFORD	GRIDLEYVILLE	TIOGA	CANDOR
GRAHAMSVILLE	SULLIVAN	NEVERSINK	GRIFFIN	HAMILTON	WELLS
GRANBY CTR.	OSWEGO	GRANBY	GRIFFIN CORS.	DELAWARE	MIDDLETOWN
GRAND GORGE STA.	DELAWARE	ROXBURY	GRIFFITH	CHAUTAUQUA	ELLERY
GRAND VIEW	HERKIMER	FRANKFORT	GRIFFITHS CORS.	WYOMING	PIKE
GRAND VIEW BEACH	MONROE	GREECE	GRINDSTONE	JEFFERSON	CLAYTON
GRAND VIEW PK.	ERIE	HAMBURG	GRINDSTONE ISLAND	JEFFERSON	CLAYTON
GRAND VIEW-ON-HUDSON V.	ROCKLAND	ORANGETOWN	GRISWOLD	GENESEE	DARIEN
			GRISWOLD	CHAUTAUQUA	ARKWRIGHT
GRANGER	ONTARIO	GORHAM	GRISWOLD STA.	GENESEE	DARIEN
GRANGER	ALLEGANY	GRANGER	GROOMS	SARATOGA	CLIFTON PARK
GRANGERVILLE	SARATOGA	SARATOGA	GROOMS CORS.	CHEMUNG	BIG FLATS
GRANITE	ULSTER	ROCHESTER	GROOMS CORS.	SARATOGA	CLIFTON PARK
GRANITE SPRGS.	WESTCHESTER	SOMERS	GROOVILLE	SULLIVAN	ROCKLAND
GRANITEVILLE	RICHMOND	NYC	GROTON CITY	TOMPKINS	GROTON
GRANT	CHAUTAUQUA	HARMONY	GROTON V.	TOMPKINS	GROTON
GRANT	HERKIMER	RUSSIA	GROTTO	TOMPKINS	GROTON
GRANT C.	ST. LAWRENCE	RUSSELL	GROVE	ALLEGANY	GROVE
GRANT C.	RICHMOND	NYC	GROVE	HAMILTON	LONG LAKE
GRANT PARK	NASSAU	HEMPSTEAD	GROVE BANK	ESSEX	CROWN POINT
GRANT STA.	CHAUTAUQUA	HARMONY	GROVE HOUSE	HAMILTON	LONG LAKE
GRANTS HOLLOW	RENSSELAER	SCHAGHTICOKE	GROVE SPRGS.	STEUBEN	WAYNE
GRANVILLE V.	WASHINGTON	GRANVILLE	GROVE SPRGS.	ONEIDA	VERONA
GRAPEVILLE	GREENE	NEW BALTIMORE	GROVENOR CORS.	SCHOHARIE	CARLISLE
GRAPHITE	WARREN	HAGUE	GROVEVILLE	WESTCHESTER	CORTLANDT
GRASSLANDS	WESTCHESTER	MT. PLEASANT	GROVEVILLE	DUTCHESS	FISHKILL
GRASSLANDS HOSP.	WESTCHESTER	MT. PLEASANT	GUILDERLAND	ALBANY	GUILDERLAND
GRASSMERE	RICHMOND	NYC	GUILDERLAND CTR.	ALBANY	GUILDERLAND
GRASSY HOLLOW	SUFFOLK	E. HAMPTON	GUILFORD	CHENANGO	GUILFORD
GRASSY POINT	ROCKLAND	STONY POINT	GUILFORD	ULSTER	GARDINER
GRAVES	ALLEGANY	WILLING	GUILFORD CTR.	CHENANGO	GUILFORD
GRAVESEND	KINGS	NYC	GULF HEAD	LEWIS	TURIN
GRAVESEND BEACH	KINGS	NYC	GULF HEAD STA.	LEWIS	TURIN
GRAVESVILLE	HERKIMER	RUSSIA	GULF SUMMIT	BROOME	SANFORD
GRAY	HERKIMER	OHIO	GULICK	ONTARIO	SO. BRISTOL
GRAY	HERKIMER	NORWAY	GULL BAY	WASHINGTON	PUTNAM
GRAY CORS.	SARATOGA	HALFMOON	GULPH	HERKIMER	FRANKFORT
GRAYMOOR	PUTNAM	PHILIPSTOWN	GUNN CORS.	JEFFERSON	CLAYTON
GREAT BEND	JEFFERSON	CHAMPION	GUNNSONS	ESSEX	CROWN POINT
GREAT FALLS	GREENE	CATSKILL	GURN SPRINGS	SARATOGA	MILTON
GREAT KILLS	RICHMOND	NYC	GUYMARD	ORANGE	MT. HOPE
GREAT MEADOW CORR. FAC.	WASHINGTON	FORT ANN	GUYMARD STA.	ORANGE	MT. HOPE
GREAT NECK V.	NASSAU	NO. HEMPSTEAD	GUYUNOGA	YATES	JERUSALEM
GREAT NECK V.	NASSAU	N. HEMPSTEAD	GYPSUM	ONTARIO	MANCHESTER
GREAT NECK ESTATES V.	NASSAU	N. HEMPSTEAD			
GREAT NECK PLAZA V.	NASSAU	N. HEMPSTEAD		-H-	
GREAT RIVER	SUFFOLK	ISLIP	HADLEY	SARATOGA	HADLEY
GREAT VALLEY	CATTARAUGUS	GREAT VALLEY	HAGAMAN V.	MONTGOMERY	AMSTERDAM
GREECE	MONROE	GREECE	HAGEDORN MILLS	SARATOGA	PROVIDENCE
GREEN	ONTARIO	GORHAM	HAGERMAN	SUFFOLK	BROOKHAVEN
GREEN ACRES	NASSAU	HEMPSTEAD	HAGUE	WARREN	HAGUE
			HAILESBORO	ST. LAWRENCE	FOWLER
GREEN CORS.	ALLEGANY	INDEPENDENCE	HAINES CORS. STA.	GREENE	HUNTER
GREEN HAVEN	DUTCHESS	BEEKMAN	HAINES FALLS	GREENE	HUNTER
GREEN HAVEN STA.	DUTCHESS	BEEKMAN	HALCOTT CTR.	GREENE	HALCOTT
GREEN ISLAND V.	ALBANY	GREEN ISLAND	HALCOTTVILLE	DELAWARE	MIDDLETOWN
GREEN LAKE	FULTON	CAROGA	HALE EDDY	DELAWARE	DEPOSIT
GREEN LAWN	SUFFOLK	HUNTINGTON	HALESITE	SUFFOLK	HUNTINGTON
GREEN POINT	KINGS	NYC	HALF ACRE	CAYUGA	AURELIUS
GREEN RIDGE	RICHMOND	NYC	HALF HOLLOW	SUFFOLK	HUNTINGTON
GREEN RIVER	COLUMBIA	HILLSDALE	HALFMOON	SARATOGA	HALFMOON
GREEN VALLEY	CLINTON	MOOERS	HALL	CATTARAUGUS	RED HOUSE
GREEN'S LOG.	ONTARIO	GORHAM	HALL	ONTARIO	SENECA
GREEN'S STA.	ONTARIO	GORHAM	HALL CORS.	JEFFERSON	ANTWERP
GREENBORO	OSWEGO	REDFIELD	HALL CORS.	SENECA	COVERT
GREENBUSH	SCHOHARIE	FULTON	HALLOCK ACRES	SUFFOLK	SMITHTOWN
GREENBUSH	RENSSELAER	E. GREENBUSH	HALLS CORS.	SCHUYLER	READING
GREENBUSH	SCHOHARIE	COBLESKILL	HALLS CORS.	WYOMING	ORANGEVILLE
GREENE CORS. STA.	ONEIDA	ROME C.	HALLS MILLS	SULLIVAN	NEVERSINK
GREENE SETTLEMENT	JEFFERSON	ADAMS	HALLSPORT	ALLEGANY	WILLING
GREENE V.	CHENANGO	GREENE	HALLSVILLE	MONTGOMERY	MINDEN
GREENFIELD	SARATOGA	GREENFIELD	HALSEY VALLEY	TIOGA	TIOGA
GREENFIELD PARK	ULSTER	WAWARSING	HALSEY VALLEY	TIOGA	BARTON
GREENFIELD STA.	SARATOGA	GREENFIELD	HALSEYVILLE	TOMPKINS	ULYSSES
GREENHURST	CHAUTAUQUA	ELLERY	HALSTEAD	COLUMBIA	ANCRAM
GREENPORT V.	SUFFOLK	SOUTHOLD	HAMBLETTVILLE	DELAWARE	DEPOSIT
GREENVALE	NASSAU	NO. HEMPSTEAD	HAMBURG STA.	ERIE	HAMBURG

55

NAME	COUNTY	TOWN
HAMBURG V.	ERIE	HAMBURG
HAMBURG-ON-LAKE	ERIE	HAMBURG
HAMDEN	DELAWARE	HAMDEN
HAMILTON BEACH	QUEENS	NYC
HAMILTON CTR.	MADISON	HAMILTON
HAMILTON STA.	MADISON	HAMILTON
HAMILTON V.	MADISON	HAMILTON
HAMILTONVILLE	ALBANY	GUILDERLAND
HAMLET	CHAUTAUQUA	VILLENOVA
HAMLIN	MONROE	HAMLIN
HAMMOND CORS. STA.	ESSEX	CROWN POINT
HAMMOND V.	ST.LAWRENCE	HAMMOND
HAMMONDSPORT V.	STEUBEN	URBANA
HAMMONDVILLE	ESSEX	CROWN POINT
HAMPSHIRE	STEUBEN	JASPER
HAMPTON	WASHINGTON	HAMPTON
HAMPTON	RENSSELAER	E. GREENBUSH
HAMPTON BAYS	SUFFOLK	SOUTHAMPTON
HAMPTON MANOR	RENSSELAER	E. GREENBUSH
HAMPTON PARK	SUFFOLK	SOUTHAMPTON
HAMPTONBURG	ORANGE	HAMPTONBURG
HAMPTONBURG STA.	ORANGE	HAMPTONBURG
HANCOCK JCT.	DELAWARE	HANCOCK
HANCOCK STA.	DELAWARE	HANCOCK
HANCOCK V.	DELAWARE	HANCOCK
HANKINS V.	SULLIVAN	FREMONT
HANLEY CORS.	DELAWARE	MIDDLETOWN
HANNACROIX	GREENE	NEW BALTIMORE
HANNAWA FALLS	ST.LAWRENCE	PIERREPONT
HANNIBAL CTR.	OSWEGO	HANNIBAL
HANNIBAL V.	OSWEGO	HANNIBAL
HANOVER CT. HSE.	ONEIDA	MARSHALL
HANOVER CTR.	CHAUTAUQUA	HANOVER
HAPPY VALLEY	OSWEGO	ALBION
HARBOR	HERKIMER	FRANKFORT
HARBOR BARGE CANAL	HERKIMER	FRANKFORT
HARBOR ISLE	NASSAU	HEMPSTEAD
HARBOR STA.	HERKIMER	FRANKFORT
HARD SCRABBLE	CLINTON	SARANAC
HARD SCRABBLE	SUFFOLK	E. HAMPTON
HARDENBURGH	ULSTER	HARDENBURGH
HARDY	WYOMING	GAINESVILLE
HARFORD	CORTLAND	HARFORD
HARFORD MILLS	CORTLAND	HARFORD
HARKNESS	CLINTON	AUSABLE
HARLEM VALLEY PSYCHIATRIC CT	DUTCHESS	DOVER
HARLEMVILLE	COLUMBIA	HILLSDALE
HARMON-ON-HUDSON	WESTCHESTER	CORTLANDT
HARPERSFIELD	DELAWARE	HARPERSFIELD
HARPERSFIELD CTR.	DELAWARE	HARPERSFIELD
HARPURSVILLE	BROOME	COLESVILLE
HARPURSVILLE STA.	BROOME	COLESVILLE
HARRIETSTOWN	FRANKLIN	HARRIETSTOWN
HARRIGAN CORS.	CLINTON	ELLENBURG
HARRIMAN V.	ORANGE	MONROE
HARRIS	SULLIVAN	THOMPSON
HARRIS HILL	ERIE	CLARENCE
HARRIS ROAD	ORLEANS	CARLTON
HARRISBURG	CATTARAUGUS	ALLEGANY
HARRISBURG	LEWIS	HARRISBURG
HARRISBURG	WARREN	STONY CREEK
HARRISVILLE V.	LEWIS	DIANA
HARROWER	MONTGOMERY	AMSTERDAM
HARRYSBURG	CHAUTAUQUA	DUNKIRK
HART LOT	ONONDAGA	ELBRIDGE
HARTFIELD	CHAUTAUQUA	CHAUTAUQUA
HARTFORD	WASHINGTON	HARTFORD
HARTLAND CORNERS	NIAGARA	HARTLAND
HARTMAN	WARREN	LAKE LUZERNE
HARTSDALE	WESTCHESTER	GREENBURGH
HARTSVILLE CTR.	STEUBEN	HARTSVILLE
HARTWELL STA.	FRANKLIN	FRANKLIN
HARTWICK	OTSEGO	HARTWICK
HARTWICK SEMINARY	OTSEGO	HARTWICK
HARTWOOD	SULLIVAN	FORESTBURGH
HARVARD	DELAWARE	HANCOCK
HARVEY	ONTARIO	PHELPS
HASBROOKS	HAMILTON	LONG LAKE
HASBROUCK	SULLIVAN	FALLSBURG
HASKEL FLATS	CATTARAUGUS	HINSDALE
HASKINVILLE	STEUBEN	FREMONT
HASTINGS	OSWEGO	HASTINGS
HASTINGS CTR.	OSWEGO	HASTINGS
HASTINGS-ON-HUDSON V	WESTCHESTER	GREENBURGH
HAUPPAUGE	SUFFOLK	SMITHTOWN
HAUPPAUGE	SUFFOLK	ISLIP
HAVEN	SULLIVAN	MAMAKATING
HAVERSTRAW V.	ROCKLAND	HAVERSTRAW
HAVILAND HOLLOW	PUTNAM	PATTERSON
HAWKES	ALLEGANY	WILLING
HAWKEYE	CLINTON	BLACK BROOK
HAWKINSVILLE	ONEIDA	BOONVILLE
HAWLEY STA.	DELAWARE	HAMDEN
HAWLEYTON	BROOME	BINGHAMTON
HAWTHORNE	WESTCHESTER	MT. PLEASANT

NAME	COUNTY	TOWN
HAYGROUND	SUFFOLK	SOUTHAMPTON
HAYMAKER	CATTARAUGUS	OLEAN
HAYNERVILLE	RENSSELAER	BRUNSWICK
HAYNES	CHENANGO	NORWICH
HAYT CORS.	SENECA	ROMULUS
HAZEL	SULLIVAN	ROCKLAND
HAZZARDVILLE	BROOME	WINDSOR
HEAD OF SOUTH BAY	WASHINGTON	FORT ANN
HEAD OF THE HARBOR V.	SUFFOLK	SMITHTOWN
HEATH HILL CORS.	FRANKLIN	DICKINSON
HEATHCOTE V.	WESTCHESTER	SCARSDALE
HEATHERHILL ST. PARK	SUFFOLK	E. HAMPTON
HEBRON	WASHINGTON	HEBRON
HECLA WORKS	ONEIDA	WESTMORELAND
HECTOR	SCHUYLER	HECTOR
HECTOR STA.	SCHUYLER	HECTOR
HEDDENS	TOMPKINS	LANSING
HEDGESVILLE	STEUBEN	WOODHULL
HELDERBURG	ALBANY	NEW SCOTLAND
HELEN HAYES HOSPITAL	ROCKLAND	W. HAVERSTRAW V.
HELENA	ST.LAWRENCE	BRASHER
HELMBURG	ORANGE	TUXEDO
HEMLOCK	LIVINGSTON	LIVONIA
HEMPSTEAD	ROCKLAND	RAMAPO
HEMPSTEAD V.	NASSAU	HEMPSTEAD
HEMSTREET PARK	RENSSELAER	SCHAGHTICOKE
HENDERSON	HERKIMER	WARREN
HENDERSON	JEFFERSON	HENDERSON
HENDERSON HARBOR	JEFFERSON	HENDERSON
HENDY CREEK	CHEMUNG	SOUTHPORT
HENRIETTA	MONROE	HENRIETTA
HENRIETTA STA.	MONROE	HENRIETTA
HENSONVILLE	GREENE	WINDHAM
HERKIMER HOMESTEAD	HERKIMER	DANUBE
HERKIMER V.	HERKIMER	HERKIMER
HERMAN M. BIGGS MEM. HOSP	TOMPKINS	ITHACA C.
HERMITAGE	WYOMING	WETHERSFIELD
HERMON V.	ST.LAWRENCE	HERMON
HERRICKS	NASSAU	NO. HEMPSTEAD
HERRING STA.	JEFFERSON	WILNA
HERRINGS V.	JEFFERSON	WILNA
HERRINGTON CORS.	CHEMUNG	ERIN
HERTEL	ERIE	BUFFALO C.
HERVEY STREET	GREENE	DURHAM
HESS INN	HAMILTON	INLET
HESS RD. STA.	NIAGARA	NEWFANE
HESSVILLE	MONTGOMERY	MINDEN
HEUVELTON V.	ST.LAWRENCE	OSWEGATCHIE
HEWITTVILLE	ST.LAWRENCE	POTSDAM
HEWLETT	NASSAU	HEMPSTEAD
HEWLETT BAY PARK V.	NASSAU	HEMPSTEAD
HEWLETT HARBOR V.	NASSAU	HEMPSTEAD
HEWLETT NECK V.	NASSAU	HEMPSTEAD
HEWLETT POINT	NASSAU	HEMPSTEAD
HIAWATHA	TIOGA	OWEGO
HIAWATHA STA.	TIOGA	OWEGO
HIBERNIA	DUTCHESS	CLINTON
HICKORY BUSH	ULSTER	ROSENDALE
HICKORY CORS.	NIAGARA	LOCKPORT
HICKS	CHEMUNG	BALDWIN
HICKS BEACH	QUEENS	NYC
HICKSPOINT	ONTARIO	SO. BRISTOL
HICKSVILLE	NASSAU	OYSTER BAY
HIDECKER	CATTARAUGUS	RED HOUSE
HIGGINS	ALLEGANY	CENTERVILLE
HIGGINS BAY	HAMILTON	ARIETTA
HIGGINS BEACH	ALLEGANY	CENTERVILLE
HIGGINSVILLE	ONEIDA	VERONA
HIGH BRIDGE	BRONX	NYC
HIGH FALLS	ST.LAWRENCE	CANTON
HIGH FALLS	ULSTER	MARBLETOWN
HIGH FALLS PARK	ULSTER	ROSENDALE
HIGH FLATS	ST.LAWRENCE	PARISHVILLE
HIGH MARKET	LEWIS	W. TURIN
HIGH MILLS	SCHENECTADY	GLENVILLE
HIGH WOODS	ULSTER	SAUGERTIES
HIGHLAND	ULSTER	LLOYD
HIGHLAND FALLS V.	ORANGE	HIGHLANDS
HIGHLAND LAKE	SULLIVAN	HIGHLAND
HIGHLAND MILLS	COLUMBIA	CLAVERACK
HIGHLAND MILLS	ORANGE	WOODBURY
HIGHLAND STA.	PUTNAM	PHILIPSTOWN
HIGHLAND-ON-LAKE	ERIE	HAMBURG
HIGHMOUNT	ULSTER	SHANDAKEN
HIGHSTREET	WARREN	THURMAN
HIGHUP	STEUBEN	TROUPSBURG
HIGHVIEW	SULLIVAN	MAMAKATING
HILLBURN V.	ROCKLAND	RAMAPO
HILLCREST	BROOME	FENTON
HILLCREST	ROCKLAND	RAMAPO
HILLSBORO	ONEIDA	CAMDEN
HILLSDALE	COLUMBIA	HILLSDALE
HILLSDALE	WASHINGTON	GRANVILLE
HILLSIDE	ONEIDA	WESTERN
HILLSIDE	WYOMING	EAGLE

Alphabetical List of Cities, Villages and Hamlets
Showing Location by County and Town
PART TWO

NAME	COUNTY	TOWN
HILLSIDE	COLUMBIA	HILLSDALE
HILLSIDE	SULLIVAN	LUMBERLAND
HILLSIDE LAKE	DUTCHESS	E. FISHKILL
HILTON BEACH	MONROE	PARMA
HILTON V.	MONROE	PARMA
HIMROD	YATES	MILO
HIMROD JCT.	YATES	MILO
HINCKLEY	ONEIDA	REMSEN
HINCKLEY	ONEIDA	TRENTON
HINCKLEY	HERKIMER	RUSSIA
HINDSBURG	ORLEANS	MURRAY
HINKLYVILLE	MONROE	PARMA
HINMANSVILLE	OSWEGO	SCHROEPPEL
HINSDALE	ONONDAGA	SALINA
HINSDALE	CATTARAUGUS	HINSDALE
HITTOWN	STEUBEN	CATON
HOAG CORS.	RENSSELAER	NASSAU
HOBART V.	DELAWARE	STAMFORD
HODGEVILLE	NIAGARA	PENDLETON
HODGEVILLE STA.	NIAGARA	PENDLETON
HOFFMAN	NIAGARA	PENDLETON
HOFFMAN STA.	NIAGARA	PENDLETON
HOFFMANS	SCHENECTADY	GLENVILLE
HOFFMANS FERRY STA.	SCHENECTADY	GLENVILLE
HOFFMEISTER	HAMILTON	MOREHOUSE
HOGANSBURG	FRANKLIN	BOMBAY
HOLBROOK	SUFFOLK	BROOKHAVEN
HOLBROOK	SUFFOLK	ISLIP
HOLCOMB V.	ONTARIO	E. BLOOMFIELD
HOLCOMBVILLE	WARREN	JOHNSBURG
HOLLAND	ERIE	HOLLAND
HOLLAND PATENT V.	ONEIDA	TRENTON
HOLLEY V.	ORLEANS	MURRAY
HOLLOWVILLE	COLUMBIA	CLAVERACK
HOLMES	PUTNAM	KENT
HOLMES	DUTCHESS	E. FISHKILL
HOLMES	DUTCHESS	PAWLING
HOLMES HILL	ST.LAWRENCE	STOCKHOLM
HOLMESVILLE	CHENANGO	NEW BERLIN
HOLMESVILLE	CHENANGO	NORWICH
HOLTSVILLE	SUFFOLK	BROOKHAVEN
HOMER V.	CORTLAND	HOMER
HOMER V.	CORTLAND	CORTLANDVILLE
HOMOWACK	SULLIVAN	MAMAKATING
HONEOYE	ONTARIO	RICHMOND
HONEOYE CORS.	ALLEGANY	BOLIVAR
HONEOYE FALLS V.	MONROE	MENDON
HONEOYE LAKE	ONTARIO	RICHMOND
HONEYVILLE	JEFFERSON	ADAMS
HONK HILL	ULSTER	WAWARSING
HONNEDAGA	HERKIMER	OHIO
HONNEDAGA	ONEIDA	REMSEN
HONNEDAGA STA.	ONEIDA	REMSEN
HOOK	WASHINGTON	ARGYLE
HOOKER	LEWIS	MONTAGUE
HOOPER	BROOME	UNION
HOOPER VALLEY	TIOGA	NICHOLS
HOOSICK	RENSSELAER	HOOSICK
HOOSICK FALLS V.	RENSSELAER	HOOSICK
HOOSICK JCT.	RENSSELAER	HOOSICK
HOPE	HAMILTON	HOPE
HOPE CTR.	HAMILTON	HOPE
HOPE FALLS	HAMILTON	HOPE
HOPE FARM	DUTCHESS	PLEASANT VALLEY
HOPE VALLEY	HAMILTON	HOPE
HOPEWELL	ORANGE	CRAWFORD
HOPEWELL	ONTARIO	HOPEWELL
HOPEWELL CTR.	ONTARIO	HOPEWELL
HOPEWELL JCT.	DUTCHESS	E. FISHKILL
HOPKINTON	ST.LAWRENCE	HOPKINTON
HOPSON DIST.	HERKIMER	SALISBURY
HORICON	WARREN	HORICON
HORNBY	STEUBEN	HORNBY
HORNBY FORKS	STEUBEN	HORNBY
HORNELL C.	STEUBEN	HORNELL C.
HORNELLSVILLE JCT.	ALLEGANY	BURNS
HORSEHEADS STA.	CHEMUNG	HORSEHEADS
HORSEHEADS V.	CHEMUNG	HORSEHEADS
HORSESHOE	ST.LAWRENCE	PIERCEFIELD
HOPTON	DELAWARE	COLCHESTER
HORTONTOWN	DUTCHESS	E. FISHKILL
HORTONVILLE	SULLIVAN	DELAWARE
HOTEL AMPERSAND	FRANKLIN	HARRIETSTOWN
HOUGHTON	ALLEGANY	CANEADEA
HOUGHTON FARM	ORANGE	CORNWALL
HOUGHVILLE	ST.LAWRENCE	NORFOLK
HOUSEVILLE	LEWIS	TURIN
HOWARD	STEUBEN	HOWARD
HOWARD BEACH	QUEENS	NYC
HOWARDVILLE	OSWEGO	ALBION
HOWELLS	ORANGE	MT. HOPE
HOWELLS	ORANGE	WALLKILL
HOWES	BROOME	SANFORD
HOWES	WYOMING	EAGLE
HOWES CAVE	SCHOHARIE	SCHOHARIE
HOWES CAVE	SCHOHARIE	COBLESKILL
HOWLAND HOOK	RICHMOND	NYC

NAME	COUNTY	TOWN
HOWLETT HILL	ONONDAGA	ONONDAGA
HOXIES GORGE	CORTLAND	CORTLANDVILLE
HUBBARD CORS.	ONEIDA	MARSHALL
HUBBARDSVILLE	MADISON	HAMILTON
HUBBARDSVILLE STA.	MADISON	HAMILTON
HUBBARDVILLE	TIOGA	CANDOR
HUBBEL CORS.	DELAWARE	ROXBURY
HUDSON C.	COLUMBIA	HUDSON C.
HUDSON FALLS V.	WASHINGTON	KINGSBURY
HUDSON RIVER PSYCHIATRIC CT	DUTCHESS	POUGHKEEPSIE T.
HUGHSONVILLE	DUTCHESS	WAPPINGER
HUGUENOT	RICHMOND	NYC
HUGUENOT	ORANGE	DEER PARK
HULBERTON	ORLEANS	MURRAY
HULETTS LDG.	WASHINGTON	DRESDEN
HULL MILLS	DUTCHESS	STANFORD
HULLVILLE	TIOGA	OWEGO
HULSE LANDING	SUFFOLK	RIVERHEAD
HUMASTON	ONEIDA	ROME C.
HUMASTON PLAINS	ONEIDA	ROME C.
HUMASTON STA.	ONEIDA	ROME C.
HUME	ALLEGANY	HUME
HUMPHREY	CATTARAUGUS	HUMPHREY
HUMPHREY CTR.	CATTARAUGUS	HUMPHREY
HUMPHREYVILLE	COLUMBIA	CLAVERACK
HUNGERFORD CORS.	JEFFERSON	HENDERSON
HUNS LAKE	DUTCHESS	STANFORD
HUNT CORS.	CORTLAND	LAPEER
HUNT HOLLOW	ONTARIO	NAPLES
HUNTER HOME	FRANKLIN	FRANKLIN
HUNTER V.	GREENE	HUNTER
HUNTERS POINT	QUEENS	NYC
HUNTERSVILLE	WESTCHESTER	YORKTOWN
HUNTINGTON	SUFFOLK	HUNTINGTON
HUNTINGTON BAY V.	SUFFOLK	HUNTINGTON
HUNTINGTON STA.	SUFFOLK	HUNTINGTON
HUNTINGTONVILLE	JEFFERSON	WATERTOWN
HUNTS CORNER	ERIE	CLARENCE
HUNTS CORS.	CORTLAND	LAPEER
HUNTS POINT	BRONX	NYC
HUNTVILLE	SARATOGA	DAY
HURD	SULLIVAN	BETHEL
HURD CORS.	DUTCHESS	PAWLING
HURLBUTVILLE	ONEIDA	BOONVILLE
HURLEY	ULSTER	HURLEY
HURLEYVILLE	SULLIVAN	FALLSBURG
HURON	WAYNE	HURON
HYDE LAKE	JEFFERSON	THERESA
HYDE PARK	DUTCHESS	HYDE PARK
HYDE PARK	JEFFERSON	THERESA
HYDE PARK	OTSEGO	HARTWICK
HYDEVILLE	WAYNE	ARCADIA
HYNDSVILLE	SCHOHARIE	SEWARD

-I-

NAME	COUNTY	TOWN
ICE POND STA.	PUTNAM	PATTERSON
IDLEWILD	ORANGE	CORNWALL
IDLEWOOD STA.	ERIE	HAMBURG
IGERNA	WARREN	CHESTER
ILION V.	HERKIMER	GERMAN FLATS
INAVALE	ALLEGANY	WIRT
INDEPENDENCE	ALLEGANY	INDEPENDENCE
INDEX	OTSEGO	HARTWICK
INDIAN CASTLE	HERKIMER	DANUBE
INDIAN CASTLE STA.	HERKIMER	DANUBE
INDIAN FALLS	GENESEE	PEMBROKE
INDIAN FALLS	GENESEE	ALABAMA
INDIAN FIELDS	ALBANY	COEYMANS
INDIAN HEAD	GREENE	HUNTER
INDIAN HILL	PUTNAM	PUTNAM VALLEY
INDIAN HILL RD.	PUTNAM	PUTNAM VALLEY
INDIAN LAKE	HAMILTON	INDIAN LAKE
INDIAN RIVER	LEWIS	CROGHAN
INDIAN VILLAGE	ONONDAGA	ONONDAGA
INDUSTRY	MONROE	RUSH
INGHAM MILLS	HERKIMER	MANHEIM
INGHAM MILLS	FULTON	OPPENHEIM
INGHAM MILLS STA.	HERKIMER	MANHEIM
INGLESIDE	STEUBEN	PRATTSBURG
INGRAHAM	CLINTON	CHAZY
INLET	HAMILTON	INLET
INMAN	FRANKLIN	FRANKLIN
INTER'L JCT.	ERIE	BUFFALO C.
INTERLAKEN V.	SENECA	COVERT
INVERNESS	LIVINGSTON	YORK
INWOOD	NEW YORK	NYC
INWOOD	NASSAU	HEMPSTEAD
IONA ISL. STA.	ROCKLAND	STONY POINT
IONIA	ONTARIO	N. BLOOMFIELD
IRA DAVENPORT MEM HOSP	STEUBEN	URBANA
IRELAND COR.	ULSTER	GARDINER
IRELAND COR.	ALBANY	COLONIE
IRELAND MILLS	SCHUYLER	READING
IRELAND MILLS	CHENANGO	SMYRNA

NAME	COUNTY	TOWN
IRISH HILL	ESSEX	CHESTERFIELD
IRISH SETTLEMENT	CLINTON	SCHUYLER FALLS
IRISH SETTLEMENT	FULTON	OPPENHEIM
IRISH SETTLEMENT	HERKIMER	NEWPORT
IRISHTOWN	ESSEX	MINERVA
IRLANDVILLE	SCHUYLER	READING
IRON WORKS	ESSEX	MINERVA
IRONA	CLINTON	ALTONA
IRONDALE	CLINTON	SARANAC
IRONDALE	HERKIMER	SALISBURY
IRONDALE	DUTCHESS	NORTHEAST
IRONDEQUOIT	MONROE	IRONDEQUOIT
IRONDEQUOIT CLUB	HAMILTON	ARIETTA
IRONTON	ST.LAWRENCE	BRASHER
IRONVILLE	ESSEX	CROWN POINT
IROQUOIS	ERIE	COLLINS
IRVINE MILLS	CATTARAUGUS	CARROLLTON
IRVING	CHAUTAUQUA	HANOVER
IRVINGTON V.	WESTCHESTER	GREENBURGH
ISCHUA	CATTARAUGUS	ISCHUA
ISLAND HOUSE	HAMILTON	LONG LAKE
ISLAND PARK V.	NASSAU	HEMPSTEAD
ISLIP	SUFFOLK	ISLIP
ISLIP MANOR	SUFFOLK	ISLIP
ISLIP TERRACE	SUFFOLK	ISLIP
ITALY HILL	YATES	ITALY
ITALY HILL	YATES	JERUSALEM
ITHACA C.	TOMPKINS	ITHACA C.
IVANHOE	DELAWARE	MASONVILLE
IVES CORS.	RENSSELAER	POESTENKILL
IVORY	CHAUTAUQUA	CARROLL

-J-

NAME	COUNTY	TOWN
J. N. ADAM DEVELOPMENTAL CTR.	CATTARAUGUS	PERRYSBURG
JACKSON	TOMPKINS	NEWFIELD
JACKSON	WASHINGTON	JACKSON
JACKSON CORS.	DUTCHESS	MILAN
JACKSON CORS.	COLUMBIA	GALLATIN
JACKSON HEIGHTS	QUEENS	NYC
JACKSON HOLLOW	TOMPKINS	NEWFIELD
JACKSON SUMMIT	FULTON	MAYFIELD
JACKSONBURG	HERKIMER	LITTLE FALLS
JACKSONVILLE	OSWEGO	ORWELL
JACKSONVILLE	TOMPKINS	ULYSSES
JAMAICA	QUEENS	NYC
JAMERSON'S CORS.	OSWEGO	AMBOY
JAMESPORT	SUFFOLK	RIVERHEAD
JAMESTOWN C.	CHAUTAUQUA	JAMESTOWN C.
JAMESVILLE	SARATOGA	GREENFIELD
JAMESVILLE	ONONDAGA	DEWITT
JAMESVILLE	WASHINGTON	GRANVILLE
JAMISON	ERIE	ELMA
JAMISON RD.	ERIE	ELMA
JAMISON STA.	ERIE	ELMA
JANESVILLE	SCHOHARIE	SEWARD
JAQUINS	CHAUTAUQUA	CLYMER
JASPER	STEUBEN	JASPER
JASPER FIVE CORS.	STEUBEN	JASPER
JAVA	WYOMING	JAVA
JAVA CTR.	WYOMING	JAVA
JAVA VILLAGE	WYOMING	JAVA
JAY	ESSEX	JAY
JAYVILLE	ST.LAWRENCE	PITCAIRN
JEDDO	ORLEANS	RIDGEWAY
JEFFERSON	SCHOHARIE	JEFFERSON
JEFFERSON CORS.	OSWEGO	AMBOY
JEFFERSON FLATS	GREENE	CATSKILL
JEFFERSON IRON CO.	JEFFERSON	ANTWERP
JEFFERSON VALLEY	WESTCHESTER	YORKTOWN
JEFFERSONVILLE V.	SULLIVAN	CALLICOON
JENKINSTOWN	ULSTER	GARDINER
JERDEN FALLS	LEWIS	CROGHAN
JERICHO	CLINTON	ALTONA
JERICHO	NASSAU	OYSTER BAY
JERICHO	SUFFOLK	E. HAMPTON
JEROME	SCHOHARIE	JEFFERSON
JERRY	OSWEGO	HASTINGS
JERSEYFIELD	HERKIMER	SALISBURY
JERUSALEM	ALBANY	NEW SCOTLAND
JERUSALEM	CLINTON	ALTONA
JERUSALEM	ST.LAWRENCE	CANTON
JERUSALEM CORS.	ERIE	EVANS
JERUSALEM HILL	HERKIMER	FRANKFORT
JESSUP LANDING	SARATOGA	CORINTH
JESSUP SWITCH	ORANGE	GOSHEN
JEWELL	ONEIDA	VIENNA
JEWETT	GREENE	JEWETT
JEWETT CTR.	GREENE	JEWETT
JEWETTVILLE	JEFFERSON	MOUNSFIELD
JOCKEY HILL	ULSTER	KINGSTON
JOE INDIAN	ST.LAWRENCE	PARISHVILLE
JOHNSBURG	WARREN	JOHNSBURG
JOHNSON	ORANGE	MINISINK
JOHNSON CITY V.	BROOME	UNION
JOHNSON CREEK	NIAGARA	HARTLAND

NAME	COUNTY	TOWN
JOHNSONBURG	WYOMING	SHELDON
JOHNSONBURG	WYOMING	ORANGEVILLE
JOHNSONTOWN	ROCKLAND	HAVERSTRAW
JOHNSONVILLE	RENSSELAER	PITTSTOWN
JOHNSTOWN C.	FULTON	JOHNSTOWN C.
JOHNSTOWN	COLUMBIA	LIVINGSTON
JOHNSVILLE	DUTCHESS	E. FISHKILL
JONES CORS.	TOMPKINS	GROTON
JONESPOINT	ROCKLAND	STONY POINT
JONESVILLE	SARATOGA	CLIFTON PARK
JORDON V.	ONONDAGA	ELBRIDGE
JORDANS	STEUBEN	WHEELER
JORDANVILLE	HERKIMER	WARREN
JOSCELYN	SULLIVAN	ROCKLAND
JOSHUA ROCK	WARREN	QUEENSBURY
JOY	WAYNE	SODUS
JUNIOR REPUBLIC	TOMPKINS	DRYDEN
JUNIUS	SENECA	JUNIUS
JUNIUS	ONTARIO	PHELPS
JUNIUS CORS.	SENECA	JUNIUS

-K-

NAME	COUNTY	TOWN
KAATERSKILL	GREENE	HUNTER
KAATERSKILL FALLS	GREENE	HUNTER
KAATERSKILL JCT.	GREENE	HUNTER
KAATERSKILL STA.	GREENE	HUNTER
KAISERTOWN	ORANGE	MONTGOMERY
KALURAH	ST.LAWRENCE	PITCAIRN
KARNER	ALBANY	COLONIE
KASOAG	OSWEGO	WILLIAMSTOWN
KAST BRIDGE	HERKIMER	HERKIMER
KAST BRIDGE STA.	HERKIMER	HERKIMER
KASTERVILLE	LEWIS	LYONSDALE
KATONAH	WESTCHESTER	BEDFORD
KATRINE	ULSTER	ULSTER
KATSBAAN	ULSTER	SAUGERTIES
KATTELVILLE	BROOME	CHENANGO
KATTSKILL BAY	WARREN	QUEENSBURY
KAUNEONGA L.	SULLIVAN	BETHEL
KECK CTR.	FULTON	JOHNSTOWN
KEEFER CORS.	ALBANY	COEYMANS
KEENE	ESSEX	KEENE
KEENE CTR.	ESSEX	KEENE
KEENE STA.	ST.LAWRENCE	ROSSIE
KEENE VALLEY	ESSEX	KEENE
KEENE'S MILLS	JEFFERSON	ANTWERP
KEENES SETT.	CORTLAND	CUYLER
KEENEY	CORTLAND	CUYLER
KEEPAWA	HAMILTON	LONG LAKE
KEESE MILLS	FRANKLIN	BRIGHTON
KEESEVILLE V.	CLINTON	AUSABLE
KEESEVILLE V.	ESSEX	CHESTERFIELD
KELLOGGSVILLE	CAYUGA	NILES
KELLY CORS.	DELAWARE	MIDDLETOWN
KELPYTOWN	LEWIS	LEYDEN
KELSEY	DELAWARE	TOMPKINS
KEMPTON	FRANKLIN	DUANE
KENDAIA	SENECA	ROMULUS
KENDALL	CHEMUNG	CATLIN
KENDALL	ORLEANS	KENDALL
KENDALL MILLS	MONROE	HAMLIN
KENDREWS	ST.LAWRENCE	DE KALB
KENMORE V.	ERIE	KENMORE
KENNEDY	CHAUTAUQUA	POLAND
KENNEDY CORS.	TOMPKINS	ENFIELD
KENNETH	WARREN	QUEENSBURY
KENOZA LAKE	SULLIVAN	DELAWARE
KENSICO	WESTCHESTER	MT. PLEASANT
KENSICO CTR.	WESTCHESTER	MT. PLEASANT
KENSICO MANOR	WESTCHESTER	MT. PLEASANT
KENSINGTON	ERIE	BUFFALO C.
KENSINGTON V.	NASSAU	N. HEMPSTEAD
KENT	ORLEANS	CARLTON
KENT CLIFFE	PUTNAM	KENT
KENWELL	HAMILTON	INLET
KENWOOD	ALBANY	ALBANY C.
KENWOOD JCT.	ALBANY	ALBANY C.
KENYONVILLE	ORLEANS	CARLTON
KERHONKSON	ULSTER	WAWARSING
KERN	YATES	JERUSALEM
KERRYS	DELAWARE	TOMPKINS
KETCHUM CORS.	SARATOGA	STILLWATER
KEUKA	STEUBEN	WAYNE
KEUKA COLLEGE	YATES	JERUSALEM
KEUKA MILLS	YATES	MILO
KEUKA PARK	YATES	JERUSALEM
KEW GARDENS	QUEENS	NYC
KEYS MILL	FRANKLIN	SANTA CLARA
KIAMESHA	SULLIVAN	THOMPSON
KIAMESHA LAKE	SULLIVAN	THOMPSON
KIANTONE	CHAUTAUQUA	KIANTONE
KIDDEPS	SENECA	OVID
KILDARE	ST.LAWRENCE	HOPKINTON
KILDARE STA.	FRANKLIN	ALTAMONT
KILL BUCK	CATTARAUGUS	GREAT VALLEY
KILLAWOG	BROOME	LISLE

NAME	COUNTY	TOWN
KIMBALL MILL	LEWIS	DIANA
KINDERHOOK LAKE	COLUMBIA	KINDERHOOK
KINDERHOOK V.	COLUMBIA	KINDERHOOK
KING CORS.	CHAUTAUQUA	CLYMER
KING FERRY	CAYUGA	GENOA
KING FERRY STA.	CAYUGA	GENOA
KING SETT.	CHENANGO	NO. NORWICH
KING STA.	SARATOGA	WILTON
KINGS	SARATOGA	GREENFIELD
KINGS HIGHWAY	KINGS	NYC
KINGS PARK	SUFFOLK	SMITHTOWN
KINGS PARK PSYCHIATRIC CTR.	SUFFOLK	SMITHTOWN
KINGS POINT V.	NASSAU	N. HEMPSTEAD
KINGS STA.	SARATOGA	GREENFIELD
KINGSBORO STA.	FULTON	JOHNSTOWN
KINGSBRIDGE	BRONX	NYC
KINGSBURY	WASHINGTON	KINGSBURY
KINGSTON	SUFFOLK	E. HAMPTON
KINGSTON C.	ULSTER	KINGSTON C.
KINNEY FOUR CORS.	OSWEGO	HANNIBAL
KIPPS	ORANGE	HAMPTONBURG
KIPPS STA.	ORANGE	HAMPTONBURG
KIRBYTOWN	ORANGE	WAWAYANDA
KIRK	CHENANGO	PLYMOUTH
KIRKLAND	ONEIDA	KIRKLAND
KIRKS CROSSING	MONROE	GREECE
KIRKVILLE	ONONDAGA	MANLIUS
KIRKWOOD	BROOME	KIRKWOOD
KIRKWOOD CTR.	BROOME	KIRKWOOD
KIRSCHNERVILLE	LEWIS	NEW BREMEN
KISKATOM	GREENE	CATSKILL
KITCABONECK	SUFFOLK	SOUTHAMPTON
KITCHAWAN	WESTCHESTER	YORKTOWN
KLINE	MONTGOMERY	FLORIDA
KLONDIKE	JEFFERSON	WORTH
KNAPP CREEK	CATTARAUGUS	ALLEGANY
KNAPP STA.	ST. LAWRENCE	STOCKHOLM
KNAPPS	ST. LAWRENCE	STOCKHOLM
KNAPPVILLE	FULTON	STRATFORD
KNIGHTS	FULTON	CAROGA
KNOWELHURST	WARREN	STONY CREEK
KNOWELSVILLE	ORLEANS	RIDGEWAY
KNOWERSVILLE	ALBANY	GUILDERLAND
KNOX	ALBANY	KNOX
KNOXBORO	ONEIDA	AUGUSTA
KORTRIGHT	DELAWARE	KORTRIGHT
KORTRIGHT STA.	DELAWARE	KORTRIGHT
KOSTERVILLE	LEWIS	LYONSDALE
KOUWENHOVENS STA.	KINGS	NYC
KREISCHERVILLE	RICHMOND	NYC
KRINGSBASH	FULTON	OPPENHEIM
KRIPPLE BUSH	ULSTER	MARBLETOWN
KRUM CORNER	TOMPKINS	ULYSSES
KRUMVILLE	ULSTER	OLIVE
KUCKVILLE	ORLEANS	CARLTON
KUNEYTOWN	SENECA	FAYETTE
KUSHAGUA	FRANKLIN	FRANKLIN
KYSORVILLE	LIVINGSTON	W. SPARTA

-L-

NAME	COUNTY	TOWN
LACKAWACK	ULSTER	WAWARSING
LACKAWANNA C.	ERIE	LACKAWANNA C.
LACONA V.	OSWEGO	SANDY CREEK
LADENTOWN	ROCKLAND	RAMAPO
LADLETON	ULSTER	DENNING
LAFARGEVILLE	JEFFERSON	ORLEANS
LAFAYETTE	ONONDAGA	LAFAYETTE
LAFAYETTE	TOMPKINS	GROTON
LAFAYETTEVILLE	DUTCHESS	MILAN
LAGRANGE	WYOMING	COVINGTON
LAGRANGE	ORANGE	HAMPTONBURG
LAGRANGEVILLE	DUTCHESS	LAGRANGE
LAIDLAW	CATTARAUGUS	FARMERSVILLE
LAIRDSVILLE	ONEIDA	WESTMORELAND
LAKE ARBUTUS	ESSEX	NEWCOMB
LAKE BEACH	MONROE	IRONDEQUOIT
LAKE BLUFF	WAYNE	HURON
LAKE BONAPARTE	LEWIS	DIANA
LAKE BONAPARTE STA.	LEWIS	DIANA
LAKE CARMEL	PUTNAM	KENT
LAKE CLEAR	FRANKLIN	HARRIETSTOWN
LAKE CLEAR JCT.	FRANKLIN	HARRIETSTOWN
LAKE COLBEY	FRANKLIN	HARRIETSTOWN
LAKE DELAWARE	DELAWARE	BOVINA
LAKE DESOLATION	SARATOGA	GREENFIELD
LAKE ERIE BEACH	ERIE	EVANS
LAKE GEORGE	WARREN	LAKE GEORGE
LAKE GEORGE ASSEM.	WARREN	QUEENSBURY
LAKE GEORGE V.	WARREN	LAKE GEORGE
LAKE GROVE V.	SUFFOLK	BROOKHAVEN
LAKE HILL	ULSTER	WOODSTOCK
LAKE HOUSE	HAMILTON	LONG LAKE
LAKE HUNTINGTON	SULLIVAN	COCHECTON
LAKE KATONAH	WESTCHESTER	LEWISBORO
LAKE KATRINE	ULSTER	ULSTER
LAKE KUSHAQUA	FRANKLIN	FRANKLIN

NAME	COUNTY	TOWN
LAKE KUSHAQUA STA.	FRANKLIN	FRANKLIN
LAKE LILA	HAMILTON	LONG LAKE
LAKE LUZEPNE	WARREN	LAKE LUZERNE
LAKE ONEIDA BEACH	MADISON	SULLIVAN
LAKE PEEKSKILL	PUTNAM	PUTNAM VALLEY
LAKE PLACID CLUB	ESSEX	NO. ELBA
LAKE PLACID V.	ESSEX	N. ELBA
LAKE PLEASANT	HAMILTON	LAKE PLEASANT
LAKE RIDGE	TOMPKINS	LANSING
LAKE RIDGE STA.	TOMPKINS	LANSING
LAKE RONKONOMA	SUFFOLK	BROOKHAVEN
LAKE SHORE RD.	ERIE	HAMBURG
LAKE STATION	ORANGE	WARWICK
LAKE SUCCESS V.	NASSAU	N. HEMPSTEAD
LAKE VIEW	ERIE	HAMBURG
LAKE WACCABUC	WESTCHESTER	LEWISBORO
LAKELAND	SUFFOLK	ISLIP
LAKEMONT	YATES	STARKEY
LAKEPORT	MADISON	SULLIVAN
LAKEROAD	NIAGARA	SOMERSET
LAKESIDE	ORLEANS	CARLTON
LAKESIDE	WAYNE	ONTARIO
LAKESIDE STA.	WAYNE	ONTARIO
LAKEVIEW	NASSAU	HEMPSTEAD
LAKEVILLE	LIVINGSTON	LIVONIA
LAKEVILLE	WASHINGTON	GREENWICH
LAKEWOOD	SULLIVAN	FREMONT
LAKEWOOD V.	CHAUTAUQUA	BUSTI
LAMBERTON	CHAUTAUQUA	POMFRET
LAMBS CORS.	ALBANY	WESTERLO
LAMONT	WYOMING	PIKE
LAMONTVILLE	ULSTER	MARBLETOWN
LANCASTER V.	ERIE	LANCASTER
LANESBURG	LEWIS	MARTINSBURG
LANESVILLE	GREENE	HUNTER
LANGDON	BROOME	KIRKWOOD
LANGDON CORS.	ST. LAWRENCE	CANTON
LANGDON CORS.	WASHINGTON	KINGSBURY
LANGFORD	ERIE	NO. COLLINS
LANSING	OSWEGO	SCRIBA
LANSING	TOMPKINS	LANSING
LANSING STA.	TOMPKINS	LANSING
LANSINGBURG	RENSSELAER	TROY C.
LANSINGVILLE	TOMPKINS	LANSING
LANSINGVILLE	DELAWARE	HAMDEN
LAONA	CHAUTAUQUA	POMFRET
LAPEER	CORTLAND	LAPEER
LAPHAM	CLINTON	PERU
LAPHAM MILLS	CLINTON	PERU
LARCHMONT V.	WESTCHESTER	MAMARONECK
LASSELLSVILLE	FULTON	EPHRATAH
LATHAM	ALBANY	COLONIE
LATHAMS CORS.	CHENANGO	GUILFORD
LATINTOWN	ULSTER	MARLBOROUGH
LATTINGTOWN V.	NASSAU	OYSTER BAY
LAUREL	SUFFOLK	SOUTHOLD
LAUREL	SUFFOLK	RIVERHEAD
LAUREL HILL	QUEENS	NYC
LAUREL HOLLOW V.	NASSAU	OYSTER BAY
LAUREL HOUSE	GREENE	HUNTER
LAUREL HOUSE STA.	GREENE	HUNTER
LAURENS V.	OTSEGO	LAURENS
LAVA	SULLIVAN	TUSTEN
LAWRENCE	SCHUYLER	CATHARINE
LAWRENCE STA.	GREENE	CATSKILL
LAWRENCE V.	NASSAU	HEMPSTEAD
LAWRENCEVILLE	GREENE	CATSKILL
LAWRENCEVILLE	STEUBEN	LINDLEY
LAWRENCEVILLE	ULSTER	ROSENDALE
LAWRENCEVILLE	ST. LAWRENCE	LAWRENCE
LAWTONS	ERIE	NO. COLLINS
LAWYERSVILLE	SCHOHARIE	SEWARD
LAWYERVILLE	SCHOHARIE	COBLESKILL
LE RAYSVILLE	JEFFERSON	LE RAY
LE ROY CORS.	SULLIVAN	NEVERSINK
LE ROY V.	GENESEE	LE ROY
LEAD MINES	ST. LAWRENCE	ROSSIE
LEBANON	MADISON	LEBANON
LEBANON LAKE	SULLIVAN	LUMBERLAND
LEBANON SPRINGS	COLUMBIA	NEW LEBANON
LEBOEUFS	FRANKLIN	SANTA CLARA
LEDYARD	CAYUGA	VENICE
LEDYARD	CAYUGA	LEDYARD
LEE	ONEIDA	LEE
LEE	WASHINGTON	CAMBRIDGE
LEE CENTER	ONEIDA	LEE
LEE STATION	WASHINGTON	CAMBRIDGE
LEEDS	GREENE	CATSKILL
LEEDSVILLE	DUTCHESS	AMENIA
LEEK	CATTARAUGUS	MACHIAS
LEESVILLE	SCHOHARIE	SHARON
LEFEVER FALLS	ULSTER	ROSENDALE
LEHIGH	GENESEE	DARIEN
LEHIGH JCT.	MONROE	WHEATLAND
LEIBHARDT	ULSTER	ROCHESTER
LEICESTER V.	LIVINGSTON	LEICESTER
LEISHER MILL	LEWIS	LEWIS

NAME	COUNTY	TOWN	NAME	COUNTY	TOWN
LENA	OTSEGO	NEW LISBON	LLOYD NECK	SUFFOLK	HUNTINGTON
LENOX	MADISON	LENOX	LOBDELL	CLINTON	SARANAC
LENOX BASIN	MADISON	LENOX	LOCH MULLER	ESSEX	SCHROON
LENT	DUTCHESS	CLINTON	LOCH SHELDRAKE	SULLIVAN	FALLSBURG
LENTVILLE	OTSEGO	MIDDLEFIELD	LOCK BERLIN	WAYNE	GALEN
LEON	CATTARAUGUS	LEON	LOCKE	CAYUGA	LOCKE
LEONARDSVILLE	MADISON	BROOKFIELD	LOCKLEY PARK	ERIE	HAMBURG
LEONARDSVILLE	OTSEGO	PLAINFIELD	LOCKPORT C.	NIAGARA	LOCKPORT C.
LEONTA	DELAWARE	FRANKLIN	LOCKPORT JCT.	NIAGARA	LOCKPORT
LEPTONDALE	ORANGE	NEWBURGH	LOCKPORT JCT. RAPIDS	NIAGARA	LOCKPORT
LESLIE	NIAGARA	ROYALTON	LOCKSEY PK.	ERIE	HAMBURG
LESTER	BROOME	WINDSOR	LOCKWOOD	TIOGA	BARTON
LESTERSHIRE	BROOME	UNION	LOCKWOOD	CHEMUNG	VAN ETTEN
LETCHWORTH PK.	WYOMING	GENESEE FALLS	LOCUST GROVE	LEWIS	LEYDEN
LETCHWORTH VIL DEVEL	ROCKLAND	HAVERSTRAW	LOCUST GROVE	NASSAU	OYSTER BAY
CTR			LOCUST TREE	NIAGARA	ROYALTON
LEURENKILL	ULSTER	WAWARSING	LOCUST VALLEY	NASSAU	OYSTER BAY
LEVANNA	CAYUGA	LEDYARD	LODI CTR.	SENECA	LODI
LEVANT	CHAUTAUQUA	POLAND	LODI LDG.	SENECA	LODI
LEVANT	CHAUTAUQUA	ELLICOTT	LODI V.	SENECA	LODI
LEVITTOWN	NASSAU	HEMPSTEAD	LOGAN	SCHUYLER	HECTOR
LEWBEACH	SULLIVAN	ROCKLAND	LOGTOWN	ORANGE	GREENVILLE
LEWIS	ESSEX	LEWIS	LOMDA	DUTCHESS	E. FISHKILL
LEWIS STA.	ONTARIO	HOPEWELL	LONG BEACH C.	NASSAU	LONG BEACH C.
LEWIS TOWERS FORGE	ESSEX	LEWIS	LONG BEACH NORTH	NASSAU	HEMPSTEAD
LEWISBORO	WESTCHESTER	LEWISBORO	LONG BOW	ST. LAWRENCE	PARISHVILLE
LEWISBURG V.	ULSTER	LLOYD	LONG BRANCH	ONONDAGA	SALINA
LEWISBURG	LEWIS	DIANA	LONG COVE	SUFFOLK	BROOKHAVEN
LEWISTON HEIGHTS	NIAGARA	LEWISTON	LONG EDDY	SULLIVAN	FREMONT
LEWISTON HGTS. STA.	NIAGARA	LEWISTON	LONG FLAT	DELAWARE	HANCOCK
LEWISTON V.	NIAGARA	LEWISTON	LONG ISLAND CITY	QUEENS	NYC
LEXINGTON	GREENE	LEXINGTON	LONG LAKE	HAMILTON	LONG LAKE
LEYDEN	LEWIS	LEYDEN	LONG LAKE WEST	HAMILTON	LONG LAKE
LIBERTY POLE	LIVINGSTON	SPRINGWATER	LONG LAKE WEST STA.	HAMILTON	LONG LAKE
LIBERTY V.	SULLIVAN	LIBERTY	LONG NECK	RICHMOND	NYC
LIBERTYVILLE	ULSTER	GARDINER	LONG POINT	YATES	TORREY
LIDO BEACH	NASSAU	HEMPSTEAD	LONG POINT PARK	JEFFERSON	LYME
LILY DALE	CHAUTAUQUA	POMFRET	LONG SAULT IS.	ST. LAWRENCE	MASSENA
LIMA V.	LIVINGSTON	LIMA	LONGS CORS.	YATES	JERUSALEM
LIME LAKE	CATTARAUGUS	MACHIAS	LONGWOOD	GENESEE	DARIEN
LIME ROCK	GENESEE	LEROY	LOOMIS	DELAWARE	WALTON
LIMERICK	JEFFERSON	BROWNVILLE	LOOMIS	DELAWARE	TOMPKINS
LIMESTONE V.	CATTARAUGUS	CARROLLTON	LOOMIS	SULLIVAN	LIBERTY
LIMESTREET	GREENE	ATHENS	LOON LAKE	STEUBEN	WAYLAND
LINCKLAEN	CHENANGO	LINCKLAEN	LOON LAKE	FRANKLIN	FRANKLIN
LINCKLAEN CTR.	CHENANGO	LINCKLAEN	LOON LAKE STA.	FRANKLIN	FRANKLIN
LINCOLN	WAYNE	WALWORTH	LOONEYVILLE	ERIE	LANCASTER
LINCOLN PK.	MONROE	ROCHESTER	LORDVILLE	DELAWARE	HANCOCK
LINCOLNDALE	WESTCHESTER	SOMERS	LORENA	ONEIDA	ROME C.
LINDEN	GENESEE	BETHANY	LORING	CORTLAND	CORTLANDVILLE
LINDENHURST V.	SUFFOLK	BABYLON	LORRAINE	JEFFERSON	LORRAINE
LINDLEY	STEUBEN	LINDLEY	LOST VILLAGE	ST. LAWRENCE	OSWEGATCHIE
LINLITHGO	COLUMBIA	LIVINGSTON	LOTVILLE	FULTON	OPPENHEIM
LINLITHGO STA.	COLUMBIA	LIVINGSTON	LOUDONVILLE	ALBANY	COLONIE
LINOLEUMVILLE	RICHMOND	NYC	LOUISVILLE	ST. LAWRENCE	LOUISVILLE
LINWOOD	LIVINGSTON	YORK	LOUNSBERRY	TIOGA	NICHOLS
LINWOOD	SARATOGA	DAY	LOW HAMPTON	WASHINGTON	HAMPTON
LISBON	ST. LAWRENCE	LISBON	LOW PT. STA.	DUTCHESS	WAPPINGER
LISBON CTR.	ST. LAWRENCE	LISBON	LOWELL	ONEIDA	WESTMORELAND
LISBON STA.	ST. LAWRENCE	LISBON	LOWER CINCINNATUS	CORTLAND	CINCINNATUS
LISHASKILL	ALBANY	COLONIE	LOWER IRON WKS.	ESSEX	NEWCOMB
LISLE V.	BROOME	LISLE	LOWER JAY	ESSEX	JAY
LITCHFIELD	FRANKLIN	ALTAMONT	LOWER LANDING	GREENE	COXSACKIE
LITCHFIELD	HERKIMER	LITCHFIELD	LOWER PINE VALLEY	CHEMUNG	VETERAN
LITCHFIELD	TIOGA	NICHOLS	LOWER ST. REGIS LAKE	FRANKLIN	BRIGHTON
LITCHFIELD STA.	TIOGA	NICHOLS	LOWERRE	WESTCHESTER	YONKERS
LITHGOW	DUTCHESS	WASHINGTON	LOWES CORS.	SULLIVAN	NEVERSINK
LITTLE AMERICA	CHAUTAUQUA	NO. HARMONY	LOWMAN	CHEMUNG	CHEMUNG
LITTLE BOW	ST. LAWRENCE	GOUVERNEUR	LOWVILLE LDG.	LEWIS	LOWVILLE
LITTLE BOW CORS.	ST. LAWRENCE	GOUVERNEUR	LOWVILLE V.	LEWIS	LOWVILLE
LITTLE BRITAIN	HERKIMER	LITTLE FALLS	LUCE LANDING	SUFFOLK	RIVERHEAD
LITTLE BRITAIN	ORANGE	NEW WINDSOR	LUDINGTONVILLE	PUTNAM	KENT
LITTLE CANADA	GENESEE	BETHANY	LUDLOWVILLE	TOMPKINS	LANSING
LITTLE FALLS C.	HERKIMER	LITTLE FALLS C.	LUDWIG	TOMPKINS	DRYDEN
LITTLE GENESEE	ALLEGANY	GENESEE	LUMBERLAND	SULLIVAN	LUMBERLAND
LITTLE HOLLOW	CAYUGA	GENOA	LUMMISVILLE	WAYNE	HURON
LITTLE JOHN SETT.	OSWEGO	REDFIELD	LUTHER	RENSSELAER	E. GREENBUSH
LITTLE LAKES	HERKIMER	WARREN	LUTHERANVILLE	SCHOHARIE	SUMMIT
LITTLE NECK	QUEENS	NYC	LUZON STA.	SULLIVAN	FALLSBURG
LITTLE REST	DUTCHESS	WASHINGTON	LYCOMING	OSWEGO	SCRIBA
LITTLE RIVER	ST. LAWRENCE	CANTON	LYKERS	MONTGOMERY	ROOT
LITTLE VALLEY CREEK	CATTARAUGUS	LITTLE VALLEY	LYNBROOK V.	NASSAU	HEMPSTEAD
LITTLE VALLEY V.	CATTARAUGUS	LITTLE VAL.	LYNDON CTR.	CATTARAUGUS	LYNDON
LITTLE WESTKILL	GREENE	PRATTSVILLE	LYNDONVILLE V.	ORLEANS	YATES
LITTLE YORK	ORANGE	WARWICK	LYNN	STEUBEN	PRATTSBURG
LITTLE YORK	SCHOHARIE	CARLISLE	LYON MOUNTAIN	CLINTON	DANNEMORA
LITTLE YORK	CORTLAND	HOMER	LYONS FALLS STA.	LEWIS	W. TURIN
LITTLE YORK	DELAWARE	WALTON	LYONS FALLS V.	LEWIS	WEST TURIN
LITTLEVILLE	ONTARIO	HOPEWELL	LYONS FALLS V.	LEWIS	LYONSDALE
LIVERPOOL V.	ONONDAGA	SALINA	LYONS LAKE	RENSSELAER	NASSAU
LIVINGSTON	COLUMBIA	LIVINGSTON	LYONS V.	WAYNE	LYONS
LIVINGSTON MANOR	SULLIVAN	ROCKLAND	LYONSDALE	LEWIS	LYONSDALE
LIVINGSTONVILLE	SCHOHARIE	BROOME	LYONSVILLE	ULSTER	MARBLETOWN
LIVONIA CTR.	LIVINGSTON	LIVONIA	LYSANDER	ONONDAGA	LYSANDER
LIVONIA V.	LIVINGSTON	LIVONIA			
LLOYD	ULSTER	LLOYD			
LLOYD HARBOR V.	SUFFOLK	HUNTINGTON			

NAME	COUNTY	TOWN
	-M-	
MABBETTSVILLE	DUTCHESS	WASHINGTON
MABIE STA.	NIAGARA	ROYALTON
MACEDON CTR.	WAYNE	MACEDON
MACEDON V.	WAYNE	MACEDON
MACHIAS	CATTARAUGUS	MACHIAS
MACINTIRE IR. WKS.	ESSEX	MINERVA
MACOMB	ST.LAWRENCE	MACOMB
MADAWASKA	FRANKLIN	SANTA CLARA
MADISON BARRACKS	JEFFERSON	HOUNSFIELD
MADISON V.	MADISON	MADISON
MADRID	ST.LAWRENCE	MADRID
MADRID SPGS.	ST.LAWRENCE	MADRID
MAHOPAC	PUTNAM	CARMEL
MAHOPAC FALLS	PUTNAM	CARMEL
MAINE	CATTARAUGUS	PORTVILLE
MAINE	BROOME	MAINE
MAINS MILLS	MADISON	BROOKFIELD
MALCOLM	SENECA	JUNIUS
MALDEN BRIDGE	COLUMBIA	CHATHAM
MALDEN-ON-HUDSON	ULSTER	SAUGERTIES
MALLORY	OSWEGO	HASTINGS
MALLORY STA.	OSWEGO	HASTINGS
MALLORYVILLE	TOMPKINS	DRYDEN
MALONE CORS.	ONEIDA	FLORENCE
MALONE V.	FRANKLIN	MALONE
MALTA	SARATOGA	MALTA
MALTA BRIDGE	SARATOGA	MALTA
MALTAVILLE	SARATOGA	MALTA
MALVERNE PARK	NASSAU	HEMPSTEAD
MALVERNE V.	NASSAU	HEMPSTEAD
MAMARONECK V.	WESTCHESTER	MAMARONECK
MAMARONECK V.	WESTCHESTER	RYE
MANCHESTER BRIDGE	DUTCHESS	POUGHKEEPSIE
MANCHESTER BRIDGE	DUTCHESS	LAGRANGE
MANCHESTER CTR.	ONTARIO	MANCHESTER
MANCHESTER V.	ONTARIO	MANCHESTER
MANHASSET	NASSAU	NO. HEMPSTEAD
MANHATTAN BEACH	KINGS	NYC
MANHATTAN PK.	WESTCHESTER	GREENBURGH
MANHEIM	HERKIMER	MANHEIM
MANHEIM CTR.	HERKIMER	MANHEIM
MANITOU	PUTNAM	PHILIPSTOWN
MANITOU BEACH	MONROE	GREECE
MANLIUS V.	ONONDAGA	MANLIUS
MANNINGVILLE	BROOME	LISLE
MANNSVILLE V.	JEFFERSON	ELLISBURG
MANNY CORS.	MONTGOMERY	AMSTERDAM
MANOR HAVEN V.	NASSAU	N. HEMPSTEAD
MANOR KILL	SCHOHARIE	CONESVILLE
MANORTON	COLUMBIA	LIVINGSTON
MANORVILLE	SUFFOLK	BROOKHAVEN
MAPES	ALLEGANY	WILLING
MAPES CORS.	ORANGE	GOSHEN
MAPLE FLATS	ONEIDA	VIENNA
MAPLE GROVE	OTSEGO	BUTTERNUTS
MAPLE GROVE	QUEENS	NYC
MAPLE GROVE STA.	QUEENS	NYC
MAPLE HILL	OSWEGO	WILLIAMSTOWN
MAPLE HILL	ULSTER	ROSENDALE
MAPLE RIDGE	LEWIS	MARTINSBURG
MAPLE SPRINGS	CHAUTAUQUA	ELLERY
MAPLE STREET	NIAGARA	WILSON
MAPLE VALLEY	OTSEGO	WESTFORD
MAPLE VIEW	OSWEGO	MEXICO
MAPLEDALE	ULSTER	HARDENBURGH
MAPLEDALE	ONEIDA	BRIDGEWATER
MAPLEHURST	CATTARAUGUS	HINSDALE
MAPLES	CATTARAUGUS	MANSFIELD
MAPLETON	CAYUGA	FLEMING
MAPLETON STA.	NIAGARA	PENDLETON
MAPLETOWN	MONTGOMERY	CANAJOHARIE
MAPLETOWN	RENSSELAER	HOOSICK
MAPLEWOOD	ALBANY	COLONIE
MAPLEWOOD	SULLIVAN	THOMPSON
MARATHON V.	CORTLAND	MARATHON
MARBLETOWN	WAYNE	ARCADIA
MARBLETOWN	ULSTER	MARBLETOWN
MARCELLUS FALLS	ONONDAGA	MARCELLUS
MARCELLUS V.	ONONDAGA	MARCELLUS
MARCY	ONEIDA	MARCY
MARCY PSYCHIATRIC CENTER	ONEIDA	MARCY
MARENGO	WAYNE	GALEN
MARGARETVILLE V.	DELAWARE	MIDDLETOWN
MARIAVILLE	SCHENECTADY	DUANESBURG
MARIETTA	ONONDAGA	MARCELLUS
MARILLA	ERIE	MARILLA
MARINERS HARBOR	RICHMOND	NYC
MARION	WAYNE	MARION
MARIPOSA	CHENANGO	LINCKLAEN
MARKET	DUTCHESS	STANFORD
MARKHAM	CATTARAUGUS	DAYTON
MARKHAMVILLE	ESSEX	WILMINGTON
MARLBORO	ULSTER	MARLBOROUGH
MARLORVILLE	DUTCHESS	WAPPINGER
MARSHALL	ONEIDA	MARSHALL

NAME	COUNTY	TOWN
MARSHALLS	STEUBEN	WHEELER
MARSHFIELD	ERIE	NO. COLLINS
MARSHVILLE	MONTGOMERY	CANAJOHARIE
MARTIN CCRS.	HERKIMER	NEWPORT
MARTINDALE	COLUMBIA	CLAVERACK
MARTINDALE CORS.	WASHINGTON	WHITE CREEK
MARTINDALE DEPOT	COLUMBIA	CLAVERACK
MARTINS CORS.	HERKIMER	NEWPORT
MARTINSBURG	LEWIS	MARTINSBURG
MARTINSBURG STA.	LEWIS	MARTINSBURG
MARTVILLE	CAYUGA	STERLING
MARVIN	CHAUTAUQUA	FRENCH CR.
MARYLAND	OTSEGO	MARYLAND
MASONVILLE	DELAWARE	MASONVILLE
MASPETH	QUEENS	NYC
MASSAPEQUA	NASSAU	OYSTER BAY
MASSAPEQUA PK. V.	NASSAU	OYSTER BAY
MASSENA CTR.	ST.LAWRENCE	MASSENA
MASSENA PT.	ST.LAWRENCE	MASSENA
MASSENA SPGS.	ST.LAWRENCE	MASSENA
MASSENA SPGS. STA.	ST.LAWRENCE	MASSENA
MASSENA V.	ST.LAWRENCE	MASSENA
MASTIC	SUFFOLK	BROOKHAVEN
MASTIC BEACH	SUFFOLK	BROOKHAVEN
MATINECOCK V.	NASSAU	OYSTER BAY
MATTEAWAN	DUTCHESS	BEACON C.
MATTITUCK	SUFFOLK	SOUTHOLD
MATTYDALE	ONONDAGA	SALINA
MAYBROOK JCT.	ORANGE	MONTGOMERY
MAYBROOK V.	ORANGE	MONTGOMERY
MAYFIELD STA.	FULTON	MAYFIELD
MAYFIELD V.	FULTON	MAYFIELD
MAYS MILL	YATES	MILO
MAYVILLE V.	CHAUTAUQUA	CHAUTAUQUA
MAYWOOD	ALBANY	COLONIE
MCCLURE SETT.	BROOME	SANFORD
MCCOLLOMS	FRANKLIN	BRIGHTON
MCCONNELL'S CORS.	ONEIDA	MARSHALL
MCCONNELLSVILLE	ONEIDA	ANNSVILLE
MCCONNELLSVILLE	ONEIDA	VIENNA
MCCONNELLSVILLE CORS.	ONEIDA	ANNSVILLE
MCDONOUGH	CHENANGO	MCDONOUGH
MCDOUGALL	SENECA	VARICK
MCGOWAN	HERKIMER	FRANKFORT
MCGRAW	STEUBEN	W. UNION
MCGRAW V.	CORTLAND	CORTLANDVILLE
MCINTOSH BRIDGE	HERKIMER	OHIO
MCINTYRE	DUTCHESS	STANFORD
MCINTYRES SETT.	SCHUYLER	CATHARINE
MCKEEL CORS.	PUTNAM	PHILIPSTOWN
MCKEEVER	HERKIMER	WEBB
MCKEY	SCHOHARIE	GILBOA
MCKINISTRY	CATTARAUGUS	YORKSHIRE
MCKINLEY	MONTGOMERY	PALATINE
MCKINNEY	TOMPKINS	LANSING
MCKOONS CROSSING	HERKIMER	COLUMBIA
MCKOWNVILLE	ALBANY	GUILDERLAND
MCLEAN	TOMPKINS	GROTON
MCLEAN	TOMPKINS	DRYDEN
MCMILLIN CORS.	ONTARIO	CANANDAIGUA
MCNAIR STA.	LIVINGSTON	W. SPARTA
MCNALLS	NIAGARA	ROYALTON
MEACHAM	FRANKLIN	DUANE
MEADOW GLEN	SUFFOLK	SMITHTOWN
MEADOWBROOK	ORANGE	CORNWALL
MEADOWDALE	ALBANY	GUILDERLAND
MEADOWMERE	NASSAU	HEMPSTEAD
MEADS CORS.	PUTNAM	KENT
MEADS CREEK	STEUBEN	CAMPBELL
MECHANIC	DUTCHESS	WASHINGTON
MECHANICSTOWN	ORANGE	WALLKILL
MECHANICVILLE C.	SARATOGA	MECHANICVILLE C.
MECKLENBURG	SCHUYLER	HECTOR
MECO	FULTON	JOHNSTOWN
MECOX	SUFFOLK	SOUTHAMPTON
MEDFORD	SUFFOLK	BROOKHAVEN
MEDINA V.	ORLEANS	RIDGEWAY
MEDINA V.	ORLEANS	SHELBY
MEDUSA	ALBANY	RENSSELAERVILLE
MEDWAY	GREENE	NEW BALTIMORE
MEEKERVILLE	ONEIDA	FORESTPORT
MELINZGAH	DUTCHESS	FISHKILL
MELLENVILLE	COLUMBIA	CLAVERACK
MELODY LAKE	SULLIVAN	THOMPSON
MELROSE	RENSSELAER	SCHAGHTICOKE
MELROSE	BRONX	NYC
MELROSE PARK	CAYUGA	OWASCO
MELVILLE	SUFFOLK	HUNTINGTON
MELVIN HILL	ONTARIO	PHELPS
MEMPHIS	ONONDAGA	VAN BUREN
MEMPHIS	ONONDAGA	CAMILLUS
MENANDS V.	ALBANY	COLONIE
MENDON	MONROE	MENDON
MENDON CTR.	MONROE	MENDON
MENO PARK	FRANKLIN	SANTA CLARA
MERCHANTVILLE	STEUBEN	THURSTON

NAME	COUNTY	TOWN	NAME	COUNTY	TOWN
MEREDITH	DELAWARE	MEREDITH	MINEOLA V.	NASSAU	N. HEMPSTEAD
MEREDITH HOLL.	DELAWARE	MEREDITH	MINERAL SPGS.	SCHOHARIE	COBLESKILL
MERIDALE	DELAWARE	MEREDITH	MINERVA	ESSEX	MINERVA
MERIDIAN V.	CAYUGA	CATO	MINEVILLE	ESSEX	MORIAH
MERRICK	NASSAU	HEMPSTEAD	MINNEHAHA	HERKIMER	WEBB
MERRICKVILLE	DELAWARE	FRANKLIN	MINNETTO STA.	OSWEGO	MINETTO
MERRICKVILLE	FRANKLIN	FRANKLIN	MINNEWASKA	ULSTER	GARDINER
MERRIEWOLD PARK	SULLIVAN	FORESTBURGH	MINOA V.	ONONDAGA	MANLIUS
MERRIFIELD	CAYUGA	SCIPIO	MINOT CORS.	HERKIMER	SCHUYLER
MERRILL	CLINTON	ELLENBURG	MINOTT	HERKIMER	SCHUYLER
MERRILLVILLE	MADISON	LINCOLN	MINSTEED	WAYNE	ARCADIA
MERRILLVILLE	FRANKLIN	FRANKLIN	MITCHELL	ONTARIO	PHELPS
MERRITT CORS.	OSWEGO	PARISH	MITCHELLS CORS.	ORANGE	MONTGOMERY
MERRITTS CORS.	WESTCHESTER	NEW CASTLE	MITCHELLVILLE	STEUBEN	WHEELER
MERTENSIA	ONTARIO	FARMINGTON	MIZZENTOP	DUTCHESS	PAWLING
MERTENSIA STA.	ONTARIO	FARMINGTON	MODEL CITY	NIAGARA	LEWISTON
MESSENGERVILLE	CORTLAND	VIRGIL	MODEL CITY STA.	NIAGARA	LEWISTON
METCALF	OSWEGO	HANNIBAL	MODELTOWN	NIAGARA	LEWISTON
METHOL	DELAWARE	HANCOCK	MODENA	ULSTER	PLATTEKILL
METROPOLITAN	QUEENS	NYC	MOFFITSVILLE	CLINTON	SARANAC
METTACAHONTS	ULSTER	ROCHESTER	MOGADORE	GENESEE	PEMBROKE
MEXICO V.	OSWEGO	MEXICO	MOHAWK HILL	LEWIS	W. TURIN
MEYER HARBOR	NASSAU	HEMPSTEAD	MOHAWK STA.	SCHENECTADY	GLENVILLE
MICHIGAN CORS.	ORANGE	WALLKILL	MOHAWK V.	HERKIMER	GER. FLATS
MID-ORANGE CORRECTIONAL FAC.	ORANGE	WARWICK	MOHAWKVILLE	SCHENECTADY	ROTTERDAM
MIDDLE BRANCH	LEWIS	DIANA	MOHEGAN	WESTCHESTER	YORKTOWN
MIDDLE FALLS	WASHINGTON	GREENWICH	MOHEGAN LAKE	WESTCHESTER	YORKTOWN
MIDDLE GRANVILLE	WASHINGTON	GRANVILLE	MOHEGAN LAKE	WESTCHESTER	CORTLANDT
MIDDLE GROVE	SARATOGA	GREENFIELD	MOHONK LAKE	ULSTER	NEW PALTZ
MIDDLE HOPE	ORANGE	NEWBURGH	MOHONK LAKE	ULSTER	MARBLETOWN
MIDDLE ISLAND	SUFFOLK	BROOKHAVEN	MOIRA	FRANKLIN	MOIRA
MIDDLE KILNS	CLINTON	BLACK BROOK	MOLASSES CORS.	FRANKLIN	FRANKLIN
MIDDLE PATENT	WESTCHESTER	NO. CASTLE	MOLINO	OSWEGO	ORWELL
MIDDLE SETTLEMENT	ONEIDA	NEW HARTFORD	MOLYNEUX CORS.	NIAGARA	CAMBRIA
MIDDLE SPRITE	FULTON	STRATFORD	MOMBACCUS	ULSTER	ROCHESTER
MIDDLE VILLAGE	QUEENS	NYC	MOHGAUP	SULLIVAN	LUMBERLAND
MIDDLE VILLAGE	OTSEGO	SPRINGFIELD	MONGAUP VALLEY	SULLIVAN	BETHEL
MIDDLEBURG V.	SCHOHARIE	MIDDLEBURG	MONROE V.	ORANGE	MONROE
MIDDLEFIELD	OTSEGO	MIDDLEFIELD	MONS CORS.	JEFFERSON	WILNA
MIDDLEFIELD CTR.	OTSEGO	MIDDLEFIELD	MONSEY	ROCKLAND	RAMAPO
MIDDLEPORT	MADISON	LEBANON	MONTAGUE	LEWIS	MONTAGUE
MIDDLEPORT V.	NIAGARA	ROYALTON	MONTAUK	SUFFOLK	E. HAMPTON
MIDDLEPORT V.	NIAGARA	HARTLAND	MONTAUK PL.	SUFFOLK	E. HAMPTON
MIDDLEROAD CH.	JEFFERSON	RUTLAND	MONTEREY	SCHUYLER	ORANGE
MIDDLESEX	YATES	MIDDLESEX	MONTEZUMA	CAYUGA	MONTEZUMA
MIDDLETOWN C.	ORANGE	MIDDLETOWN C.	MONTEZUMA STA.	CAYUGA	MONTEZUMA
MIDDLETOWN PSYCHIATRIC CTR.	ORANGE	MIDDLETOWN C.	MONTGOMERY V.	ORANGE	MONTGOMERY
			MONTICELLO	OTSEGO	RICHFIELD
MIDDLEVILLE	SUFFOLK	SMITHTOWN	MONTICELLO V.	SULLIVAN	THOMPSON
MIDDLEVILLE V.	HERKIMER	FAIRFIELD	MONTOUR FALLS V.	SCHUYLER	DIX
MIDDLEVILLE V.	HERKIMER	NEWPORT	MONTOUR FALLS V.	SCHUYLER	MONTOUR
MIDLAND BEACH	RICHMOND	NYC	MONTROSE	WESTCHESTER	CORTLANDT
MIDWAY	TOMPKINS	LANSING	MONTVILLE	CAYUGA	MORAVIA
			MONTVILLE	ROCKLAND	STONY POINT
MIDWAY	CHAUTAUQUA	ELLERY	MONTY'S BRIDGE	WARREN	QUEENSBURY
MIDWAY PARK	CHAUTAUQUA	ELLERY	MOODNA	ORANGE	NEW WINDSOR
MIDWAY PARK	ORANGE	WALLKILL	MOODY	FRANKLIN	ALTAMONT
MILAN	DUTCHESS	MILAN	MOOERS FORKS	CLINTON	MOOERS
MILESES	SULLIVAN	FREMONT	MOOERS JCT.	CLINTON	MOOERS
MILESTRIP	MADISON	FENNER	MOOERS V.	CLINTON	MOOERS
MILFORD CTR.	OTSEGO	MILFORD	MOOLEYVILLE	SARATOGA	CORINTH
MILFORD V.	OTSEGO	MILFORD	MOONS	CHAUTAUQUA	CHARLOTTE
MILITARY TURNPIKE	CLINTON	PLATTSBURG	MOORE CORS.	ONEIDA	MARSHALL
MILL GROVE	CATTARAUGUS	PORTVILLE	MOORE SETT.	DELAWARE	ROXBURY
MILL GROVE	ERIE	ALDEN	MOORES MILLS	DUTCHESS	LAGRANGE
MILL HOOK	ULSTER	ROCHESTER	MOOSE RIVER	LEWIS	LYONSDALE
MILL NECK V.	NASSAU	OYSTER BAY	MORAINE	ALLEGANY	BURNS
MILL POINT	MONTGOMERY	GLEN	MORAVIA V.	CAYUGA	MORAVIA
MILLBROOK V.	DUTCHESS	WASHINGTON	MOREHOUSE	HAMILTON	MOREHOUSE
MILLEN BAY	JEFFERSON	CAPE VINCENT	MORELAND	SCHUYLER	DIX
MILLER CORS.	MONTGOMERY	FLORIDA	MORELAND STA.	SCHUYLER	DIX
MILLER CORS.	RENSSELAER	NASSAU	MORESVILLE	DELAWARE	ROXBURY
MILLER PLACE	SUFFOLK	BROOKHAVEN	MORETON FARM	MONROE	OGDEN
MILLERS	ORLEANS	YATES	MOREVILLE	SCHOHARIE	JEFFERSON
MILLERS MILLS	HERKIMER	COLUMBIA	MORGANVILLE	GENESEE	STAFFORD
MILLERSPORT	ERIE	CLARENCE	MORIAH	ESSEX	MORIAH
MILLERTON V.	DUTCHESS	NORTHEAST	MORIAH CTR.	ESSEX	MORIAH
MILLPORT V.	CHEMUNG	VETERAN	MORLEY	ST. LAWRENCE	CANTON
MILLS CORNERS	FULTON	BROADALBIN	MORRIS CORS.	MONTGOMERY	FLORIDA
MILLS MILLS	ALLEGANY	HUME	MORRIS PARK	QUEENS	NYC
MILLSBURG	ORANGE	WALLKILL	MORRIS V.	OTSEGO	MORRIS
MILLSBURG	ORANGE	WAWAYANDA	MORRISANIA	BRONX	NYC
MILLSBURG	ORANGE	MINISINK	MORRISONVILLE	CLINTON	PLATTSBURG
MILLTOWN	PUTNAM	SOUTHEAST	MORRISONVILLE	CLINTON	SCHUYLER FALLS
MILLVILLE	ORLEANS	SHELBY	MORRISTOWN V.	ST. LAWRENCE	MORRISTOWN
MILLWOOD	WESTCHESTER	NEW CASTLE	MORRISVILLE STA.	MADISON	EATON
MILO	YATES	MILO	MORRISVILLE V.	MADISON	EATON
MILO CTR.	YATES	MILO	MORSE	OSWEGO	PALERMO
MILO MILLS	YATES	MILO	MORSE MILLS	CAYUGA	MORAVIA
MILO STA.	YATES	MILO	MORSETON	SULLIVAN	ROCKLAND
MILTON	ULSTER	MARLBOROUGH	MORSEVILLE	SCHOHARIE	JEFFERSON
MILTON CTR.	SARATOGA	MILTON	MORTIMER	MONROE	HENRIETTA
MINA	CHAUTAUQUA	MINA	MORTON	MONROE	HAMLIN
MINA CORS.	CHAUTAUQUA	MINA	MORTON	ORLEANS	KENDALL
MINAVILLE	MONTGOMERY	FLORIDA	MORTON CORS.	ERIE	CONCORD
MINDEN	MONTGOMERY	MINDEN	MOSCOW	LIVINGSTON	LEICESTER
MINDENVILLE	MONTGOMERY	MINDEN	MOSCOW HILL	MADISON	BROOKFIELD

NAME	COUNTY	TOWN
MOSES KILL	WASHINGTON	FORT EDWARD
MOSHERVILLE	SARATOGA	GALWAY
MOSS STREET	WASHINGTON	KINGSBURY
MOTT HAVEN	BRONX	NYC
MOTTVILLE	ONONDAGA	SKANEATELES
MOUNT AIRY	WESTCHESTER	CORTLANDT
MOUNT ARAB	ST. LAWRENCE	PIERCEFIELD
MOUNT CARMEL	BROOME	SANFORD
MOUNT CARMEL	BROOME	WINDSOR
MOUNT CARMEL SCHOOL DISTRICT	BROOME	WINDSOR
MOUNT HOPE	ORANGE	MT. HOPE
MOUNT HOPE	WESTCHESTER	GREENBURGH
MOUNT HOUSE	GREENE	HUNTER
MOUNT IVY	ROCKLAND	HAVERSTRAW
MOUNT KISCO V.	WESTCHESTER	MT. KISCO
MOUNT LEBANON	COLUMBIA	NEW LEBANON
MOUNT LORETTA	RICHMOND	NYC
MOUNT MARION	ULSTER	SAUGERTIES
MOUNT MCGREGOR	SARATOGA	WILTON
MOUNT MORRIS V.	LIVINGSTON	MT. MORRIS
MOUNT PLEASANT	OSWEGO	VOLNEY
MOUNT PLEASANT	WESTCHESTER	MT. PLEASANT
MOUNT PLEASANT	SARATOGA	GREENFIELD
MOUNT PROSPER	SULLIVAN	MAMAKATING
MOUNT READ	MONROE	GREECE
MOUNT RIGA	DUTCHESS	NORTHEAST
MOUNT RODERICK	CORTLAND	TAYLOR
MOUNT ST. VINCENT	BRONX	NYC
MOUNT SINAI	SUFFOLK	BROOKHAVEN
MOUNT TREMPER	ULSTER	SHANDAKEN
MOUNT UPTON	CHENANGO	GUILFORD
MOUNT VALLEY	ULSTER	SHAWANGUNK
MOUNT VERNON	OTSEGO	LAURENS
MOUNT VERNON C.	WESTCHESTER	MT. VERNON C.
MOUNT VERNON-ON-THE-LAKE	ERIE	HAMBURG
MOUNT VIEW FARM	FRANKLIN	HARRIETSTOWN
MOUNT VISION	OTSEGO	LAURENS
MOUNTAIN DALE	SULLIVAN	FALLSBURG
MOUNTAIN HOUSE	GREENE	HUNTER
MOUNTAIN HOUSE RD.	GREENE	CATSKILL
MOUNTAIN VIEW	FRANKLIN	BELLMONT
MOUNTAINVILLE	ORANGE	CORNWALL
MUD CREEK	CHAUTAUQUA	POLAND
MUD CREEK	CATTARAUGUS	RANDOLPH
MUD HILL	OSWEGO	AMBOY
MUD LAKE	LEWIS	LEWIS
MUD LOCK	CAYUGA	AURELIUS
MUITZEKILL	RENSSELAER	SCHODACK
MUMFORD	MONROE	WHEATLAND
MUNDALE	DELAWARE	HAMDEN
MUNNS	MADISON	STOCKBRIDGE
MUNNS STA.	MADISON	STOCKBRIDGE
MUNNSVILLE STA.	MADISON	STOCKBRIDGE
MUNNSVILLE V.	MADISON	STOCKBRIDGE
MUNSEY PARK V.	NASSAU	N. HEMPSTEAD
MUNSON	NASSAU	HEMPSTEAD
MUNSONS CORNERS	CORTLAND	CORTLANDVILLE
MUNSONVILLE	FULTON	MAYFIELD
MURRAY	ORLEANS	MURRAY
MURRAY CORS.	COLUMBIA	HILLSDALE
MURRAY HILL	LIVINGSTON	MT. MORRIS
MURRAYISLE	JEFFERSON	CLAYTON
MUTTONTOWN V.	NASSAU	OYSTER BAY
MYERS	TOMPKINS	LANSING
MYERS CORS.	DUTCHESS	WAPPINGER

-N-

NAME	COUNTY	TOWN
N. C. CROSSING	ONTARIO	PHELPS
NANTICOKE	BROOME	NANTICOKE
NANUET	ROCKLAND	CLARKSTOWN
NAPANOCH	ULSTER	WAWARSING
NAPEAGUE BEACH	SUFFOLK	E. HAMPTON
NAPLES V.	ONTARIO	NAPLES
NAPOLI	CATTARAUGUS	NAPOLI
NARROWSBURG	SULLIVAN	TUSTEN
NASHVILLE	CHAUTAUQUA	HANOVER
NASSAU MILLS	RENSSELAER	NASSAU
NASSAU V.	RENSSELAER	NASSAU
NATIONAL MONUMENT	NIAGARA	PORTER
NATURAL BRIDGE	JEFFERSON	WILNA
NATURAL DAM	ST. LAWRENCE	GOUVERNEUR
NAUMBURG	LEWIS	CROGHAN
NAUVOO	JEFFERSON	ANTWERP
NAVARINO	ONONDAGA	ONONDAGA
NEDROW	ONONDAGA	ONONDAGA
NEELYTOWN	ORANGE	HAMPTONBURG
NEHASANE	HAMILTON	LONG LAKE
NEHASANE STA.	HAMILTON	LONG LAKE
NELLISTON V.	MONTGOMERY	PALATINE
NELSON	MADISON	NELSON
NELSON CORS.	PUTNAM	PHILIPSTOWN
NELSONVILLE V.	PUTNAM	PHILLIPSTOWN
NEPERA PARK	WESTCHESTER	YONKERS C.
NEPONSIT	QUEENS	NYC

NAME	COUNTY	TOWN
NEPPERHAN	WESTCHESTER	YONKERS C.
NESCONSET	SUFFOLK	SMITHTOWN
NETHERWOOD	DUTCHESS	PLEASANT VALLEY
NEVERSINK	SULLIVAN	NEVERSINK
NEVIS	COLUMBIA	CLERMONT
NEW ALBION	CATTARAUGUS	NEW ALBION
NEW BALTIMORE	GREENE	NEW BALTIMORE
NEW BALTIMORE STA.	GREENE	NEW BALTIMORE
NEW BERLIN CTR.	CHENANGO	NEW BERLIN
NEW BERLIN JCT.	CHENANGO	GUILFORD
NEW BERLIN STA.	CHENANGO	NEW BERLIN
NEW BERLIN V.	CHENANGO	NEW BERLIN
NEW BOSTON	LEWIS	PINCKNEY
NEW BREMEN	LEWIS	NEW BREMEN
NEW BRIDGE	ST. LAWRENCE	CLARE
NEW BRIGHTON	RICHMOND	NYC
NEW BRITAIN	COLUMBIA	NEW LEBANON
NEW CASSEL	NASSAU	NO. HEMPSTEAD
NEW CASTLE	WESTCHESTER	NEW CASTLE
NEW CITY	ROCKLAND	CLARKSTOWN
NEW CITY	ROCKLAND	RAMAPO
NEW CONCORD	COLUMBIA	CHATHAM
NEW DORP	RICHMOND	NYC
NEW FORGE	COLUMBIA	TAGHKANIC
NEW HACKENSACK	DUTCHESS	WAPPINGER
NEW HAMBURG	DUTCHESS	POUGHKEEPSIE
NEW HAMPTON	ORANGE	WAWAYANDA
NEW HARTFORD STA.	ONEIDA	NEW HARTFORD
NEW HARTFORD V.	ONEIDA	NEW HARTFORD
NEW HAVEN	OSWEGO	NEW HAVEN
NEW HEMPSTEAD	ROCKLAND	RAMAPO
NEW HOPE	CAYUGA	NILES
NEW HURLEY	ULSTER	SHAWANGUNK
NEW HYDE PARK V.	NASSAU	HEMPSTEAD
NEW HYDE PARK V.	NASSAU	N. HEMPSTEAD
NEW IRELAND	BROOME	MAINE
NEW KINGSTON	DELAWARE	MIDDLETOWN
NEW LEBANON	COLUMBIA	NEW LEBANON
NEW LEBANON CTR.	COLUMBIA	NEW LEBANON
NEW LISBON	OTSEGO	NEW LISBON
NEW LONDON	ONEIDA	VERONA
NEW LOTS STA.	KINGS	NYC
NEW MILFORD	ORANGE	WARWICK
NEW OHIO	BROOME	COLESVILLE
NEW OREGON	ERIE	NO. COLLINS
NEW PALTZ LDG.	ULSTER	LLOYD
NEW PALTZ V.	ULSTER	N. PALTZ
NEW PROSPECT CH.	ULSTER	SHAWANGUNK
NEW ROCHELLE C.	WESTCHESTER	NEW ROCHELLE C.
NEW RUSSIA	ESSEX	ELIZABETHTOWN
NEW SALEM	ULSTER	ESOPUS
NEW SALEM	ONTARIO	FARMINGTON
NEW SALEM	ALBANY	NEW SCOTLAND
NEW SCOTLAND	ALBANY	NEW SCOTLAND
NEW SCRANTON	ERIE	HAMBURG
NEW SCRIBA	OSWEGO	ORWELL
NEW SPRINGVILLE	RICHMOND	NYC
NEW SQUARE V.	ROCKLAND	RAMAPO
NEW SUFFOLK	SUFFOLK	SOUTHOLD
NEW SWEDEN	CLINTON	AUSABLE
NEW VERNON	ORANGE	MT. HOPE
NEW VERNON	SULLIVAN	MAMAKATING
NEW WINDSOR	ORANGE	NEW WINDSOR
NEW WOODSTOCK	MADISON	CAZENOVIA
NEW YORK	NEW YORK	NYC
NEW YORK MILLS V.	ONEIDA	WHITESTOWN
NEW YORK MILLS V.	ONEIDA	NEW HARTFORD
NYS BARGE CANAL TERM CHAMP DIV	WASHINGTON	WHITEHALL
NYS FISH HATCHERY	STEUBEN	URBANA
NYS HOME FOR VET & DEPENDENTS	CHENANGO	OXFORD
NEW YORK UPPER MILLS	ONEIDA	NEW HARTFORD
NEWARK DEVELOPMENTAL CTR	WAYNE	NEWARK
NEWARK STA.	WAYNE	ARCADIA
NEWARK V.	WAYNE	ARCADIA
NEWARK VALLEY V.	TIOGA	NEWARK VALLEY
NEWBURG	WYOMING	GAINESVILLE
NEWBURGH C.	ORANGE	NEWBURGH C.
NEWCOMB	ESSEX	NEWCOMB
NEWEIDEN	SULLIVAN	TUSTEN
NEWFANE	NIAGARA	NEWFANE
NEWFIELD	TOMPKINS	NEWFIELD
NEWFIELD STA.	TOMPKINS	NEWFIELD
NEWKIRK MILLS	FULTON	CAROGA
NEWMAN	ESSEX	NO. ELBA
NEWPORT STA.	HERKIMER	NEWPORT
NEWPORT V.	HERKIMER	NEWPORT
NEWTON	ERIE	COLLINS
NEWTON FALLS	ST. LAWRENCE	CLIFTON
NEWTON HOOK	COLUMBIA	STUYVESANT
NEWTONVILLE	ALBANY	COLONIE
NEWTOWN	QUEENS	NYC
NEWTOWN	SUFFOLK	SOUTHAMPTON
NEWVILLE	HERKIMER	DANUBE

NAME	COUNTY	TOWN	NAME	COUNTY	TOWN
NIAGARA	NIAGARA	NIAGARA	NO. GREECE	MONROE	GREECE
NIAGARA FALLS C.	NIAGARA	NIAGARA FALLS C.	NO. GREENBUSH	RENSSELAER	NO. GREENBUSH
NIAGARA JCT.	NIAGARA	LEWISTON	NO. GREENFIELD	SARATOGA	GREENFIELD
NIAGARA UNIV.	NIAGARA	LEWISTON	NO. GREENWICH	WASHINGTON	GREENWICH
NICHOL'S CORS.	SENECA	SENECA FALLS	NO. HAMDEN	DELAWARE	HAMDEN
NICHOL'S MILLS	ONEIDA	FORESTPORT	NO. HAMLIN	MONROE	HAMLIN
NICHOLS	STEUBEN	TUSCARORA	NO. HAMMOND	ST.LAWRENCE	HAMMOND
NICHOLS V.	TIOGA	NICHOLS	NO. HANNIBAL	OSWEGO	HANNIBAL
NICHOLSVILLE	ONEIDA	FORESTPORT	NO. HARMONY	CHAUTAUQUA	HARMONY
NICHOLVILLE	ST.LAWRENCE	LAWRENCE	NO. HARPERSFIELD	DELAWARE	HARPERSFIELD
NICHOLVILLE	ST.LAWRENCE	HOPKINTON	NO. HARTLAND	NIAGARA	HARTLAND
NIETS CREST	CHAUTAUQUA	NO. HARMONY	NO. HAVEN V.	SUFFOLK	SOUTHAMPTON
NILES	CAYUGA	NILES	NO. HAVERSTRAW	ROCKLAND	STONY POINT
NIMMONSBURG	BROOME	CHENANGO	NO. HEBRON	WASHINGTON	HEBRON
NINA	TOMPKINS	NEWFIELD	NO. HECTOR	SCHUYLER	HECTOR
NINE MILE POINT	CAYUGA	STERLING	NO. HECTOR STA.	SCHUYLER	HECTOR
NINETY SIX	ONEIDA	REMSEN	NO. HILLS V.	NASSAU	N. HEMPSTEAD
NINEVEH	BROOME	COLESVILLE	NO. HILLSDALE	COLUMBIA	HILLSDALE
NINEVEH JCT.	CHENANGO	AFTON	NO. HOOSICK	RENSSELAER	HOOSICK
NIOBE	CHAUTAUQUA	HARMONY	NO. HORNELL V.	STEUBEN	HORNELLSVILLE
NIOBE JCT.	CHAUTAUQUA	HARMONY	NO. HUDSON	ESSEX	NO. HUDSON
NISKAYUNA	SCHENECTADY	NISKAYUNA	NO. HURON	WAYNE	HURON
NISSEQUOGUE V.	SUFFOLK	SMITHTOWN	NO. JASPER	STEUBEN	JASPER
NIVERVILLE	COLUMBIA	KINDERHOOK	NO. JAVA	WYOMING	JAVA
NOBLEBORO	HERKIMER	OHIO	NO. JAVA STA.	WYOMING	JAVA
NOBLEVILLE	OTSEGO	NEW LISBON	NO. JAY	ESSEX	JAY
NORFOLK	ST.LAWRENCE	NORFOLK	NO. KORTRIGHT	DELAWARE	KORTRIGHT
NORMANSKILL	ALBANY	BETHLEHEM	NO. LANDING	JEFFERSON	ELLISBURG
NORMANSVILLE	ALBANY	BETHLEHEM	NO. LANSING	TOMPKINS	LANSING
NORRISVILLE	CLINTON	SCHUYLER FALLS	NO. LAWRENCE	NASSAU	HEMPSTEAD
NO. ADAMS	JEFFERSON	ADAMS	NO. LAWRENCE	ST.LAWRENCE	LAWRENCE
NO. AFTON	CHENANGO	AFTON	NO. LEROY	GENESEE	LEROY
NO. ALEXANDER	GENESEE	ALEXANDER	NO. LINDENHURST	SUFFOLK	BABYLON
NO. ALMOND	ALLEGANY	ALMOND	NO. LITCHFIELD	HERKIMER	LITCHFIELD
NO. AMBOY	OSWEGO	AMBOY	NO. LONG BEACH	NASSAU	HEMPSTEAD
NO. AMBOY	WASHINGTON	ARGYLE	NO. MASSAPEQUA	NASSAU	OYSTER BAY
NO. AMITYVILLE	SUFFOLK	BABYLON	NO. MERRICK	NASSAU	HEMPSTEAD
NO. ARGYLE	WASHINGTON	ARGYLE	NO. MILTON	SARATOGA	MILTON
NO. BABYLON	SUFFOLK	BABYLON	NO. NASSAU	RENSSELAER	NASSAU
NO. BANGOR	FRANKLIN	BANGOR	NO. NORWICH	CHENANGO	NO. NORWICH
NO. BARTON	TIOGA	BARTON	NO. OAK HILL	STEUBEN	DANSVILLE
NO. BAY	ONEIDA	VIENNA	NO. OSCEOLA	LEWIS	OSCEOLA
NO. BEACH	QUEENS	NYC	NO. PARMA	MONROE	PARMA
NO. BELLMORE	NASSAU	HEMPSTEAD	NO. PEMBROKE	GENESEE	PEMBROKE
NO. BERGEN	GENESEE	BERGEN	NO. PETERSBURG	RENSSELAER	PETERSBURG
NO. BLENHEIM	SCHOHARIE	BLENHEIM	NO. PHARSALIA	CHENANGO	PHARSALIA
NO. BLOOMFIELD	LIVINGSTON	LIMA	NO. PITCHER	CHENANGO	PITCHER
NO. BLOOMFIELD	ONTARIO	W. BLOOMFIELD	NO. READING	SCHUYLER	READING
NO. BOLTON	WARREN	BOLTON	NO. RIDGE	NIAGARA	CAMBRIA
NO. BOSTON	ERIE	BOSTON	NO. RIDGEWAY	ORLEANS	RIDGEWAY
NO. BOYLSTON	OSWEGO	BOYLSTON	NO. RIVER	WARREN	JOHNSBURG
NO. BRANCH	SULLIVAN	CALLICOON	NO. ROCKVILLE CENTRE	NASSAU	HEMPSTEAD
NO. BRIDGEWATER	ONEIDA	BRIDGEWATER	NO. ROSE	WAYNE	ROSE
NO. BROADALBIN	FULTON	BROADALBIN	NO. RUSH	MONROE	RUSH
NO. BROOKDALE	ST.LAWRENCE	STOCKHOLM	NO. RUSSELL	ST.LAWRENCE	RUSSELL
NO. BROOKFIELD	MADISON	BROOKFIELD	NO. SALEM	WESTCHESTER	NO. SALEM
NO. BROOKFIELD STA.	MADISON	BROOKFIELD	NO. SANFORD	BROOME	SANFORD
NO. BUFFALO STA.	ERIE	BUFFALO C.	NO. SCRIBA	OSWEGO	SCRIBA
NO. BURKE	FRANKLIN	BURKE	NO. SEA	SUFFOLK	SOUTHAMPTON
NO. BURT	NIAGARA	NEWFANE	NO. SETTLEMENT	GREENE	WINDHAM
NO. BYRON	GENESEE	BYRON	NO. SHELDON	WYOMING	SHELDON
NO. CAMBRIDGE	WASHINGTON	CAMBRIDGE	NO. SHENOROCK	WESTCHESTER	SOMERS
NO. CAMERON	STEUBEN	CAMERON	NO. SPENCER	TIOGA	SPENCER
NO. CASTLE	WESTCHESTER	NO. CASTLE	NO. STEPHENTOWN	RENSSELAER	STEPHENTOWN
NO. CHATHAM	COLUMBIA	CHATHAM	NO. STERLING	CAYUGA	STERLING
NO. CHEMUNG	CHEMUNG	BALDWIN	NO. STEUBEN	ONEIDA	STEUBEN
NO. CHILI	MONROE	CHILI	NO. STOCKHOLM	ST.LAWRENCE	STOCKHOLM
NO. CHITTENANGO	MADISON	SULLIVAN	NO. SUMMER HILL	CAYUGA	SEMPRONIUS
NO. CLARKSON	MONROE	HAMLIN	NO. SYRACUSE V.	ONONDAGA	CICERO
NO. CLOVE	DUTCHESS	UNION VALE	NO. SYRACUSE V.	ONONDAGA	CLAY
NO. CLYMER	CHAUTAUQUA	CLYMER	NO. TARRYTOWN V.	WESTCHESTER	MT. PLEASANT
NO. COHOCTON	STEUBEN	COHOCTON	NO. TONAWANDA C.	NIAGARA	NO. TONAWANDA C.
NO. COLESVILLE	BROOME	COLESVILLE	NO. URBANA	STEUBEN	URBANA
NO. COLLINS V.	ERIE	NO. COLLINS	NO. VALLEY STREAM	NASSAU	HEMPSTEAD
NO. COLUMBIA	HERKIMER	COLUMBIA	NO. VICTORY	CAYUGA	VICTORY
NO. CONSTANTIA	OSWEGO	CONSTANTIA	NO. VOLNEY	OSWEGO	VOLNEY
NO. CREEK	WARREN	JOHNSBURG	NO. WANTAGH	NASSAU	HEMPSTEAD
NO. CROGHAN	LEWIS	CROGHAN	NO. WESTERN	ONEIDA	WESTERN
NO. CUBA	ALLEGANY	CUBA	NO. WHITE PLAINS	WESTCHESTER	NO. CASTLE
NO. DARIEN	GENESEE	DARIEN	NO. WILMURT	HERKIMER	OHIO
NO. E. BENNINGTON	WYOMING	BENNINGTON	NO. WILNA	JEFFERSON	WILNA
NO. E. CENTER	DUTCHESS	NORTHEAST	NO. WOLCOTT	WAYNE	WOLCOTT
NO. EASTON	WASHINGTON	EASTON	NO. WOODMERE	NASSAU	HEMPSTEAD
NO. ELBA	ESSEX	NO. ELBA	NORTHAMPTON	FULTON	NORTHAMPTON
NO. ELMIRA	CHEMUNG	HORSEHEADS	NORTHBUSH	FULTON	CAROGA
NO. EVANS	ERIE	HAMBURG	NORTHFIELD	DELAWARE	WALTON
NO. EVANS	ERIE	EVANS	NORTHFIELD STA.	DELAWARE	FRANKLIN
NO. FAIRHAVEN	CAYUGA	STERLING	NORTHPORT JCT.	SUFFOLK	HUNTINGTON
NO. FENTON	BROOME	FENTON	NORTHPORT V.	SUFFOLK	HUNTINGTON
NO. FRANKFORT	HERKIMER	SCHUYLER	NORTHRUP CORS.	ST.LAWRENCE	OSWEGATCHIE
NO. FRANKLIN	DELAWARE	FRANKLIN	NORTHSIDE	SARATOGA	WATERFORD
NO. GAGE	ONEIDA	DEERFIELD	NORTHUMBERLAND	SARATOGA	NORTHUMBERLAND
NO. GAINESVILLE	WYOMING	GAINESVILLE	NORTHVILLE	SUFFOLK	RIVERHEAD
NO. GALWAY	SARATOGA	GALWAY	NORTHVILLE	CAYUGA	GENOA
NO. GERMANTOWN	COLUMBIA	GERMANTOWN	NORTHVILLE V.	FULTON	NORTHAMPTON
NO. GRANVILLE	WASHINGTON	GRANVILLE	NORTHWOOD	HERKIMER	RUSSIA
NO. GREAT RIVER	SUFFOLK	ISLIP	NORTHWOODS CLUB	ESSEX	MINERVA

NAME	COUNTY	TOWN	NAME	COUNTY	TOWN
NORTON	STEUBEN	GREENWOOD	ONTARIO CO. HOME	ONTARIO	HOPEWELL
NORTON	TOMPKINS	LANSING	ONTARIO CTR.	WAYNE	ONTARIO
NORTON HILL	GREENE	GREENVILLE	ONTEORA PK.	GREENE	HUNTER
NORTON HOLLOW	STEUBEN	GREENWOOD	OPEN MEADOWS	CHAUTAUQUA	NO. HARMONY
NORWAY	HERKIMER	NORWAY	OPPENHEIM	FULTON	OPPENHEIM
NORWICH C.	CHENANGO	NORWICH C.	OGUAGA LAKE	BROOME	SANFORD
NORWICH CORS.	HERKIMER	LITCHFIELD	ORAMEL	ALLEGANY	CANEADEA
NORWOOD V.	ST.LAWRENCE	NORFOLK	ORAN	ONONDAGA	POMPEY
NORWOOD V.	ST.LAWRENCE	POTSDAM	ORANGE FARM STA.	ORANGE	GOSHEN
NOXON	DUTCHESS	LAGRANGE	ORANGE LAKE	ORANGE	NEWBURGH
NOYACK	SUFFOLK	SOUTHAMPTON	ORANGEBURG	ROCKLAND	ORANGETOWN
NUBIA	TOMPKINS	GROTON	ORANGEPORT	NIAGARA	ROYALTON
NUMBER FOUR	LEWIS	WATSON	ORANGETOWN	SCHUYLER	ORANGE
NUNDA JCT.	LIVINGSTON	NUNDA	ORANGEVILLE	WYOMING	ORANGEVILLE
NUNDA V.	LIVINGSTON	NUNDA	ORANGEVILLE CTR.	WYOMING	ORANGEVILLE
NYACK V.	ROCKLAND	ORANGETOWN	ORCHARD HILL	WESTCHESTER	GREENBURGH
NYANDO	ST.LAWRENCE	MASSENA	ORCHARD PARK V.	ERIE	ORCHARD PARK
			OREGON	FULTON	STRATFORD
	-O-		OREGON CORS.	PUTNAM	PUTNAM VALLEY
OAK BEACH	SUFFOLK	BABYLON	ORENDORF CORS.	HERKIMER	COLUMBIA
OAK CORS.	ONTARIO	PHELPS	ORIENT	SUFFOLK	SOUTHOLD
OAK HILL	GREENE	DURHAM	ORIENTAL PARK	CHAUTAUQUA	ELLERY
OAK HILL	WYOMING	CASTILE	ORISKANY FALLS V.	ONEIDA	AUGUSTA
OAK HILL	STEUBEN	DANSVILLE	ORISKANY V.	ONEIDA	WHITESTOWN
OAK HILL	COLUMBIA	LIVINGSTON	ORLANDO	CATTARAUGUS	MANSFIELD
OAK ISLAND	ST.LAWRENCE	HAMMOND	ORLEANS	ONTARIO	PHELPS
OAK MOUNTAIN	HERKIMER	SALISBURY	ORLEANS CORS.	JEFFERSON	ORLEANS
OAK ORCHARD	ORLEANS	RIDGEWAY	ORR MILLS	ORANGE	CORNWALL
OAK ORCHARD HARBOR	ORLEANS	CARLTON	ORWELL	OSWEGO	ORWELL
OAK ORCHARD ON THE LAKE	ORLEANS	CARLTON	OSBORN	TIOGA	NICHOLS
OAK POINT	ST.LAWRENCE	HAMMOND	OSBORN BRIDGE	FULTON	NORTHAMPTON
OAK RIDGE	ULSTER	WAWARSING	OSBORNE HOLLOW	BROOME	COLESVILLE
OAK RIDGE	MONTGOMERY	CHARLESTON	OSCAWANA	WESTCHESTER	CORTLANDT
OAK SUMMIT	DUTCHESS	WASHINGTON	OSCAWANA CORS.	PUTNAM	PUTNAM VALLEY
OAKDALE	SUFFOLK	ISLIP	OSCEOLA	LEWIS	OSCEOLA
OAKDALE	BROOME	UNION	OSSIAN	LIVINGSTON	OSSIAN
OAKDALE STA.	SUFFOLK	ISLIP	OSSINING CORRECTIONAL FAC.	WESTCHESTER	OSSINING
OAKES	ULSTER	LLOYD	OSSINING V.	WESTCHESTER	OSSINING
OAKFIELD V.	GENESEE	OAKFIELD	OSWEGATCHIE	ST.LAWRENCE	FINE
OAKLAND STA.	SULLIVAN	FORESTBURGH	OSWEGATCHIE CORS.	LEWIS	DIANA
OAKLAND VALLEY	SULLIVAN	FORESTBURGH	OSWEGATCHIE SETT.	LEWIS	DIANA
OAKLEY CORS.	TIOGA	OWEGO	OSWEGO C.	OSWEGO	OSWEGO C.
OAKS CORS.	ONTARIO	PHELPS	OSWEGO FALLS	OSWEGO	FULTON C.
OAKVALE STA.	ST.LAWRENCE	HAMMOND	OTEGO V.	OTSEGO	OTEGO
OAKVILLE	OTSEGO	OTSEGO	OTIS JCT.	GREENE	CATSKILL
OAKVILLE	SUFFOLK	SOUTHAMPTON	OTISCO	ONONDAGA	OTISCO
OAKWOOD	CAYUGA	SPRINGPORT	OTISVILLE V.	ORANGE	MT. HOPE
OATKA	WYOMING	WARSAW	OTSDAWA	OTSEGO	OTEGO
OATKA	MONROE	HENRIETTA	OTSELIC	CHENANGO	OTSELIC
OBERNBURG V.	SULLIVAN	FREMONT	OTSELIC CTR.	CHENANGO	OTSELIC
OBI	ALLEGANY	GENESEE	OTTER	ST.LAWRENCE	HOPKINTON
OCCANUM	BROOME	WINDSOR	OTTER KILL	ORANGE	HAMPTONBURG
OCEAN BAY PARK	SUFFOLK	ISLIP	OTTERLAKE	ONEIDA	FORESTPORT
OCEAN BEACH V.	SUFFOLK	ISLIP	OTTO	CATTARAUGUS	OTTO
OCEAN SIDE	NASSAU	HEMPSTEAD	OTTO MILLS	OSWEGO	REDFIELD
ODESSA V.	SCHUYLER	CATHERINE	OTTSVILLE	ORANGE	MT. HOPE
OGDEN	MONROE	OGDEN	QUAQUAGA	BROOME	COLESVILLE
OGDEN CTR.	MONROE	OGDEN	OUTLET STA.	ONTARIO	PHELPS
OGDENS	DELAWARE	WALTON	OVERACKER CORS.	YATES	MIDDLESEX
OGDENSBURG C.	ST.LAWRENCE	OGDENSBURG C.	OVERLOOK	DUTCHESS	LAGRANGE
OHIO	HERKIMER	OHIO	OVID CTR.	SENECA	OVID
OHIOVILLE	ULSTER	NEW PALTZ	OVID STA.	SENECA	OVID
OLCOTT	NIAGARA	NEWFANE	OVID V.	SENECA	OVID
OLCOTT BEACH	NIAGARA	NEWFANE	OWASCO	CAYUGA	OWASCO
OLD BETH PAGE	NASSAU	OYSTER BAY	OWASCO HILL	CAYUGA	VENICE
OLD BROOKVILLE V.	NASSAU	OYSTER BAY	OWASCO LAKE	CAYUGA	FLEMING
OLD CHATHAM	COLUMBIA	CHATHAM	OWEGO V.	TIOGA	OWEGO
OLD CROTON DAM	WESTCHESTER	YORKTOWN	OWENS MILLS	CHEMUNG	CHEMUNG
OLD FALLS	SULLIVAN	FALLSBURG	OWLS HEAD	FRANKLIN	BELLMONT
OLD FIELD V.	SUFFOLK	BROOKHAVEN	OXBOW	JEFFERSON	ANTWERP
OLD FORGE	HERKIMER	WEBB	OXFORD	ORANGE	BLOOMING GR.
OLD FURNACE	ESSEX	CROWN POINT	OXFORD DEPOT	ORANGE	BLOOMING GR.
OLD IRVING	CHAUTAUQUA	HANOVER	OXFORD V.	CHENANGO	OXFORD
OLD WESTBURY V.	NASSAU	N. HEMPSTEAD	OYSTER BAY	NASSAU	OYSTER BAY
OLD WESTBURY V.	NASSAU	OYSTER BAY	OYSTER BAY COVE V.	NASSAU	OYSTER BAY
OLEAN C.	CATTARAUGUS	OLEAN C.	OZONE PARK	QUEENS	NYC
OLIVE BRIDGE	ULSTER	OLIVE	OZONIA	FRANKLIN	FRANKLIN
OLIVEREA	ULSTER	SHANDAKEN			
OLMSTEDVILLE	ESSEX	MINERVA		-P-	
OMAR	JEFFERSON	ORLEANS	PACAMA	ULSTER	MARBLETOWN
OMI	COLUMBIA	GHENT	PADELFORD	ONTARIO	CANANDAIGUA
OMRO	CAYUGA	NILES	PAGE	CATTARAUGUS	SALAMANCA
ONCHIOTA	FRANKLIN	FRANKLIN	PAGEBROOK	CHENANGO	GREENE
ONEIDA C.	MADISON	ONEIDA C.	PAINE HOLLOW	HERKIMER	LITTLE FALLS
ONEIDA CASTLE V.	ONEIDA	VERNON	PAINTED POST V.	STEUBEN	ERWIN
ONEIDA CREEK	MADISON	LENOX	PALATINE BRIDGE V.	MONTGOMERY	PALATINE
ONEIDA LAKE	MADISON	LENOX	PALATINE CHURCH	MONTGOMERY	PALATINE
ONEIDA VALLEY	MADISON	LENOX	PALENTOWN	ULSTER	ROCHESTER
ONEIDTOWN	MADISON	SULLIVAN	PALENVILLE	GREENE	CATSKILL
ONEONTA C.	OTSEGO	ONEONTA C.	PALERMO	OSWEGO	PALERMO
ONISKETHAU	ALBANY	NEW SCOTLAND	PALISADES	ROCKLAND	ORANGETOWN
ONONDAGA HILL	ONONDAGA	ONONDAGA	PALKVILLE	CHENANGO	NORWICH
ONONDAGA VALLEY	ONONDAGA	ONONDAGA	PALMER	SARATOGA	CORINTH
ONOVILLE	CATTARAUGUS	SO. VALLEY	PALMER FALLS	SARATOGA	CORINTH
ONOVILLE STA.	CATTARAUGUS	SO. VALLEY	PALMER HILL	CLINTON	BLACK BROOK
ONTARIO	WAYNE	ONTARIO			

NAME	COUNTY	TOWN
PALMER SUMMIT	CATTARAUGUS	RED HOUSE
PALMERVILLE	ST.LAWRENCE	RUSSELL
PALMYRA V.	WAYNE	PALMYRA
PAMELIA FOUR CORS.	JEFFERSON	PAMELIA
PAMELIA STA.	JEFFERSON	PAMELIA
PANAMA STA.	CHAUTAUQUA	CLYMER
PANAMA V.	CHAUTAUQUA	HARMONY
PANTAGO	SUFFOLK	E. HAMPTON
PANTHER LAKE	OSWEGO	CONSTANTIA
PARADOX	ESSEX	SCHROON
PARDEEVILLE	ULSTER	DENNING
PARIS	ONEIDA	PARIS
PARIS HILL	ONEIDA	PARIS
PARIS STA.	ONEIDA	PARIS
PARISH	ONTARIO	NAPLES
PARISH V.	OSWEGO	PARISH
PARISHVILLE	ST.LAWRENCE	PARISHVILLE
PARISHVILLE CTR.	ST.LAWRENCE	PARISHVILLE
PARK	CHEMUNG	ERIN
PARK STA.	CHEMUNG	ERIN
PARKER	CHENANGO	GUILFORD
PARKER STA.	CHENANGO	GUILFORD
PARKERS	LEWIS	MONTAGUE
PARKERS CORS.	HERKIMER	LITCHFIELD
PARKERS GLEN	SULLIVAN	LUMBERLAND
PARKVILLE	KINGS	NYC
PARKSTON	SULLIVAN	ROCKLAND
PARKSVILLE	SULLIVAN	LIBERTY
PARKVIEW	BROOME	UNION
PARKWAY GDNS.	WESTCHESTER	GREENBURGH
PARMA	MONROE	PARMA
PARMA CTR.	MONROE	PARMA
PARTLOW	HAMILTON	LONG LAKE
PARTRIDGEVILLE	LEWIS	GREIG
PASADENA	LEWIS	LEYDEN
PASCACK	ROCKLAND	RAMAPO
PATAUKUNK	ULSTER	ROCHESTER
PATCHIN	ERIE	BOSTON
PATCHINVILLE	STEUBEN	WAYLAND
PATCHOGUE V.	SUFFOLK	BROOKHAVEN
PATRIA	SCHOHARIE	FULTON
PATTEN MILLS	WASHINGTON	KINGSBURY
PATTERSON	PUTNAM	PATTERSON
PATTERSONVILLE	SCHENECTADY	ROTTERDAM
PAUL SMITHS	FRANKLIN	BRIGHTON
PAUL SMITHS COLLEGE	FRANKLIN	BRIGHTON
PAVEMENT	ERIE	LANCASTER
PAVILION	GENESEE	PAVILION
PAVILION CTR.	GENESEE	PAVILION
PAWLING V.	DUTCHESS	PAWLING
PAYNESVILLE	ALLEGANY	WILLING
PEABROOK	DELAWARE	HANCOCK
PEACETOWN	BROOME	WINDSOR
PEACH LAKE	WESTCHESTER	NO. SALEM
PEACH ORCHARD	SCHUYLER	HECTOR
PEACH ORCHARD LDG.	SCHUYLER	HECTOR
PEAKVILLE	DELAWARE	HANCOCK
PEARL CREEK	WYOMING	COVINGTON
PEARL POINT	WASHINGTON	DRESDEN
PEARL RIVER	ROCKLAND	ORANGETOWN
PEASLEEVILLE	CLINTON	PERU
PEAT CORS.	OSWEGO	PALERMO
PECK'S CORS.	ONEIDA	MARSHALL
PECKSPORT	MADISON	EATON
PECKSPORT STA.	MADISON	EATON
PECKVILLE	DUTCHESS	E. FISHKILL
PECONIC	SUFFOLK	SOUTHOLD
PEEKAMOOSE	ULSTER	DENNING
PEEKAMOOSE LDG.	ULSTER	DENNING
PEEKSKILL C.	WESTCHESTER	PEEKSKILL C.
PEKIN	NIAGARA	LEWISTON
PEKIN	NIAGARA	CAMBRIA
PEKIN HILL	CHAUTAUQUA	FRENCH CR.
PELHAM BAY PK.	BRONX	NYC
PELHAM MANOR V.	WESTCHESTER	PELHAM
PELHAM V.	WESTCHESTER	PELHAM
PELHAMWOOD	WESTCHESTER	PELHAM
PEMBROKE	GENESEE	PEMBROKE
PENDLETON	NIAGARA	PENDLETON
PENDLETON CTR.	NIAGARA	PENDLETON
PENDLETON CTR. STA.	NIAGARA	PENDLETON
PENELOPE	BROOME	TRIANGLE
PENFIELD	MONROE	PENFIELD
PENFIELD CTR.	MONROE	PENFIELD
PENN YAN V.	YATES	BENTON
PENN YAN V.	YATES	MILO
PENNELLVILLE	OSWEGO	SCHROEPPEL
PENNY BRIDGE	QUEENS	NYC
PEORIA	WYOMING	COVINGTON
PEPACTON	DELAWARE	COLCHESTER
PERCH RIVER	JEFFERSON	BROWNVILLE
PERCIVAL	CATTARAUGUS	RED HOUSE
PERINTON	MONROE	PERINTON
PERKINSVILLE	STEUBEN	WAYLAND
PERRY CITY	SCHUYLER	HECTOR
PERRY CORS.	DUTCHESS	NORTHEAST
PERRY CTR.	WYOMING	PERRY

NAME	COUNTY	TOWN
PERRY MILLS	CLINTON	CHAMPLAIN
PERRY V.	WYOMING	CASTILE
PERRY V.	WYOMING	PERRY
PERRYSBURG V.	CATTARAUGUS	PERRYSBURG
PERRYVILLE	TIOGA	CANDOR
PERRYVILLE	MADISON	FENNER
PERRYVILLE	MADISON	LINCOLN
PERRYVILLE	MADISON	SULLIVAN
PERSIA	CATTARAUGUS	PERSIA
PERTH	FULTON	PERTH
PERU	CLINTON	PERU
PERUTON	TOMPKINS	GROTON
PERUTON STA.	TOMPKINS	GROTON
PERUVILLE	TOMPKINS	GROTON
PETER ISL. CAMP	HAMILTON	INLET
PETERBORO	MADISON	SMITHFIELD
PETERS CORS.	FULTON	BLEECKER
PETERS CORS.	ERIE	ALDEN
PETERSBURG	RENSSELAER	PETERSBURG
PETERSBURG	SCHOHARIE	FULTON
PETERSBURG JCT.	RENSSELAER	HOOSICK
PETH	CATTARAUGUS	GREAT VALLEY
PETRIE CORS.	LEWIS	WATSON
PETRIE DEVELOPMENT	HERKIMER	HERKIMER
PETROLIA	ALLEGANY	SCIO
PHARSALIA	CHENANGO	PHARSALIA
PHELPS JCT.	ONTARIO	PHELPS
PHELPS STA.	ONTARIO	PHELPS
PHELPS V.	ONTARIO	PHELPS
PHILADELPHIA V.	JEFFERSON	PHILADELPHIA
PHILIPS MILLS	CHAUTAUQUA	ELLERY
PHILLIPSBURG	ORANGE	WALLKILL
PHILLIPSPORT	SULLIVAN	MAMAKATING
PHILMONT V.	COLUMBIA	CLAVERACK
PHIPPS CORS.	FULTON	OPPENHEIM
PHOENICIA	ULSTER	SHANDAKEN
PHOENIX MILLS	OTSEGO	MIDDLEFIELD
PHOENIX STA.	OTSEGO	HARTWICK
PHOENIX V.	OSWEGO	SCHROEPPEL
PICARD BRIDGE	NIAGARA	PENDLETON
PICKETT CORS.	CLINTON	SARANAC
PICKETTVILLE	ST.LAWRENCE	PARISHVILLE
PIERCEFIELD	ST.LAWRENCE	PIERCEFIELD
PIERCEVILLE	MADISON	EATON
PIERMONT V.	ROCKLAND	ORANGETOWN
PIERREPONT	ST.LAWRENCE	PIERREPONT
PIERREPONT MANOR	JEFFERSON	ELLISBURG
PIFFARD	LIVINGSTON	YORK
PIKE FIVE CORS.	WYOMING	PIKE
PIKE V.	WYOMING	PIKE
PIKEVILLE	ALLEGANY	ALMA
PILGRIM CORS.	ORANGE	WALLKILL
PILGRIM PSYCHIATRIC CTR.	SUFFOLK	ISLIP
PILLAR PT.	JEFFERSON	BROWNVILLE
PILOT KNOB	WASHINGTON	FORT ANN
PINCKNEY	LEWIS	PINCKNEY
PINE	ONEIDA	VIENNA
PINE AIRE	SUFFOLK	ISLIP
PINE BRIDGE	WESTCHESTER	YORKTOWN
PINE BROOK	DELAWARE	WALTON
PINE BUSH	ORANGE	CRAWFORD
PINE BUSH	ULSTER	ROCHESTER
PINE CAMP	JEFFERSON	WILNA
PINE CAMP JCT.	JEFFERSON	WILNA
PINE CITY	CHEMUNG	SOUTHPORT
PINE CREEK	SCHUYLER	ORANGE
PINE GROVE	ESSEX	ELIZABETHTOWN
PINE GROVE	ULSTER	SAUGERTIES
PINE HILL V.	ULSTER	SHANDAKEN
PINE ISLAND	ORANGE	WARWICK
PINE LAKE	FULTON	CAROGA
PINE MEADOW	OSWEGO	ORWELL
PINE PLAINS	FRANKLIN	BOMBAY
PINE PLAINS	DUTCHESS	PINE PLAINS
PINE PLAINS	FRANKLIN	FORT COVINGTON
PINE VAL. STA.	CATTARAUGUS	DAYTON
PINE VALLEY	CHEMUNG	VETERAN
PINE VALLEY	CHEMUNG	CATLIN
PINE WOODS	MADISON	EATON
PINEHURST	ERIE	HAMBURG
PINELAWN	SUFFOLK	BABYLON
PINEVILLE	DELAWARE	WALTON
PINNACLE	FULTON	BLEECKER
PINNEY SETTLEMENT	LEWIS	LYONSDALE
PISECO	HAMILTON	ARIETTA
PISECO PALLEY PL.	HAMILTON	ARIETTA
PITCAIRN	ST.LAWRENCE	PITCAIRN
PITCHER	CHENANGO	PITCHER
PITCHER SPGS.	CHENANGO	PITCHER
PITTSFIELD	OTSEGO	PITTSFIELD
PITTSFORD V.	MONROE	PITTSFORD
PITTSTOWN	RENSSELAER	PITTSTOWN
PLACE COR.	GREENE	GREENVILLE
PLAINFIELD CTR.	OTSEGO	PLAINFIELD
PLAINS	ONEIDA	ROME C.
PLAINVIEW	NASSAU	OYSTER BAY

NAME	COUNTY	TOWN
PLAINVILLE	ONONDAGA	LYSANDER
PLANDOME HGHTS. V.	NASSAU	N. HEMPSTEAD
PLANDOME MANOR V.	NASSAU	N. HEMPSTEAD
PLANDOME V.	NASSAU	N. HEMPSTEAD
PLASTERVILLE	CHENANGO	NO. NORWICH
PLATO	CATTARAUGUS	E. OTTO
PLATT CLOVE	GREENE	HUNTER
PLATTEKILL	ULSTER	PLATTEKILL
PLATTSBURG C.	CLINTON	PLATTSBURG C.
PLATTSBURG BAR'KS.	CLINTON	PLATTSBURG
PLEASANT LAKE	ST. LAWRENCE	PIERCEFIELD
PLEASANT LAKE	FULTON	STRATFORD
PLEASANT PLAINS	DUTCHESS	CLINTON
PLEASANT PLAINS	RICHMOND	NYC
PLEASANT POINT	OSWEGO	NEW HAVEN
PLEASANT RIDGE	DUTCHESS	UNION VALE
PLEASANT SIDE	WESTCHESTER	CORTLANDT
PLEASANT VALLEY	STEUBEN	URBANA
PLEASANT VALLEY	DELAWARE	ANDES
PLEASANT VALLEY	TOMPKINS	GROTON
PLEASANT VALLEY	CHAUTAUQUA	SHERMAN
PLEASANT VALLEY	ONEIDA	SANGERFIELD
PLEASANT VALLEY	SCHOHARIE	FULTON
PLEASANT VALLEY	SULLIVAN	MAMAKATING
PLEASANT VALLEY	SULLIVAN	FREMONT
PLEASANT VALLEY	DUTCHESS	PLEASANT VALLEY
PLEASANTBROOK	OTSEGO	ROSEBOOM
PLEASANTDALE	RENSSELAER	SCHAGHTICOKE
PLEASANTVILLE V.	WESTCHESTER	MT. PLEASANT
PLESSIS	JEFFERSON	ALEXANDRIA
PLUM BROOK	ST. LAWRENCE	NORFOLK
PLUMADORE	FRANKLIN	FRANKLIN
PLUTARCH	ULSTER	NEW PALTZ
PLYMOUTH	CHENANGO	PLYMOUTH
POCANTICO HILLS	WESTCHESTER	MT. PLEASANT
POCATELLO	ORANGE	WALLKILL
POELSBURG	COLUMBIA	STUYVESANT
POESTENKILL	RENSSELAER	POESTENKILL
POINT AU ROCK	CLINTON	BEEKMANTOWN
POINT BREEZE	ORLEANS	CARLTON
POINT CHAUTAUQUA	CHAUTAUQUA	CHAUTAUQUA
POINT LOOKOUT	NASSAU	HEMPSTEAD
POINT O'WOODS	SUFFOLK	BROOKHAVEN
POINT PENINSULA	JEFFERSON	LYME
POINT PLEASANT	MONROE	IRONDEQUOIT
POINT ROCK	ONEIDA	LEE
POINT STOCKHOLM	CHAUTAUQUA	ELLERY
POINT VIVIAN	JEFFERSON	ALEXANDRIA
POLAND CTR.	CHAUTAUQUA	POLAND
POLAND HILL	WYOMING	BENNINGTON
POLAND V.	HERKIMER	NEWPORT
POLAND V.	HERKIMER	RUSSIA
POLKVILLE	CORTLAND	CORTLANDVILLE
POLKVILLE	CHENANGO	NORWICH
POLLY'S POND	LEWIS	LEWIS
POMONA	ROCKLAND	RAMAPO
POMONA	ROCKLAND	HAVERSTRAW
POMONA HEIGHTS	ROCKLAND	RAMAPO
POMONA V.	ROCKLAND	RAMAPO
POMPEY	ONONDAGA	POMPEY
POMPEY CTR.	ONONDAGA	POMPEY
POND EDDY	SULLIVAN	LUMBERLAND
PONDS	MONROE	GREECE
PONQUOGUE	SUFFOLK	SOUTHAMPTON
PONTIAC	ERIE	EVANS
PONY HOLLOW	TOMPKINS	NEWFIELD
POOLVILLE	MADISON	HAMILTON
POOLVILLE STA.	MADISON	HAMILTON
POPE	CATTARAUGUS	CONEWANGO
POPE HILL	CHAUTAUQUA	VILLENOVA
POPE HILL	CHAUTAUQUA	HANOVER
POPLAR RIDGE	CAYUGA	VENICE
POQUOTT V.	SUFFOLK	BROOKHAVEN
PORCAVILLE	FRANKLIN	DUANE
PORT BENJAMIN	ULSTER	WAWARSING
PORT BYRON V.	CAYUGA	MENTZ
PORT CHESTER V.	WESTCHESTER	RYE
PORT CRANE	BROOME	FENTON
PORT DICKINSON V.	BROOME	DICKINSON
PORT DOUGLAS	ESSEX	CHESTERFIELD
PORT EWEN	ULSTER	ESOPUS
PORT GIBSON	ONTARIO	MANCHESTER
PORT HENRY V.	ESSEX	MORIAH
PORT JACKSON	CLINTON	PERU
PORT JACKSON	ULSTER	ROCHESTER
PORT JEFFERSON V.	SUFFOLK	BROOKHAVEN
PORT JEFFERSON STA.	SUFFOLK	BROOKHAVEN
PORT JERVIS C.	ORANGE	PORT JERVIS C.
PORT KENDALL	ESSEX	CHESTERFIELD
PORT KENT	ESSEX	CHESTERFIELD
PORT LEYDEN	LEWIS	LYONSDALE
PORT LEYDEN V.	LEWIS	LEYDEN
PORT METCALF	JEFFERSON	CLAYTON
PORT ONTARIO	OSWEGO	RICHLAND
PORT RICHMOND	RICHMOND	NYC
PORT WASHINGTON	NASSAU	NO. HEMPSTEAD
PORT WASHINGTON N. V.	NASSAU	N. HEMPSTEAD
PORTAGEVILLE	WYOMING	GENESEE FALLS
PORTER	NIAGARA	PORTER
PORTER	WASHINGTON	HEBRON
PORTER CENTER	NIAGARA	PORTER
PORTER CORS.	SARATOGA	GREENFIELD
PORTERVILLE	ERIE	MAPILLA
PORTLAND	CHAUTAUQUA	POPTLAND
PORTLAND POINT	TOMPKINS	LANSING
PORTLANDVILLE	OTSEGO	MILFORD
PORTVILLE V.	CATTARAUGUS	PORTVILLE
POST CORS.	WASHINGTON	WHITE CREEK
POST CREEK	CHEMUNG	CATLIN
POST ROAD CRG.	RENSSELAER	SCHODACK
POTSDAM V.	ST. LAWRENCE	POTSDAM
POTTER	YATES	POTTER
POTTER HILL	RENSSELAER	HOOSICK
POTTER HILL	CORTLAND	TAYLOR
POTTER HOLLOW	ALBANY	RENSSELAERVILLE
POTTERS CORNERS	DUTCHESS	UNION VALE
POTTERSVILLE	WARREN	CHESTER
POTTERSVILLE	ULSTER	ROCHESTER
POTUNK	SUFFOLK	SOUTHAMPTON
POUGHKEEPSIE C.	DUTCHESS	POUGHKEEPSIE C.
POUGHQUAG	DUTCHESS	BEEKMAN
POUNDRIDGE	WESTCHESTER	POUNDRIDGE
POWELL HILL	ONTARIO	SO. BRISTOL
POWLEY PL.	HAMILTON	ARIETTA
PRATT	KINGS	NYC
PRATT STA.	MADISON	EATON
PRATTHAM	OSWEGO	MEXICO
PRATTS	MADISON	EATON
PRATTS HOLLOW	MADISON	EATON
PRATTSVILLE	GREENE	PRATTSVILLE
PREBLE	CORTLAND	PREBLE
PRENTISS	GREENE	ATHENS
PRESHO	STEUBEN	LINDLEY
PRESTON	CHENANGO	PRESTON
PRESTON CTR.	CHENANGO	PRESTON
PRESTON HOLLOW	ALBANY	RENSSELAERVILLE
PRINCE BAY	RICHMOND	NYC
PRINCETOWN	SCHENECTADY	PRINCETOWN
PROMISED LAND	SUFFOLK	E. HAMPTON
PROSPECT HGTS.	RENSSELAER	E. GREENBUSH
PROSPECT JCT.	ONEIDA	TRENTON
PROSPECT PK.	JEFFERSON	CLAYTON
PROSPECT STA.	ONEIDA	TRENTON
PROSPECT STREET	BROOME	BINGHAMTON C.
PROSPECT V.	ONEIDA	TRENTON
PROSSER	ALLEGANY	GENESEE
PROTECTION	ERIE	HOLLAND
PROTECTION	ERIE	SARDINIA
PROVIDENCE	SARATOGA	PROVIDENCE
PRUSSIAN SETT.	LEWIS	LEWIS
PULASKI V.	OSWEGO	RICHLAND
PULPWOOD ROCK	HAMILTON	LONG LAKE
PULTENEY	STEUBEN	PULTENEY
PULTENEYVILLE	WAYNE	WILLIAMSON
PULVER	COLUMBIA	GHENT
PUMPKIN HOLLOW	COLUMBIA	TAGHKANIC
PUMPKINHOOK	WASHINGTON	WHITE CREEK
PURDY CREEK	STEUBEN	HARTSVILLE
PURDY MILL	CLINTON	ALTONA
PURDY STA.	WESTCHESTER	NO. SALEM
PURDYS	WESTCHESTER	NO. SALEM
PURLING	GREENE	CAIRO
PUT CORS.	ULSTER	NEW PALTZ
PUTNAM	WASHINGTON	PUTNAM
PUTNAM LAKE	PUTNAM	PATTERSON
PUTNAM STA.	WASHINGTON	PUTNAM
PUTNAM VALLEY	PUTNAM	PUTNAM VALLEY
PYRITES	ST. LAWRENCE	CANTON

-Q-

NAME	COUNTY	TOWN
QUACKENKILL	RENSSELAER	GRAFTON
QUAKER BRIDGE	WESTCHESTER	CORTLANDT
QUAKER BRIDGE	CATTARAUGUS	ELKO
QUAKER BRIDGE STA.	CATTARAUGUS	ELKO
QUAKER CITY	DUTCHESS	UNION VALE
QUAKER HILL	DUTCHESS	PAWLING
QUAKER SETT.	MADISON	DERUYTER
QUAKER SPGS.	SARATOGA	SARATOGA
QUAKER STREET	SCHENECTADY	DUANESBURG
QUALITY HILL	MADISON	LENOX
QUARRYVILLE	ULSTER	SAUGERTIES
QUEECHY	COLUMBIA	CANAAN
QUEENS	QUEENS	NYC
QUEENSBORO	ORANGE	HIGHLANDS
QUEENSBORO	ORANGE	WOODBURY
QUEENSBURY	WARREN	QUEENSBURY
QUINNEVILLE	CHENANGO	GREENE
QUOGUE V.	SUFFOLK	SOUTHAMPTON

NAME	COUNTY	TOWN
	-R-	
RACEVILLE	WASHINGTON	GRANVILLE
RACKET RIVER	ST. LAWRENCE	MASSENA
RADBURN STA.	CHEMUNG	VAN ETTEN
RAILROAD MILLS	ONTARIO	VICTOR
RAINBOW	FRANKLIN	BRIGHTON
RAINBOW STA.	FRANKLIN	FRANKLIN
RALPH	CLINTON	DANNEMORA
RAMAPO	ROCKLAND	RAMAPO
RAND HILL	CLINTON	BEEKMANTOWN
RANDALL	NIAGARA	WILSON
RANDALL	MONTGOMERY	ROOT
RANDALL RD.	NIAGARA	WILSON
RANDALLS ISLAND	NEW YORK	NYC
RANDALLVILLE	MADISON	LEBANON
RANDOLPH	BROOME	WINDSOR
RANDOLPH V.	CATTARAUGUS	RANDOLPH
RANSOMVILLE	NIAGARA	PORTER
RAPIDS	NIAGARA	LOCKPORT
RAQUETTE LAKE	HAMILTON	LONG LAKE
RAQUETTE LAKE STA.	HAMILTON	LONG LAKE
RATHBONE	STEUBEN	RATHBONE
RATHBONEVILLE	STEUBEN	RATHBONE
RAVENA V.	ALBANY	COEYMANS
RAVENSWOOD	QUEENS	NYC
RAWSON	CATTARAUGUS	LYNDON
RAY	GENESEE	ALEXANDER
RAYBROOK	ESSEX	NO. ELBA
RAYMERTOWN	RENSSELAER	PITTSTOWN
RAYMOND	NIAGARA	LOCKPORT
RAYMOND HILL	NIAGARA	LOCKPORT
RAYMONDVILLE	ST. LAWRENCE	NORFOLK
RAYVILLE	COLUMBIA	CHATHAM
READ CREEK	DELAWARE	HANCOCK
READBURN	DELAWARE	HANCOCK
READING CTR.	SCHUYLER	READING
REBER	ESSEX	WILLSBORO
RECEPTION CTR.	CHEMUNG	ELMIRA C.
RECTOR	LEWIS	MONTAGUE
RECTOR CORS.	LEWIS	MONTAGUE
RED BIRD	CHAUTAUQUA	GERRY
RED CREEK	MONROE	HENRIETTA
RED CREEK V.	WAYNE	WOLCOTT
RED FALLS	GREENE	PRATTSVILLE
RED FORD	CLINTON	SARANAC
RED HILL	ULSTER	DENNING
RED HILL	SULLIVAN	MAMAKATING
RED HOOK V.	DUTCHESS	RED HOOK
RED HOUSE	CATTARAUGUS	RED HOUSE
RED HOUSE STA.	CATTARAUGUS	RED HOUSE
RED MILLS	ULSTER	SHAWANGUNK
RED MILLS	ORANGE	CRAWFORD
RED MILLS	ST. LAWRENCE	LISBON
RED MILLS	TOMPKINS	DRYDEN
RED OAK MILLS	DUTCHESS	POUGHKEEPSIE
RED ROCK	COLUMBIA	CANAAN
REDFIELD	OSWEGO	REDFIELD
REDMOND	MONROE	CLARKSON
REDMOND CORS.	MONROE	CLARKSON
REDWOOD	JEFFERSON	ALEXANDRIA
REED CORS.	LIVINGSTON	SPARTA
REED CORS.	ONTARIO	GORHAM
REEDVILLE	JEFFERSON	WILNA
REGO	QUEENS	NYC
REIDSVILLE	ALBANY	BERNE
RELIUS	CAYUGA	AURELIUS
REMINGTON CORS.	LEWIS	DIANA
REMSEN V.	ONEIDA	TRENTON
REMSEN V.	ONEIDA	REMSEN
REMSENBURG	SUFFOLK	SOUTHAMPTON
RENCHANS	STEUBEN	WHEELER
RENIFF	TIOGA	BARTON
RENSSELAER C.	RENSSELAER	RENSSELAER C.
RENSSELAER FALLS V.	ST. LAWRENCE	CANTON
RENSSELAERVILLE	ALBANY	RENSSELAERVILLE
RENWICK	TOMPKINS	ITHACA
RESORT	WAYNE	HURON
RETSOF	LIVINGSTON	YORK
RETSOF DEPOT	LIVINGSTON	YORK
RETSOF JCT.	LIVINGSTON	YORK
REVILLE SUMMIT	DUTCHESS	PAWLING
REXFORD	SARATOGA	CLIFTON PARK
REXFORD FLATS	SARATOGA	CLIFTON PARK
REXLEIGH	WASHINGTON	SALEM
REXVILLE	STEUBEN	W. UNION
REYNOLDS	RENSSELAER	SCHAGHTICOKE
REYNOLDS BASIN	NIAGARA	ROYALTON
REYNOLDS CORS.	SARATOGA	MOREAU
REYNOLDSVILLE	SCHUYLER	HECTOR
REYNOLDSVILLE STA.	DUTCHESS	PAWLING
RHINEBECK V.	DUTCHESS	RHINEBECK
RHINECLIFF	DUTCHESS	RHINEBECK
RHOADVILLE	TIOGA	CANDOR
RHODE ISLAND	CHENANGO	OTSELIC
RICARD	OSWEGO	WILLIAMSTOWN
RICE	FRANKLIN	HARRIETSTOWN
RICES	JEFFERSON	WATERTOWN

NAME	COUNTY	TOWN
RICES STA.	JEFFERSON	WATERTOWN
RICEVILLE	CATTARAUGUS	ASHFORD
RICEVILLE	FULTON	MAYFIELD
RICEVILLE STA.	CATTARAUGUS	ASHFORD
RICHBURG V.	ALLEGANY	WIRT
RICHBURG V.	ALLEGANY	BOLIVAR
RICHES CORS.	ORLEANS	ALBION
RICHFIELD	OTSEGO	RICHFIELD
RICHFIELD JCT.	ONEIDA	PARIS
RICHFIELD SPGS. V.	OTSEGO	RICHFIELD
RICHFORD	TIOGA	RICHFORD
RICHLAND	OSWEGO	RICHLAND
RICHMOND	RICHMOND	NYC
RICHMOND CORS.	GREENE	ASHLAND
RICHMOND HILL	QUEENS	NYC
RICHMOND MILLS	ONTARIO	RICHMOND
RICHMOND VAL.	RICHMOND	NYC
RICHMONDVILLE V.	SCHOHARIE	RICHMONDVILLE
RICHVILLE STA.	ST. LAWRENCE	DE KALB
RICHVILLE V.	ST. LAWRENCE	DE KALB
RIDER CORS.	MONTGOMERY	CHARLESTON
RIDER MILLS	COLUMBIA	CHATHAM
RIDGE	SUFFOLK	BROOKHAVEN
RIDGE	LIVINGSTON	MT. MORRIS
RIDGE MILLS	ONEIDA	ROME C.
RIDGE ROAD	NIAGARA	NEWFANE
RIDGEBURY	ORANGE	WAWAYANDA
RIDGELAND	MONROE	HENRIETTA
RIDGEWAY	ORLEANS	RIDGEWAY
RIDGEWAY	WESTCHESTER	WHITE PLAINS C.
RIDGEWOOD	QUEENS	NYC
RIDGEWOOD VILLA	FRANKLIN	HARRIETSTOWN
RIFTON	ULSTER	ESOPUS
RIGA	MONROE	RIGA
RIGA CTR.	MONROE	RIGA
RIKERS HOLLOW	STEUBEN	PRATTSBURG
RIO	ORANGE	DEER PARK
RIPARIUS	WARREN	JOHNSBURG
RIPLEY	CHAUTAUQUA	RIPLEY
RIPPLETON	MADISON	CAZENOVIA
RISINGVILLE	STEUBEN	THURSTON
RIVER FORKS	MADISON	BROOKFIELD
RIVER STA.	MADISON	BROOKFIELD
RIVERBANK	WARREN	BOLTON
RIVERDALE	NEW YORK	NYC
RIVERGATE	JEFFERSON	THERESA
RIVERHEAD	SUFFOLK	SOUTHAMPTON
RIVERHEAD	SUFFOLK	RIVERHEAD
RIVERSIDE	BROOME	KIRKWOOD
RIVERSIDE	WARREN	CHESTER
RIVERSIDE	TIOGA	OWEGO
RIVERSIDE	SUFFOLK	SOUTHAMPTON
RIVERSIDE	SARATOGA	STILLWATER
RIVERSIDE JCT.	CATTARAUGUS	CARROLLTON
RIVERSIDE V.	STEUBEN	CORNING
RIVERVIEW	CLINTON	SARANAC
RIVERVIEW	ALBANY	BETHLEHEM
RIVERVIEW	JEFFERSON	CAPE VINCENT
ROAKDALE	FRANKLIN	FRANKLIN
ROANOKE	GENESEE	STAFFORD
ROANOKE LDG.	SUFFOLK	RIVERHEAD
ROBERTS CORS.	JEFFERSON	HENDERSON
ROBINS ISLAND	SUFFOLK	SOUTHOLD
ROBINSON	CLINTON	ALTONA
ROBINSON MILLS	CHENANGO	OXFORD
ROBINWOOD	HAMILTON	LONG LAKE
ROCHDALE	DUTCHESS	POUGHKEEPSIE
ROCHESTER C.	MONROE	ROCHESTER C.
ROCHESTER JCT.	MONROE	MENDON
ROCHESTER	MONROE	ROCHESTER C.
PSYCHIATRIC CTR.		
ROCK	LEWIS	DIANA
ROCK CITY	COLUMBIA	CHATHAM
ROCK CITY	ALLEGANY	GENESEE
ROCK CITY	DUTCHESS	MILAN
ROCK CITY FALLS	SARATOGA	MILTON
ROCK CITY STA.	CATTARAUGUS	ALLEGANY
ROCK GLEN	WYOMING	GAINESVILLE
ROCK HILL	SULLIVAN	THOMPSON
ROCK STREAM	YATES	STARKEY
ROCK TAVERN	ORANGE	NEW WINDSOR
ROCK VALLEY	DELAWARE	HANCOCK
ROCKAWAY BCH.	QUEENS	NYC
ROCKAWAY POINT	NEW YORK	NYC
ROCKDALE	CHENANGO	GUILFORD
ROCKHURST	WARREN	QUEENSBURY
ROCKLAND	SULLIVAN	ROCKLAND
ROCKLAND PSYCHIATRIC	ROCKLAND	ORANGETOWN
CTR		
ROCKVIEW	CATTARAUGUS	ALLEGANY
ROCKVILLE	SCHOHARIE	SHARON
ROCKVILLE	ALLEGANY	BELFAST
ROCKVILLE	LEWIS	GREIG
ROCKVILLE	ORANGE	WALLKILL
ROCKVILLE CTR. V.	NASSAU	HEMPSTEAD
ROCKVILLE GLEN	ALLEGANY	BELFAST
ROCKWELL MILLS	CHENANGO	GUILFORD

68

NAME	COUNTY	TOWN
ROCKWOOD	FULTON	EPHRATAH
ROCKY BRANCH	ESSEX	JAY
ROCKY PT.	HAMILTON	LONG LAKE
ROCKY PT.	SUFFOLK	BROOKHAVEN
ROCTON	MONTGOMERY	AMSTERDAM C.
RODBOURN	CHEMUNG	VAN ETTEN
RODMAN	JEFFERSON	RODMAN
ROE PARK	WESTCHESTER	CORTLANDT
ROESSLEVILLE	ALBANY	COLONIE
ROGERS	LEWIS	CROGHAN
ROGERSFIELD	CLINTON	DANNEMORA
ROGERSVILLE	STEUBEN	DANSVILLE
ROME C.	ONEIDA	ROME C.
ROME	ESSEX	JAY
ROME DEVELOPMENTAL CENTER	ONEIDA	ROME CITY
ROMULUS	SENECA	VARICK
ROMULUS	SENECA	ROMULUS
ROMULUS CTR.	SENECA	ROMULUS
RONDAXE	HERKIMER	WEBB
RONDOUT	ULSTER	KINGSTON C.
RONE	ESSEX	JAY
RONKONKOMA	SUFFOLK	BROOKHAVEN
RONKONKOMA	SUFFOLK	ISLIP
ROOSA GAP	SULLIVAN	MAMAKATING
ROOSEVELT	NASSAU	HEMPSTEAD
ROOSEVELT CORS.	OSWEGO	SCHROEPPEL
ROOSEVELTOWN	ST.LAWRENCE	MASSENA
ROSAS	SULLIVAN	LUMBERLAND
ROSCOE	SULLIVAN	ROCKLAND
ROSE	WAYNE	ROSE
ROSE GROVE	SUFFOLK	SOUTHAMPTON
ROSE HILL	SENECA	FAYETTE
ROSE HILL	ONONDAGA	MARCELLUS
ROSE STATION	WAYNE	ROSE
ROSEBANK	RICHMOND	NYC
ROSEBOOM	OTSEGO	ROSEBOOM
ROSEDALE	WESTCHESTER	WHITE PLAINS C.
ROSEDALE	QUEENS	NYC
ROSELAND	MONROE	PENFIELD
ROSENDALE V.	ULSTER	ROSENDALE
ROSETON	ORANGE	NEWBURGH
ROSIERE	JEFFERSON	CAPE VINCENT
ROSLYN ESTATES V.	NASSAU	N. HEMPSTEAD
ROSLYN HARBOR V.	NASSAU	N. HEMPSTEAD
ROSLYN HARBOR V.	NASSAU	OYSTER BAY
ROSLYN HGHTS.	NASSAU	NO. HEMPSTEAD
ROSLYN V.	NASSAU	N. HEMPSTEAD
ROSS CORS.	BROOME	VESTAL
ROSS CORS.	LIVINGSTON	SPARTA
ROSS CROSSING	ALLEGANY	GROVE
ROSS MILLS	CHAUTAUQUA	GERRY
ROSS MILLS	CHAUTAUQUA	ELLICOTT
ROSS STATION	CHAUTAUQUA	ELLICOTT
ROSSBURG	ALLEGANY	HUME
ROSSES	LIVINGSTON	NUNDA
ROSSIE	ST.LAWRENCE	ROSSIE
ROSSMAN	COLUMBIA	STOCKPORT
ROSSMAN STA.	COLUMBIA	STOCKPORT
ROSSTOWN	CHEMUNG	SOUTHPORT
ROSSVILLE	RICHMOND	NYC
ROSWELL PK. MEMORIAL INST.	ERIE	BUFFALO C.
ROTTERDAM JCT.	SCHENECTADY	ROTTERDAM
ROTTERDAM STA.	SCHENECTADY	ROTTERDAM
ROUGH & READY	STEUBEN	GREENWOOD
ROUND LAKE V.	SARATOGA	MALTA
ROUND POND STA.	FRANKLIN	FRANKLIN
ROUND TOP	GREENE	CAIRO
ROUSES POINT V.	CLINTON	CHAMPLAIN
ROUTE 305	ALLEGANY	GENESEE
ROWLAND	DUTCHESS	CLINTON
ROXBURY	DELAWARE	ROXBURY
ROXBURY	QUEENS	NYC
ROXBURY STA.	DELAWARE	ROXBURY
ROYALTON	NIAGARA	ROYALTON
ROYALTON CTR.	NIAGARA	ROYALTON
RUBY P.O.	ULSTER	ULSTER
RUDCO	DUTCHESS	POUGHKEEPSIE
RUDESTON	HAMILTON	ARIETTA
RURAL GROVE	MONTGOMERY	ROOT
RURAL HILL	JEFFERSON	ELLISBURG
RUSH	MONROE	RUSH
RUSHFORD	ALLEGANY	RUSHFORD
RUSHVILLE	YATES	POTTER
RUSHVILLE V.	ONTARIO	GORHAM
RUSKEY	DUTCHESS	PLEASANT VALLEY
RUSS MILLS	OSWEGO	PALERMO
RUSSELL	ST.LAWRENCE	RUSSELL
RUSSELL GARDENS V.	NASSAU	N. HEMPSTEAD
RUSSELL TURNPIKE	ST.LAWRENCE	POTSDAM
RUSSIA	HERKIMER	RUSSIA
RUSSIA	CLINTON	SARANAC
RUSSIA CORS.	HERKIMER	RUSSIA
RUSSIA STA.	CLINTON	SARANAC
RUSTIG LDGE.	FRANKLIN	HARRIETSTOWN
RUTGERS STA.	ORANGE	MINISINK
RUTLAND	JEFFERSON	RUTLAND
RUTLAND CTR.	JEFFERSON	RUTLAND
RUTLEDGE	CATTARAUGUS	CONEWANGO
RUTSONVILLE	ULSTER	GARDINER
RYE C.	WESTCHESTER	RYE C.
RYNEX CORS.	SCHENECTADY	ROTTERDAM
RYNGEWOOD	TOMPKINS	DRYDEN

-S-

NAME	COUNTY	TOWN
SABAEL	HAMILTON	INDIAN LAKE
SABATTIS	HAMILTON	LONG LAKE
SABBATH DAY PARK	SUFFOLK	HUNTINGTON
SABBATH DAY PT.	WARREN	HAGUE
SACANDAGA	FULTON	NORTHAMPTON
SACANDAGA PK.	FULTON	NORTHAMPTON
SACKETS HARBOR STA.	JEFFERSON	HOUNSFIELD
SACKETS HARBOR V.	JEFFERSON	HOUNSFIELD
SACKETT LAKE	SULLIVAN	THOMPSON
SADDLE ROCK V.	NASSAU	N. HEMPSTEAD
SAG	SUFFOLK	SOUTHAMPTON
SAG HARBOR V.	SUFFOLK	EASTHAMPTON
SAG HARBOR V.	SUFFOLK	SOUTHAMPTON
SAGAMORE	WARREN	BOLTON
SAGAPONACK	SUFFOLK	SOUTHAMPTON
SAGE	TOMPKINS	LANSING
SAGE CORS.	CHENANGO	NEW BERLIN
SAGETOWN	CHEMUNG	SOUTHPORT
ST. ALBANS	QUEENS	NYC
ST. ANDREW	ORANGE	MONTGOMERY
ST. BONAVENTURE COL.	CATTARAUGUS	ALLEGANY
ST. ELMO	ULSTER	SHAWANGUNK
ST. ELMO STA.	ULSTER	SHAWANGUNK
ST. GEORGE	RICHMOND	NYC
ST. HELENA	WYOMING	CASTILE
ST. HUBERT	ESSEX	KEENE
ST. JAMES	SUFFOLK	SMITHTOWN
ST. JOHN	ROCKLAND	HAVERSTRAW
ST. JOHNLAND	ROCKLAND	HAVERSTRAW
ST. JOHNSBURG	NIAGARA	WHEATFIELD
ST. JOHNSVILLE STA.	MONTGOMERY	MINDEN
ST. JOHNSVILLE V.	MONTGOMERY	ST. JOHNSVILLE
ST. JOSEN	ULSTER	ROCHESTER
ST. JOSEPHS	SULLIVAN	FORESTBURGH
ST. JOSEPHS FARM	WESTCHESTER	CORTLANDT
ST. LAWRENCE	JEFFERSON	CAPE VINCENT
ST. LAWRENCE PSYCHIATRIC CTR.	ST.LAWRENCE	OGDENSBURG C.
ST. MARKS PL.	SUFFOLK	HUNTINGTON
ST. REGIS	FRANKLIN	BOMBAY
ST. REGIS FALLS	FRANKLIN	WAVERLY
ST. REMY	ULSTER	ESOPUS
SALA	OSWEGO	NEW HAVEN
SALAMANCA C.	CATTARAUGUS	SALAMANCA C.
SALAMANCA & BRADFORD JCT.	CATTARAUGUS	GREAT VALLEY
SALEM CTR.	WESTCHESTER	NO. SALEM
SALEM V.	WASHINGTON	SALEM
SALISBURY	HERKIMER	SALISBURY
SALISBURY CTR.	HERKIMER	SALISBURY
SALISBURY MILLS	ORANGE	BLOOMING GR.
SALMON RIVER	CLINTON	PLATTSBURG
SALMON RIVER	ORLEANS	ALBION
SALT POINT	DUTCHESS	PLEASANT VALLEY
SALT RISING	ALLEGANY	GENESEE
SALT SPRINGVILLE	OTSEGO	CHERRY VALLEY
SALT VALE	WYOMING	MIDDLEBURY
SALTAIRE V.	SUFFOLK	ISLIP
SAMMONSVILLE	FULTON	JOHNSTOWN
SAMSONVILLE	ULSTER	OLIVE
SAN REMO	SUFFOLK	SMITHTOWN
SANBORN	NIAGARA	LEWISTON
SAND FLATS	MONTGOMERY	MOHAWK
SAND HILL	OTSEGO	UNADILLA
SAND LAKE	RENSSELAER	SAND LAKE
SANDBURG	SULLIVAN	FALLSBURG
SANDS POINT V.	NASSAU	N. HEMPSTEAD
SANDUSKY	CATTARAUGUS	FREEDOM
SANDY CREEK V.	OSWEGO	SANDY CREEK
SANDY CREEK	OSWEGO	SANDY CREEK
SANDY HILL	WASHINGTON	KINGSBURY
SANFORD	BROOME	SANFORD
SANFORD CORS.	JEFFERSON	LE RAY
SANFORD STA.	JEFFERSON	LE RAY
SANFORDVILLE	ST.LAWRENCE	STOCKHOLM
SANGERFIELD	ONEIDA	SANGERFIELD
SANITARIA SPGS.	BROOME	COLESVILLE
SANTA CLARA	FRANKLIN	SANTA CLARA
SARANAC	CLINTON	SARANAC
SARANAC CLUB	FRANKLIN	HARRIETSTOWN
SARANAC INN	FRANKLIN	SANTA CLARA
SARANAC INN STA.	FRANKLIN	SANTA CLARA
SARANAC INN STA.	FRANKLIN	HARRIETSTOWN
SARANAC JCT.	FRANKLIN	HARRIETSTOWN
SARANAC LAKE V.	ESSEX	N. ELBA & ST. ARMAND
SARANAC LAKE V.	FRANKLIN	HARRIETSTOWN
SARATOGA SPGS. C.	SARATOGA	SARATOGA SPGS. C.

NAME	COUNTY	TOWN	NAME	COUNTY	TOWN
SARDINIA	ERIE	SARDINIA	SHAKERS	ALBANY	COLONIE
SAUGERTIES MANOR	ULSTER	SAUGERTIES	SHALETON	ERIE	HAMBURG
SAUGERTIES V.	ULSTER	SAUGERTIES	SHANDAKEN	ULSTER	SHANDAKEN
SAUNDERS	STEUBEN	W. UNION	SHANDELEE	SULLIVAN	CALLICOON
SAUQUOIT V.	ONEIDA	PARIS	SHARON	SCHOHARIE	SHARON
SAVANNAH V.	WAYNE	SAVANNAH	SHARON CTR.	SCHOHARIE	SHARON
SAVILTON	ORANGE	NEWBURGH	SHARON HILL	SCHOHARIE	SHARON
SAVONA V.	STEUBEN	BATH	SHARON SPGS. SPA	SCHOHARIE	SHARON
SAWENS	GENESEE	DARIEN	SHARON SPGS. V.	SCHOHARIE	SHARON
SAWKILL	ULSTER	KINGSTON	SHARON STA.	DUTCHESS	NORTHEAST
SAWYER	ORLEANS	CARLTON	SHARON STA.	DUTCHESS	AMENIA
SAXTON	ULSTER	SAUGERTIES	SHAW CORS.	FULTON	CAROGA
SAYLES CORS.	CAYUGA	SEMPRONIUS	SHAWANGUNK	ULSTER	SHAWANGUNK
SAYVILLE	SUFFOLK	ISLIP	SHAWNEE	NIAGARA	WHEATFIELD
SCARSDALE V.	WESTCHESTER	SCARSDALE	SHEAF CORS.	HERKIMER	SCHUYLER
SCHAGHTICOKE HILL	RENSSELAER	SCHAGHTICOKE	SHEDS	MADISON	DERUYTER
SCHAGHTICOKE V.	RENSSELAER	SCHAGHTICOKE	SHEDS CORS.	MADISON	DERUYTER
SCHELL'S BUSH	HERKIMER	HERKIMER	SHEDS CORS. STA.	MADISON	DERUYTER
SCHENECTADY C.	SCHENECTADY	SCHENECTADY C.	SHEEP CORS.	HERKIMER	SCHUYLER
SCHENEVUS V.	OTSEGO	MARYLAND	SHEEPSHEAD BAY	KINGS	NYC
SCHEUTZEN PK.	QUEENS	NYC	SHEKOMEKO	DUTCHESS	NORTHEAST
SCHODACK	RENSSELAER	SCHODACK	SHELBY BASIN	ORLEANS	SHELBY
SCHODACK CTR.	RENSSELAER	SCHODACK	SHELBY CTR.	ORLEANS	SHELBY
SCHODACK DEPOT	RENSSELAER	SCHODACK	SHELDON	WYOMING	SHELDON
SCHODACK LDG.	RENSSELAER	SCHODACK	SHELDON CTR.	WYOMING	SHELDON
SCHOHARIE JCT.	SCHOHARIE	ESPERANCE	SHELDONVILLE	WYOMING	SHELDON
SCHOHARIE V.	SCHOHARIE	SCHOHARIE	SHELDRAKE	SENECA	OVID
SCHOONMAKER	CATTARAUGUS	RED HOUSE	SHELDRAKE SPGS.	SENECA	OVID
SCHROON	ESSEX	SCHROON	SHELDRAKE STA.	SENECA	OVID
SCHROON FALLS	ESSEX	SCHROON	SHELTER ISLAND	SUFFOLK	SHELTER ISLAND
SCHROON LAKE	ESSEX	SCHROON	SHELTER VALLEY	MADISON	CAZENOVIA
SCHULTZVILLE	DUTCHESS	CLINTON	SHELVING ROCK	WASHINGTON	FORT ANN
SCHUYLER	ESSEX	CHESTERFIELD	SHENANDOAH	DUTCHESS	E. FISHKILL
SCHUYLER FALLS	CLINTON	SCHUYLER FALLS	SHENROCK	WESTCHESTER	SOMERS
SCHUYLER JCT.	HERKIMER	SCHUYLER	SHERBURNE FOUR CORS.	CHENANGO	PLYMOUTH
SCHUYLER LK.	OTSEGO	EXETER	SHERBURNE V.	CHENANGO	SHERBURNE
SCHUYLERVILLE V.	SARATOGA	SARATOGA	SHERIDAN TOWN HALL	CHAUTAUQUA	SHERIDAN
SCIO	ALLEGANY	SCIO	SHERMAN	FULTON	CAROGA
SCIOTA	CLINTON	CHAZY	SHERMAN CORS.	ESSEX	CROWN POINT
SCIPIO	CAYUGA	SCIPIO	SHERMAN CTR.	CHAUTAUQUA	SHERMAN
SCIPIO CTR.	CAYUGA	SCIPIO	SHERMAN V.	CHAUTAUQUA	SHERMAN
SCIPIOVILLE	CAYUGA	SCIPIO	SHERRILL C.	ONEIDA	SHERRILL C.
SCONONDOA	ONEIDA	VERONA	SHERRUCK	DELAWARE	TOMPKINS
SCOTCH BUSH	MONTGOMERY	FLORIDA	SHERWOOD	CAYUGA	SCIPIO
SCOTCH BUSH	FULTON	EPHRATAH	SHERWOOD PK.	RENSSELAER	E. GREENBUSH
SCOTCH CHURCH	SCHENECTADY	DUANESBURG	SHIN CREEK	SULLIVAN	ROCKLAND
SCOTCH CHURCH	MONTGOMERY	FLORIDA	SHIN HOLLOW	ORANGE	DEER PARK
SCOTCHTOWN	ORANGE	WALLKILL	SHINHOPPLE	DELAWARE	COLCHESTER
SCOTIA V.	SCHENECTADY	GLENVILLE	SHINNECOCK	SUFFOLK	SOUTHAMPTON
SCOTT	CORTLAND	SCOTT	SHINNECOCK HILLS	SUFFOLK	SOUTHAMPTON
SCOTT CORS.	SENECA	OVID	SHIRLEY	SUFFOLK	BROOKHAVEN
SCOTT CORS.	CATTARAUGUS	HINSDALE	SHIRLEY	ERIE	NO. COLLINS
SCOTTMINIS	ORANGE	TUXEDO	SHOKAN	ULSTER	OLIVE
SCOTTSBURG	LIVINGSTON	SPARTA	SHONGO	CATTARAUGUS	SALAMANCA
SCOTTSVILLE STA.	MONROE	WHEATLAND	SHONGO	ALLEGANY	WILLING
SCOTTSVILLE V.	MONROE	WHEATLAND	SHOOKVILLE	DUTCHESS	MILAN
SCRANTON	ERIE	HAMBURG	SHORE ACRES	CHAUTAUQUA	ELLERY
SCRIBA	OSWEGO	SCRIBA	SHOREHAM V.	SUFFOLK	BROOKHAVEN
SCUTTLE HOLE	SUFFOLK	SOUTHAMPTON	SHORT BEACH	NASSAU	HEMPSTEAD
SEA BREEZE	MONROE	IRONDEQUOIT	SHORT TRACT	ALLEGANY	GRANGER
SEA CLIFF V.	NASSAU	OYSTER BAY	SHORTSVILLE V.	ONTARIO	MANCHESTER
SEA GATE	KINGS	NYC	SHRUB OAK	WESTCHESTER	YORKTOWN
SEAFORD	NASSAU	HEMPSTEAD	SHUETOWN	LEWIS	LYONSDALE
SEAFORD HARBOR	NASSAU	HEMPSTEAD	SHUMLA	CHAUTAUQUA	POMFRET
SEAGER	ULSTER	HARDENBURGH	SHUNPIKE	DUTCHESS	WASHINGTON
SEAMAN'S CORS.	ONTARIO	NAPLES	SHURTLEFF	JEFFERSON	THERESA
SEARINGTOWN	NASSAU	NO. HEMPSTEAD	SHUSHAN	WASHINGTON	SALEM
SEARSBURG	SCHUYLER	HECTOR	SHUTTER CORS.	SCHOHARIE	WRIGHT
SEARSVILLE	ORANGE	CRAWFORD	SHUTTS CORS.	SCHOHARIE	COBLESKILL
SEASIDE	RICHMOND	NYC	SIBLEYVILLE	MONROE	MENDON
SEAVIEW	SUFFOLK	ISLIP	SIDNEY CTR.	DELAWARE	SIDNEY
SECOND MILO	YATES	MILO	SIDNEY CTR.	DELAWARE	MASONVILLE
SEELY CREEK	CHEMUNG	SOUTHPORT	SIDNEY V.	DELAWARE	SIDNEY
SELDEN	SUFFOLK	BROOKHAVEN	SIERKS CROSSING	WYOMING	ATTICA
SELKIRK	ALBANY	BETHLEHEM	SILLS CORS.	CAYUGA	GENOA
SELKIRK	OSWEGO	RICHLAND	SILOAM	MADISON	SMITHFIELD
SELKIRK SHORES ST.PK.	OSWEGO	RICHLAND	SILVER BAY	WARREN	HAGUE
			SILVER CREEK V.	CHAUTAUQUA	HANOVER
SEMPRONIUS	CAYUGA	SEMPRONIUS	SILVER LAKE	ORANGE	WALLKILL
SEMPRONIUS HILL	CAYUGA	SEMPRONIUS	SILVER LAKE	WYOMING	CASTILE
SENECA CASTLE	ONTARIO	SENECA	SILVER LAKE	CLINTON	BLACK BROOK
SENECA FALLS V.	SENECA	SENECA FALLS	SILVER LK. ASSEM.	WYOMING	CASTILE
SENECA JCT.	SENECA	SENECA FALLS	SILVER LK. STA.	WYOMING	CASTILE
SENECA MILLS	YATES	MILO	SILVER SPGS. V.	WYOMING	GAINESVILLE
SENECA MILLS STA.	YATES	MILO	SILVERHILL	ST. LAWRENCE	RUSSELL
SENECA PK.	MONROE	IRONDEQUOIT	SILVERNAIL	COLUMBIA	GALLATIN
SENECA RIVER STA.	WAYNE	SAVANNAH	SIMONS HILL	STEUBEN	WOODHULL
SENNETT	CAYUGA	SENNETT	SIMPSONVILLE	DELAWARE	DAVENPORT
SETAUKET	SUFFOLK	BROOKHAVEN	SINCLAIRVILLE STA.	CHAUTAUQUA	GERRY
SEVENTH LK. HOTEL	HAMILTON	INLET	SINCLAIRVILLE V.	CHAUTAUQUA	CHARLOTTE
SEVERANCE	ESSEX	SCHROON	SINCLAIRVILLE V.	CHAUTAUQUA	GERRY
SEWARD	SCHOHARIE	SEWARD	SISSONVILLE	ST. LAWRENCE	POTSDAM
SHADIGEE	ORLEANS	YATES	SKANEATELES FALLS	ONONDAGA	SKANEATELES
SHADY	ULSTER	WOODSTOCK	SKANEATELES V.	ONONDAGA	SKANEATELES
SHAKER CROSSING	LIVINGSTON	LEICESTER	SKINNERS FALLS	SULLIVAN	COCHECTON
SHAKER PLACE	HAMILTON	ARIETTA	SKINNERVILLE	ST. LAWRENCE	STOCKHOLM
SHAKER VILLAGE	COLUMBIA	NEW LEBANON	SLAB BRIDGE	FRANKLIN	FRANKLIN

NAME	COUNTY	TOWN	NAME	COUNTY	TOWN
SLAB CITY	ST.LAWRENCE	POTSDAM	S. CANDOR	TIOGA	CANDOR
SLATE HILL	ORANGE	WAWAYANDA	S. CANISTEO	STEUBEN	CANISTEO
SLATERVILLE SPGS.	TOMPKINS	CAROLINE	S. CANTON	ST.LAWRENCE	CANTON
SLATEVILLE	WASHINGTON	HEBRON	S. CENTERVILLE	ORANGE	WAWAYANDA
SLEIGHTSBURG	ULSTER	ESOPUS	S. CHAMPION	JEFFERSON	CHAMPION
SLINGERLANDS	ALBANY	BETHLEHEM	S. CHILI	MONROE	CHILI
SLITER	RENSSELAER	SAND LAKE	S. COLUMBIA	HERKIMER	COLUMBIA
SLOAN V.	ERIE	CHEEKTOWAGA	S. CORINTH	SARATOGA	CORINTH
SLOANE	ALBANY	GUILDERLAND	S. CORNING V.	STEUBEN	CORNING
SLOANSVILLE	SCHOHARIE	ESPERANCE	S. CORTLAND	CORTLAND	CORTLANDVILLE
SLOATS CORS.	ORANGE	MONTGOMERY	S. CUYLER	CORTLAND	CUYLER
SLOATSBURG V.	ROCKLAND	RAMAPO	S. DANBY	TOMPKINS	DANBY
SLYBORO	WASHINGTON	GRANVILLE	S. DAYTON V.	CATTARAUGUS	DAYTON
SMALLWOOD	SULLIVAN	BETHEL	S. DURHAM	GREENE	DURHAM
SMARTVILLE	OSWEGO	BOYLSTON	S. EASTON	WASHINGTON	EASTON
SMITH BASIN	WASHINGTON	KINGSBURY	S. EDMESTON STA.	CHENANGO	COLUMBUS
SMITH CORS.	ALBANY	RENSSELAERVILLE	S. EDWARDS	ST.LAWRENCE	EDWARDS
SMITH CORS.	HERKIMER	STARK	S. ERIN	CHEMUNG	ERIN
SMITH CORS.	FULTON	JOHNSTOWN	S. FALLSBURG	SULLIVAN	FALLSBURG
SMITH CORS.	ORANGE	GREENVILLE	S. FARMINGDALE	NASSAU	OYSTER BAY
SMITH CORS.	WYOMING	WETHERSFIELD	S. FLORAL PK. V.	NASSAU	HEMPSTEAD
SMITH CORS.	COLUMBIA	STOCKPORT	S. GALWAY	SARATOGA	GALWAY
SMITH LDG.	LEWIS	LOWVILLE	S. GILBOA	SCHOHARIE	GILBOA
SMITH LDG.	GREENE	CATSKILL	S. GILBOA STA.	SCHOHARIE	GILBOA
SMITH MILLS	CHAUTAUQUA	HANOVER	S. GLENS FALLS V.	SARATOGA	MOREAU
SMITH VALLEY	SCHUYLER	HECTOR	S. GRANBY	OSWEGO	GRANBY
SMITH VILLAGE	ORANGE	MINISINK	S. GRANVILLE	WASHINGTON	GRANVILLE
SMITHBORO	TIOGA	TIOGA	S. GREAT RIVER	SUFFOLK	ISLIP
SMITHFIELD	DUTCHESS	AMENIA	S. GREECE	MONROE	GREECE
SMITHTOWN	SARATOGA	HALFMOON	S. GREENFIELD	SARATOGA	GREENFIELD
SMITHTOWN	SUFFOLK	SMITHTOWN	S. GREIGSVILLE	LIVINGSTON	YORK
SMITHTOWN BRANCH	SUFFOLK	SMITHTOWN	S. HAMILTON	MADISON	HAMILTON
SMITHTOWN LDG.	SUFFOLK	SMITHTOWN	S. HAMMOND	ST.LAWRENCE	HAMMOND
SMITHVILLE	JEFFERSON	ADAMS	S. HANNIBAL	OSWEGO	HANNIBAL
SMITHVILLE	GENESEE	ALABAMA	S. HARRISBURG	LEWIS	HARRISBURG
SMITHVILLE	SARATOGA	SARATOGA	S. HARTFORD	WASHINGTON	HARTFORD
SMITHVILLE	JEFFERSON	HENDERSON	S. HARTWICK	OTSEGO	HARTWICK
SMITHVILLE CTR.	CHENANGO	SMITHVILLE	S. HEMPSTEAD	NASSAU	HEMPSTEAD
SMITHVILLE FLATS	CHENANGO	SMITHVILLE	S. HORICON	WARREN	HORICON
SMITHVILLE P.O.	JEFFERSON	ADAMS	S. HOWARD	STEUBEN	HOWARD
SMITHVILLE STA.	GENESEE	ALABAMA	S. HUNTINGTON	SUFFOLK	HUNTINGTON
SMYRNA CTR.	CHENANGO	SMYRNA	S. JAMESPORT	SUFFOLK	RIVERHEAD
SMYRNA V.	CHENANGO	SMYRNA	S. JEFFERSON	SCHOHARIE	JEFFERSON
SNODY DOCK	WASHINGTON	DRESDEN	S. JUNCTION	CLINTON	PLATTSBURG
SNOOKS CORS.	MONTGOMERY	FLORIDA	S. KORTRIGHT	DELAWARE	KORTRIGHT
SNOWDON	OTSEGO	OTSEGO	S. LANSING	TOMPKINS	LANSING
SNYDER	TOMPKINS	DRYDEN	S. LEBANON	MADISON	LEBANON
SNYDER	TIOGA	CANDOR	S. LIMA	LIVINGSTON	LIMA
SNYDER	ERIE	AMHERST	S. LIVONIA	LIVINGSTON	LIVONIA
SNYDER CORS.	RENSSELAER	POESTENKILL	S. MANOR	SUFFOLK	BROOKHAVEN
SNYDER CORS.	RENSSELAER	NO. GREENBUSH	S. MEXICO	OSWEGO	MEXICO
SNYDERS LAKE	RENSSELAER	NO. GREENBUSH	S. MILLEROOK	DUTCHESS	WASHINGTON
SNYDERVILLE	COLUMBIA	GALLATIN	S. MONSEY	ROCKLAND	RAMAPO
SODOM	WARREN	JOHNSBURG	S. NEW BERLIN	CHENANGO	NEW BERLIN
SODOM	PUTNAM	SOUTHEAST	S. NEW BERLIN	OTSEGO	MORRIS
SODUS CTR.	WAYNE	SODUS	S. NEW HAVEN	OSWEGO	NEW HAVEN
SODUS POINT V.	WAYNE	SODUS	S. NYACK V.	ROCKLAND	ORANGETOWN
SODUS V.	WAYNE	SODUS	S. ONONDAGA	ONONDAGA	ONONDAGA
SOLA BELLA	ESSEX	SCHROON	S. OTSELIC	CHENANGO	OTSELIC
SOLON	CORTLAND	SOLON	S. OWEGO	TIOGA	OWEGO
SOLON POND	CORTLAND	SOLON	S. OXFORD	CHENANGO	OXFORD
SOLSVILLE	MADISON	MADISON	S. PARK	MONROE	BRIGHTON
SOLVAY V.	ONONDAGA	GEDDES	S. PLYMOUTH	CHENANGO	PLYMOUTH
SOMERS	WESTCHESTER	SOMERS	S. PULTENEY	STEUBEN	PULTENEY
SOMERS CTR.	WESTCHESTER	SOMERS	S. RUSSELL	ST.LAWRENCE	RUSSELL
SOMERSET	NIAGARA	SOMERSET	S. RUTLAND	JEFFERSON	RUTLAND
SOMERVILLE	ST.LAWRENCE	ROSSIE	S. SALEM	WESTCHESTER	LEWISBORO
SONYEA	LIVINGSTON	GROVELAND	S. SAND LAKE	RENSSELAER	SAND LAKE
SOULE	CAYUGA	SENNETT	S. SCHENECTADY	SCHENECTADY	ROTTERDAM
SOUND AVE.	SUFFOLK	RIVERHEAD	S. SCHODACK	RENSSELAER	SCHODACK
SOUND BEACH	SUFFOLK	BROOKHAVEN	S. SCHROON	ESSEX	SCHROON
S. ADDISON	STEUBEN	TUSCARORA	S. SCRIBA	OSWEGO	SCRIBA
S. ALABAMA	GENESEE	ALABAMA	S. SODUS	WAYNE	SODUS
S. ALBANY	ALBANY	BETHLEHEM	S. SOMERSET	NIAGARA	SOMERSET
S. ALBION	ORLEANS	ALBION	S. SPAFFORD	ONONDAGA	SPAFFORD
S. AMENIA	DUTCHESS	AMENIA	S. STOCKTON	CHAUTAUQUA	STOCKTON
S. APALACHIN	TIOGA	OWEGO	S. THURSTON	STEUBEN	THURSTON
S. ARGYLE	WASHINGTON	ARGYLE	S. TRENTON	ONEIDA	TRENTON
S. ATTICA	WYOMING	ATTICA	S. TROUPSBURG	STEUBEN	TROUPSBURG
S. AVON	LIVINGSTON	AVON	S. UNADILLA	DELAWARE	SIDNEY
S. BANGOR	FRANKLIN	BANGOR	S. UNADILLA STA.	DELAWARE	SIDNEY
S. BARRE	ORLEANS	BARRE	S. VALLEY	OTSEGO	ROSEBOOM
S. BAY	MADISON	LENOX	S. VANDALIA STA.	CATTARAUGUS	CARROLLTON
S. BAY	WASHINGTON	DRESDEN	S. VESTAL	BROOME	VESTAL
S. BEACH	RICHMOND	NYC	S. WALES	ERIE	WALES
S. BERNE	ALBANY	BERNE	S. WARSAW	WYOMING	WARSAW
S. BETHLEHEM	ALBANY	BETHLEHEM	S. WESTBURY	NASSAU	HEMPSTEAD
S. BOLIVAR	ALLEGANY	BOLIVAR	S. WESTERLO	ALBANY	WESTERLO
S. BOMBAY	FRANKLIN	BOMBAY	S. WILSON	NIAGARA	WILSON
S. BRADFORD	STEUBEN	BRADFORD	S. WOODS	SULLIVAN	THOMPSON
S. BRISTOL	ONTARIO	SO. BRISTOL	S. WORCESTER	OTSEGO	WORCESTER
S. BROOKFIELD	MADISON	BROOKFIELD	SOUTHAMPTON V.	SUFFOLK	SOUTHAMPTON
S. BUTLER	WAYNE	BUTLER	SOUTHERN CENTRAL JCT.	TIOGA	TIOGA
S. BYRON	GENESEE	BYRON	SOUTHFIELD	ORANGE	TUXEDO
S. CAIRO	GREENE	CAIRO	SOUTHOLD	SUFFOLK	SOUTHOLD
S. CAMBRIDGE	WASHINGTON	CAMBRIDGE			
S. CAMERON	STEUBEN	CAMERON	SOUTHPORT	SUFFOLK	SOUTHAMPTON

NAME	COUNTY	TOWN
SOUTHPORT	CHEMUNG	SOUTHPORT
SOUTHVILLE	ST. LAWRENCE	STOCKHOLM
SOWERBY CORS.	WYOMING	CASTILE
SPAFFORD	ONONDAGA	SPAFFORD
SPARKILL	ROCKLAND	ORANGETOWN
SPARROW BUSH	ORANGE	DEER PARK
SPARTA	LIVINGSTON	SPARTA
SPAULDING FURN.	COLUMBIA	GALLATIN
SPECULATOR V.	HAMILTON	LK. PLEASANT
SPEEDVILLE	TOMPKINS	CAROLINE
SPEIGELTOWN	RENSSELAER	SCHAGHTICOKE
SPELLMANS	DUTCHESS	BEEKMAN
SPENCER CORS.	DUTCHESS	NORTHEAST
SPENCER SETT.	ONEIDA	WESTMORELAND
SPENCER SPGS.	TIOGA	SPENCER
SPENCER STA.	TIOGA	SPENCER
SPENCER SUMMIT	TIOGA	SPENCER
SPENCER V.	TIOGA	SPENCER
SPENCERPORT V.	MONROE	OGDEN
SPENCERTOWN	COLUMBIA	AUSTERLITZ
SPEONK	SUFFOLK	SOUTHAMPTON
SPERRYVILLE	LEWIS	WATSON
SPIER FALLS	SARATOGA	CORINTH
SPINNERVILLE	HERKIMER	COLUMBIA
SPLIT ROCK	ONONDAGA	ONONDAGA
SPOONER COR.	OTSEGO	PLAINFIELD
SPRAGUETOWN	WASHINGTON	GREENWICH
SPRAGUEVILLE	ST. LAWRENCE	ROSSIE
SPRAGUEVILLE	JEFFERSON	ANTWERP
SPRAKERS	MONTGOMERY	ROOT
SPRAKERS BASIN	MONTGOMERY	ROOT
SPRAKERS STA.	MONTGOMERY	PALATINE
SPRING BROOK	ERIE	ELMA
SPRING BROOK STA.	ERIE	ELMA
SPRING COVE	FRANKLIN	SANTA CLARA
SPRING GLEN	SULLIVAN	MAMAKATING
SPRING GLEN	ULSTER	WAWARSING
SPRING LAKE	DUTCHESS	RED HOOK
SPRING LAKE STA.	DUTCHESS	RED HOOK
SPRING MILLS	ALLEGANY	INDEPENDENCE
SPRING VALLEY	ROCKLAND	RAMAPO
SPRING VALLEY V.	ROCKLAND	RAMAPO
SPRING VALLEY V.	ROCKLAND	CLARKSTOWN
SPRINGBROOK	DELAWARE	COLCHESTER
SPRINGFIELD	OTSEGO	SPRINGFIELD
SPRINGFIELD	QUEENS	NYC
SPRINGFIELD CTR.	OTSEGO	SPRINGFIELD
SPRINGFIELD GARDENS	QUEENS	NYC
SPRINGLAND	QUEENS	NYC
SPRINGPORT STA.	CAYUGA	SPRINGPORT
SPRINGS	SUFFOLK	E. HAMPTON
SPRINGTOWN	ULSTER	NEW PALTZ
SPRINGVILLE	SUFFOLK	SOUTHAMPTON
SPRINGVILLE V.	ERIE	CONCORD
SPRINGWATER	LIVINGSTON	SPRINGWATER
SPROUT BROOK	MONTGOMERY	CANAJOHARIE
SPROUT CREEK	DUTCHESS	LAGRANGE
SPRUCE HILL	ESSEX	LEWIS
SPRUCETON	GREENE	LEXINGTON
SPUYTEN DUYVIL	BRONX	NYC
SPY LAKE	HAMILTON	ARIETTA
SQUIRETOWN	SUFFOLK	SOUTHAMPTON
STAATSBURG	DUTCHESS	HYDE PARK
STACY BASIN	ONEIDA	VERONA
STAFFORD	GENESEE	STAFFORD
STAFFORD CORS.	ST. LAWRENCE	PARISHVILLE
STAMFORD V.	DELAWARE	STAMFORD
STAMFORD V.	DELAWARE	HARPERSFIELD
STANARD CORS.	ALLEGANY	WILLING
STANARDS	ALLEGANY	WILLING
STANERO	CHENANGO	OTSELIC
STANDISH	CLINTON	SARANAC
STANDISH	FRANKLIN	BELLMONT
STANDISH STA.	CLINTON	DANNEMORA
STANFORDVILLE	DUTCHESS	STANFORD
STANLEY	ONTARIO	SENECA
STANNARD CORS.	ALLEGANY	WELLSVILLE
STANTON HILL	GREENE	NEW BALTIMORE
STANWIX	ONEIDA	ROME C.
STAPLETON	RICHMOND	NYC
STAR	CLINTON	ELLENBURG
STAR LAKE	ST. LAWRENCE	FINE
STAR LAKE INN	ST. LAWRENCE	FINE
STARBUCKVILLE	WARREN	CHESTER
STARKVILLE	HERKIMER	STARK
STARLIGHT	SULLIVAN	THOMPSON
STARR FARM	CHAUTAUQUA	ELLERY
STATE AGRIC. & IND. SCHOOL, IND.	MONROE	RUSH
STATE BRIDGE	ONEIDA	VERONA
STATE CAMP	WESTCHESTER	CORTLANDT
STATE FAIR GROUNDS	ONONDAGA	GEDDES
STATE LINE	DUTCHESS	NORTHEAST
STATE LINE	COLUMBIA	CANAAN
STATE LINE JCT.	CHEMUNG	SOUTHPORT
STATE LINE STA.	DUTCHESS	NORTHEAST
STATE PARK	LIVINGSTON	OSSIAN

NAME	COUNTY	TOWN
STATE RANGER SCHOOL	ST. LAWRENCE	FINE
STATE ROAD	ALLEGANY	ANGELICA
STATE VOCATIONAL INSTITUTION	GREENE	COXSACKIE
STATELINE	BROOME	WINDSOR
STATEN IS.	RICHMOND	NYC
STEAMBURG	CATTARAUGUS	COLD SPRING
STEDMAN	CHAUTAUQUA	NO. HARMONY
STEINWAY	QUEENS	NYC
STELLA	BROOME	DICKINSON
STELLA MINES OR STELLAVILLE	ST. LAWRENCE	DE KALB
STELLA NIAGARA	NIAGARA	LEWISTON
STEPHENS MILLS	STEUBEN	FREMONT
STEPHENSVILLE	ALBANY	COEYMANS
STEPHENTOWN	RENSSELAER	STEPHENTOWN
STEPHENTOWN CTR.	RENSSELAER	STEPHENTOWN
STERLING	CAYUGA	STERLING
STERLING FOREST	ORANGE	WARWICK
STERLING MINES	ORANGE	WARWICK
STERLING STA.	CAYUGA	STERLING
STERLING VALLEY	CAYUGA	STERLING
STERLINGBURG	JEFFERSON	ANTWERP
STERLINGBUSH	LEWIS	DIANA
STERLINGVILLE	JEFFERSON	PHILADELPHIA
STERLINGVILLE STA.	JEFFERSON	PHILADELPHIA
STERNBERG	ST. LAWRENCE	FINE
STETSONVILLE	OTSEGO	NEW LISBON
STEUBEN	ONEIDA	STEUBEN
STEUBEN VALLEY	ONEIDA	STEUBEN
STEVENS	CATTARAUGUS	RED HOUSE
STEVENS MILLS	STEUBEN	FREMONT
STEVENSON	ESSEX	WESTPORT
STEWART	SCHOHARIE	JEFFERSON
STEWART CORS.	OSWEGO	SCHROEPPEL
STEWART CORS.	STEUBEN	PULTENEY
STEWART MANOR V.	NASSAU	HEMPSTEAD
STICKNEY BRIDGE	ESSEX	JAY
STICKNEYS	STEUBEN	WHEELER
STILESVILLE	DELAWARE	DEPOSIT
STILLWATER	OSWEGO	ORWELL
STILLWATER	HERKIMER	WEBB
STILLWATER CTR.	SARATOGA	STILLWATER
STILLWATER V.	SARATOGA	STILLWATER
STISSING	DUTCHESS	STANFORD
STITTVILLE	ONEIDA	MARCY
STOCKBRIDGE	MADISON	STOCKBRIDGE
STOCKBRIDGE STA.	MADISON	STOCKBRIDGE
STOCKHOLM & STK. CTR.	ST. LAWRENCE	STOCKHOLM
STOCKPORT	COLUMBIA	STOCKPORT
STOCKPORT CTR. STA.	COLUMBIA	STOCKPORT
STOCKPORT STA.	DELAWARE	HANCOCK
STOCKTON	CHAUTAUQUA	STOCKTON
STOCKWELL	ONEIDA	SANGERFIELD
STOKES	ONEIDA	LEE
STONE ARABIA	MONTGOMERY	PALATINE
STONE BRIDGE	SCHOHARIE	CONESVILLE
STONE CHURCH	GENESEE	BERGEN
STONE DAM	ALLEGANY	WILLING
STONE FALLS	LIVINGSTON	NO. DANSVILLE
STONE HILL	OSWEGO	WILLIAMSTOWN
STONE HOUSE	DUTCHESS	PAWLING
STONE MILLS	JEFFERSON	ORLEANS
STONE RIDGE	MONTGOMERY	ROOT
STONE RIDGE P.O.	ULSTER	MARBLETOWN
STONECO	DUTCHESS	POUGHKEEPSIE
STONER LAKE	FULTON	CAROGA
STONEY BROOK JCT.	CATTARAUGUS	RED HOUSE
STONY BROOK	SUFFOLK	BROOKHAVEN
STONY CLOVE STA.	GREENE	HUNTER
STONY CREEK	WARREN	STONY CREEK
STONY CREEK STA.	WARREN	STONY CREEK
STONY FORD	ORANGE	HAMPTONBURG
STONY FORD STA.	ORANGE	WALLKILL
STONY HILL	ALBANY	NEW SCOTLAND
STONY HOLLOW	ULSTER	KINGSTON
STONY HOLLOW	ULSTER	ULSTER
STONY ISLAND	JEFFERSON	HOUNSFIELD
STONY POINT	ROCKLAND	STONY POINT
STONY POINT	JEFFERSON	HENDERSON
STORM KING P.O.	PUTNAM	PHILIPSTOWN
STORM KING STA.	PUTNAM	PHILIPSTOWN
STORMVILLE	DUTCHESS	E. FISHKILL
STOTTVILLE	COLUMBIA	STOCKPORT
STOW	CHAUTAUQUA	NO. HARMONY
STOWELL COR.	JEFFERSON	HOUNSFIELD
STRAIT CORS.	TIOGA	TIOGA
STRATFORD	FULTON	STRATFORD
STRATFORD	HERKIMER	SALISBURY
STRATTON	TOMPKINS	NEWFIELD
STRICKLAND CORS.	JEFFERSON	PHILADELPHIA
STRONGTOWN	SULLIVAN	LIBERTY
STROUGH	JEFFERSON	THERESA
STRYKERSVILLE	WYOMING	SHELDON
STRYKERVILLE	WYOMING	JAVA
STRYKERVILLE	SCHOHARIE	CONESVILLE

Alphabetical List of Cities, Villages and Hamlets
Showing Location by County and Town
PART TWO

NAME	COUNTY	TOWN
STUART CORS.	CAYUGA	VENICE
STURGEON POINT	ERIE	EVANS
STUPTEVANT LDG.	YATES	JERUSALEM
STUYVESANT	COLUMBIA	STUYVESANT
STUYVESANT FALLS	COLUMBIA	STUYVESANT
SUFFERN	ROCKLAND	RAMAPO
SUFFERN V.	ROCKLAND	RAMAPO
SUFFOLK DEVELOPMENTAL CTR.	SUFFOLK	HUNTINGTON
SUFFOLK DOWNS	SUFFOLK	SOUTHAMPTON
SUGAR BUSH	FRANKLIN	FRANKLIN
SUGAR HILL	SCHUYLER	ORANGE
SUGARLOAF	ORANGE	CHESTER
SUGARLOAF	GREENE	HUNTER
SUGARTOWN	CATTARAUGUS	HUMPHREY
SULLIVAN	MADISON	SULLIVAN
SULLIVAN STA.	MADISON	SULLIVAN
SULLIVANVILLE	CHEMUNG	VETERAN
SULPHUR SPA.	FULTON	JOHNSTOWN
SULPHUR SPA. JCT.	FULTON	JOHNSTOWN
SULPHUR SPGS.	JEFFERSON	HOUNSFIELD
SUMMER HILL	CAYUGA	SUMMER HILL
SUMMERDALE	CHAUTAUQUA	CHAUTAUQUA
SUMMERVILLE	MONROE	IRONDEQUOIT
SUMMIT	DELAWARE	FRANKLIN
SUMMIT	TOMPKINS	DANBY
SUMMIT	SCHOHARIE	SUMMIT
SUMMIT	ALLEGANY	CUBA
SUMMIT	CHENANGO	OXFORD
SUMMIT PK.	ERIE	BUFFALO C.
SUMMIT PK.	ROCKLAND	RAMAPO
SUMMIT STA.	SARATOGA	WILTON
SUMMIT STA.	WASHINGTON	CAMBRIDGE
SUMMITVILLE	SULLIVAN	MAMAKATING
SUN	FRANKLIN	BURKE
SUNDOWN	ULSTER	DENNING
SUNKEN MEADOW	SUFFOLK	SMITHTOWN
SUNMOUNT	FRANKLIN	ALTAMONT
SUNMOUNT DEVELOPMENTAL CTR.	FRANKLIN	ALTAMONT
SUNNYSIDE	QUEENS	NYC
SUNNYSIDE BCH.	MONROE	HAMLIN
SUNRISE TERRACE	BROOME	DICKINSON
SUNSET	WESTCHESTER	CORTLANDT
SUNSIDE	GREENE	DURHAM
SURPRISE	GREENE	GREENVILLE
SUSPENSION BRIDGE	NIAGARA	NIAGARA FALLS C.
SUYDAM	COLUMBIA	GALLATIN
SWAIN	ALLEGANY	GROVE
SWAIN JCT.	ALLEGANY	GROVE
SWALE	STEUBEN	CANISTEO
SWAMP SIDING	TIOGA	SPENCER
SWAN LAKE	SULLIVAN	LIBERTY
SWANCOTT MILLS	LEWIS	LEWIS
SWARTOUTVILLE	DUTCHESS	WAPPINGER
SWAPTWOOD	CHEMUNG	VAN ETTEN
SHASTIKA	CLINTON	BLACK BROOK
SWEDEN	MONROE	SWEDEN
SWEDEN CTR.	MONROE	SWEDEN
SWEEBERS LANE	MONTGOMERY	CANAJOHARIE
SWEETS	CHENANGO	COLUMBUS
SWORMSVILLE	ERIE	CLARENCE
SWORMVILLE	ERIE	AMHERST
SYLVA	ULSTER	PLATTEKILL
SYLVAN BEACH V.	ONEIDA	VIENNA
SYLVAN FALLS	ST.LAWRENCE	HOPKINTON
SYLVAN LAKE	DUTCHESS	BEEKMAN
SYLVANDALE	GREENE	NEW BALTIMORE
SYOSSET	NASSAU	OYSTER BAY
SYRACUSE C.	ONONDAGA	SYRACUSE C.

-T-

NAME	COUNTY	TOWN
TABASCO	ULSTER	ROCHESTER
TABERG	ONEIDA	ANNSVILLE
TABOLT CORS.	ORANGE	MONTGOMERY
TABORS CORS.	LIVINGSTON	SPRINGWATER
TABORTON	RENSSELAER	SAND LAKE
TACOMA	DELAWARE	MASONVILLE
TAGGART	STEUBEN	URBANA
TAGHKANIC	COLUMBIA	TAGHKANIC
TAHAWUS	ESSEX	NEWCOMB
TALCOTTS CORS.	CAYUGA	LEDYARD
TALCOTTS CORS.	CAYUGA	VENICE
TALCOTVILLE	LEWIS	LEYDEN
TALCVILLE	ST.LAWRENCE	EDWARDS
TALLETTE	CHENANGO	COLUMBUS
TALLMAN	ROCKLAND	RAMAPO
TAMARACK GARDENS	WESTCHESTER	RYE
TANNER CORS.	JEFFERSON	ALEXANDRIA
TANNERS	COLUMBIA	ANCRAM
TANNEPSLATE	GREENE	HUNTER
TANNERSVILLE V.	GREENE	HUNTER
TAPPAN	ROCKLAND	ORANGETOWN
TARRYTOWN V.	WESTCHESTER	GREENBURG
TAUGHANNOCK	TOMPKINS	LANSING
TAUGHANNOCK FALLS	TOMPKINS	ULYSSES

NAME	COUNTY	TOWN
TAUNTON	ONONDAGA	ONONDAGA
TAYLOR	CORTLAND	TAYLOR
TAYLOR CTR.	COPTLAND	TAYLOR
TAYLOR HOLLOW	ERIE	COLLINS
TAYLOR VALLEY	COPTLAND	TAYLOR
TEATOWN	WESTCHESTER	CORTLANDT
TEBO	FRANKLIN	DICKINSON
TEED CORS.	LIVINGSTON	LEICESTER
TEKANE	FRANKLIN	FRANKLIN
TEN MILE RIVER VILLAGE	SULLIVAN	TUSTEN
TENNANAL LAKE	SULLIVAN	FREMONT
TERRACE PK.	ST.LAWRENCE	MORRISTOWN
TERRY CORS.	CHEMUNG	VETERAN
TERRY CORS.	PUTNAM	KENT
TERRYVILLE	SUFFOLK	BROOKHAVEN
TEXAS	OSWEGO	MEXICO
TEXAS	LEWIS	CROGHAN
TEXAS VALLEY	CORTLAND	MARATHON
THATEP CORS.	FRANKLIN	BURKE
THE ARROW HEAD	HAMILTON	INLET
THE BRANCH V.	SUFFOLK	SMITHTOWN
THE CAPE	ULSTER	SHAWANGUNK
THE ELBOW	WARREN	HORICON
THE GLEN	WARREN	JOHNSBURG
THE JUNCTION	CLINTON	DANNEMORA
THE PINES	LIVINGSTON	LEICESTER
THE PLAINS	ST.LAWRENCE	FINE
THE RAUNT STA.	QUEENS	NYC
THE SAGAMORE	HAMILTON	LONG LAKE
THE UNION	CLINTON	PERU
THE VLY	ULSTER	MARBLETOWN
THE WAYSIDE	FRANKLIN	HARRIETSTOWN
THENDARA	HERKIMER	WEBB
THERESA STA.	JEFFERSON	THERESA
THERESA V.	JEFFERSON	THERESA
THIELLS	ROCKLAND	HAVERSTRAW
THIRTYMILE PT.	NIAGARA	SOMERSET
THOMAS	CLINTON	DANNEMORA
THOMAS CORS.	SCHENECTADY	GLENVILLE
THOMAS CORS.	CATTARAUGUS	ASHFORD
THOMAS SETT.	JEFFERSON	ADAMS
THOMASTON V.	NASSAU	N. HEMPSTEAD
THOMPSON CORS.	ONTARIO	VICTOR
THOMPSON LAKE	ALBANY	BERNE
THOMPSON RIDGE	ORANGE	CRAWFORD
THOMPSON STA.	WAYNE	LYONS
THOMPSONVILLE	SULLIVAN	THOMPSON
THOMSON	WASHINGTON	GREENWICH
THOMSON CORS.	ONEIDA	FLORENCE
THORN CORS.	CLINTON	MOOERS
THORN HILL	ONONDAGA	MARCELLUS
THORNVILLE	DUTCHESS	MILAN
THORNWOOD	WESTCHESTER	MT. PLEASANT
THOUSAND IS. PK.	JEFFERSON	ORLEANS
THREE MILE BAY	JEFFERSON	LYME
THREE MILE BAY STA.	JEFFERSON	LYME
THREE MILE HARBOR	SUFFOLK	E. HAMPTON
THROGS NECK	BRONX	NYC
THROOP	CAYUGA	THROOP
THURMAN	WARREN	THURMAN
THURSO	JEFFERSON	CLAYTON
THURSTON	STEUBEN	THURSTON
TIANA	SUFFOLK	SOUTHAMPTON
TIASHOKE	RENSSELAER	HOOSICK
TICONDEROGA V.	ESSEX	TICONDEROGA
TIERNAN RIDGE	ST.LAWRENCE	NORFOLK
TILLSON	ULSTER	ROSENDALE
TILLY FOSTER	PUTNAM	SOUTHEAST
TIOGA CTR.	TIOGA	TIOGA
TIONA	BROOME	MAINE
TIP TOP	ALLEGANY	ALFRED
TIPLADY	WASHINGTON	HEBRON
TIPLADY CORS.	WASHINGTON	HEBRON
TITUSVILLE	DUTCHESS	LAGRANGE
TITUSVILLE	FRANKLIN	MALONE
TIVOLI	DUTCHESS	RED HOOK
TIVOLI V.	DUTCHESS	RED HOOK
TODDSVILLE	WESTCHESTER	CORTLANDT
TODDSVILLE	OTSEGO	HARTWICK
TOHAWUS CLUB	ESSEX	NEWCOMB
TOMHANNOCK	RENSSELAER	PITTSTOWN
TOMKINS COVE	ROCKLAND	STONY POINT
TOMPKINS CORS.	CHEMUNG	CATLIN
TOMPKINS CORS.	PUTNAM	PUTNAM VALLEY
TOMPKINS CORS.	WESTCHESTER	NEW CASTLE
TOMPKINSVILLE	RICHMOND	NYC
TOMPSON	SENECA	JUNIUS
TONAWANDA C.	ERIE	TONAWANDA C.
TOTTENVILLE	RICHMOND	NYC
TOWERS FORGE	ESSEX	LEWIS
TOWERVILLE CORS.	CHAUTAUQUA	GERRY
TOWLESVILLE	STEUBEN	HOWARD
TOWN LINE	ERIE	LANCASTER
TOWN LINE	ERIE	ALDEN
TOWN LINE STA.	ERIE	LANCASTER
TOWN PUMP	MONROE	OGDEN

NAME	COUNTY	TOWN
TOWNERS	PUTNAM	PATTERSON
TOWNSEND	SCHUYLER	DIX
TOWNSENDVILLE	SENECA	LODI
TRACY CREEK	BROOME	VESTAL
TRANSIT BRIDGE	ALLEGANY	BELFAST
TRAVERS CORS.	DUTCHESS	CLINTON
TRAVIS	RICHMOND	NYC
TRAVIS CORS.	PUTNAM	PHILIPSTOWN
TREADWELL	DELAWARE	FRANKLIN
TREADWELLS MILLS	CLINTON	PLATTSBURG
TREMAINE CORS.	JEFFERSON	RODMAN
TREMAINES	JEFFERSON	RODMAN
TREMONT	BRONX	NYC
TRENTON CAMP GROUNDS	ONEIDA	TRENTON
TRENTON FALLS	ONEIDA	TRENTON
TRENTON FALLS STA.	HERKIMER	RUSSIA
TRESTLE	CHENANGO	GUILFORD
TRIANGLE	BROOME	TRIANGLE
TRIBES HILL	MONTGOMERY	AMSTERDAM
TRIBES HILL	MONTGOMERY	MOHAWK
TRIONDS	WASHINGTON	GREENWICH
TRIPOLI	CORTLAND	CUYLER
TROMBLEES	FRANKLIN	HARRIETSTOWN
TROUPSBURG	STEUBEN	TROUPSBURG
TROUT BROOK	DELAWARE	HANCOCK
TROUT BROOK STA.	DELAWARE	HANCOCK
TROUT CREEK	DELAWARE	TOMPKINS
TROUT RIVER	FRANKLIN	CONSTABLE
TROUTBURG	MONROE	HAMLIN
TROY C.	RENSSELAER	TROY C.
TRUAX STA.	MONTGOMERY	AMSTERDAM
TRUMANSBURG LDG.	SENECA	COVERT
TRUMANSBURG V.	TOMPKINS	ULYSSES
TRUMANVILLE	RENSSELAER	HOOSICK
TRUMBULL CORS.	TOMPKINS	NEWFIELD
TRUTHVILLE	WASHINGTON	GRANVILLE
TRUXTON	CORTLAND	TRUXTON
TUCKAHOE	SUFFOLK	SOUTHAMPTON
TUCKAHOE V.	WESTCHESTER	E. CHESTER
TUCKERS CORNERS	ULSTER	PLATTEKILL
TULLY V.	ONONDAGA	TULLY
TUNESASSA	CATTARAUGUS	ELKO
TUNNEL	BROOME	COLESVILLE
TUPPER LAKE JCT.	FRANKLIN	ALTAMONT
TUPPER LAKE JCT. FAUST	FRANKLIN	ALTAMONT
TUPPER LAKE V.	FRANKLIN	ALTAMONT
TURIN V.	LEWIS	TURIN
TURNWOOD	ULSTER	HARDENBURGH
TUSCARORA	BROOME	WINDSOR
TUSCARORA	LIVINGSTON	MT. MORRIS
TUSTEN	SULLIVAN	TUSTEN
TUSTEN STA.	SULLIVAN	TUSTEN
TUTHILL	ULSTER	GARDINER
TUTTLE	ONTARIO	FARMINGTON
TUXEDO	ORANGE	TUXEDO
TUXEDO PK. V.	ORANGE	TUXEDO
TUXEDO STA.	ORANGE	TUXEDO
TWELVE CORS.	MONROE	BRIGHTON
TWELVE CORS.	CAYUGA	NILES
TWILIGHT PK.	GREENE	HUNTER
TWIN ORCHARDS	BROOME	VESTAL
TYLERTOWN	SULLIVAN	COCHECTON
TYLERVILLE	JEFFERSON	RUTLAND
TYNER	CHENANGO	SMITHVILLE
TYRE	SENECA	TYRE
TYRONE	SCHUYLER	TYRONE

-U-

NAME	COUNTY	TOWN
ULSTER HGHTS.	ULSTER	WAWARSING
ULSTER LANDING	ULSTER	ULSTER
ULSTER PK.	ULSTER	ESOPUS
ULSTERVILLE	ULSTER	SHAWANGUNK
UNADILLA	DELAWARE	SIDNEY
UNADILLA CTR.	OTSEGO	UNADILLA
UNADILLA FORKS	OTSEGO	PLAINFIELD
UNADILLA FORKS STA.	OTSEGO	PLAINFIELD
UNADILLA V.	OTSEGO	UNADILLA
UNCAS	HAMILTON	LONG LAKE
UNCAS RD.	HAMILTON	INLET
UNDERHILL	WESTCHESTER	YORKTOWN
UNION	MADISON	CAZENOVIA
UNION	BROOME	UNION
UNION CENTER	BROOME	UNION
UNION CHURCH	ALBANY	NEW SCOTLAND
UNION CORNERS	GENESEE	PAVILION
UNION CORNERS	LIVINGSTON	W. SPARTA
UNION CORNERS	WESTCHESTER	EASTCHESTER
UNION CORNERS	COLUMBIA	LIVINGSTON
UNION CORNERS	DUTCHESS	HYDE PARK
UNION FALLS	CLINTON	BLACK BROOK
UNION HILL	MONROE	WEBSTER
UNION HILL STA.	WAYNE	ONTARIO
UNION MILLS	FULTON	BROADALBIN
UNION PLACE	SUFFOLK	SOUTHAMPTON
UNION SCHOOL AREA	ORANGE	CRAWFORD

NAME	COUNTY	TOWN
UNION SOCIETY	GREENE	WINDHAM
UNION SPRINGS V.	CAYUGA	SPRINGPORT
UNION SQUARE	OSWEGO	MEXICO
UNION VALLEY	CHENANGO	BAINBRIDGE
UNION VALLEY	CHENANGO	PITCHER
UNION VALLEY	CORTLAND	TAYLOR
UNIONDALE	NASSAU	HEMPSTEAD
UNIONPORT	BRONX	NYC
UNIONVILLE	JEFFERSON	RODMAN
UNIONVILLE	SULLIVAN	NEVERSINK
UNIONVILLE	ST. LAWRENCE	POTSDAM
UNIONVILLE	ALBANY	NEW SCOTLAND
UNIONVILLE V.	ONTARIO	PHELPS
UNIONVILLE V.	ORANGE	MINISINK
UNIVERSITY HGHTS.	NEW YORK	NYC
UPPER BROOKVILLE V.	NASSAU	OYSTER BAY
UPPER CHATEAUGAY LK.	CLINTON	DANNEMORA
UPPER GRAND VIEW	ROCKLAND	ORANGETOWN
UPPER GREEN RIVER	COLUMBIA	AUSTERLITZ
UPPER IRON WORKS	ESSEX	NEWCOMB
UPPER JAY	ESSEX	JAY
UPPER KILNS	CLINTON	BLACK BROOK
UPPER LANDING	GREENE	COXSACKIE
UPPER LISLE	BROOME	TRIANGLE
UPPER MILLS	SUFFOLK	RIVERHEAD
UPPER NYACK V.	ROCKLAND	CLARKSTOWN
UPPER RED HOOK	DUTCHESS	RED HOOK
UPPER SARANAC	FRANKLIN	SANTA CLARA
UPPER ST. JOHNSVILLE	MONTGOMERY	ST. JOHNSVILLE
UPPER ST. REGIS	FRANKLIN	HARRIETSTOWN
UPPER TUCKAHOE	WESTCHESTER	EASTCHESTER
UPPERVILLE	CHENANGO	SMYRNA
UPSON CORNERS	OSWEGO	PALERMO
UPTON	SUFFOLK	BROOKHAVEN
UPTON LAKE	DUTCHESS	STANFORD
URBANA	STEUBEN	URBANA
USHER	SARATOGA	HALFMOON
UTICA C.	ONEIDA	UTICA C.
UTICA PSYCHIATRIC CENTER	ONEIDA	UTICA C.
UTOPIA	ALLEGANY	WIRT

-V-

NAME	COUNTY	TOWN
VAILS GATE	ORANGE	NEW WINDSOR
VAILS MILLS	FULTON	MAYFIELD
VALATIE V.	COLUMBIA	KINDERHOOK
VALCOUR	CLINTON	PERU
VALCOUR ISLANDS	CLINTON	PERU
VALENTINE	CATTARAUGUS	RANDOLPH
VALHALLA	WESTCHESTER	MT. PLEASANT
VALLEY BROOK	MONTGOMERY	MINDEN
VALLEY COTTAGES	ROCKLAND	CLARKSTOWN
VALLEY FALLS V.	RENSSELAER	PITTSTOWN
VALLEY FALLS V.	RENSSELAER	SCHAGHTICOKE
VALLEY MILLS	MADISON	STOCKBRIDGE
VALLEY STREAM V.	NASSAU	HEMPSTEAD
VALLEY VIEW	YATES	MIDDLESEX
VALLONIA SPGS.	BROOME	COLESVILLE
VALOIS	SCHUYLER	HECTOR
VAN BUREN	CHAUTAUQUA	POMFRET
VAN BUREN	ONONDAGA	VAN BUREN
VAN BUREN PT.	CHAUTAUQUA	POMFRET
VAN BURENVILLE	ORANGE	WALLKILL
VAN CORTLANDT	BRONX	NYC
VAN CORTLANDVILLE	WESTCHESTER	CORTLANDT
VAN ETTEN JCT.	CHEMUNG	VAN ETTEN
VAN ETTEN V.	CHEMUNG	VAN ETTEN
VAN ETTENVILLE	CHEMUNG	VAN ETTEN
VAN HOESEN STA.	RENSSELAER	SCHODACK
VAN NEST	BRONX	NYC
VAN NOSTRAND CROSS	ALLEGANY	GROVE
VAN VLEET	STEUBEN	TUSCARORA
VAN VRANKEN	FULTON	BROADALBIN
VAN VRANKEN CORS.	FULTON	BROADALBIN
VAN WAGNER	DUTCHESS	POUGHKEEPSIE
VAN WIES	ALBANY	BETHLEHEM
VANBUREN	OSWEGO	VOLNEY
VANDALIA	CATTARAUGUS	ALLEGANY
VANDALIA	CATTARAUGUS	CARROLLTON
VANDERMARK ROAD	ALLEGANY	WARD
VANDEUSENVILLE	MONTGOMERY	CANAJOHARIE
VANHORNESVILLE	HERKIMER	STARK
VARIAN MILLS	WESTCHESTER	CORTLANDT
VARICK	SENECA	VARICK
VARNA	TOMPKINS	DRYDEN
VARYSBURG	WYOMING	SHELDON
VASSAR COLLEGE	DUTCHESS	POUGHKEEPSIE
VAUGHNS	WASHINGTON	KINGSBURY
VAUGHNS CORS.	WASHINGTON	KINGSBURY
VEGA	DELAWARE	ROXBURY
VENICE	CAYUGA	VENICE
VENICE CTR.	CAYUGA	VENICE
VENUS	STEUBEN	W. UNION
VERBANK	DUTCHESS	UNION VALE
VERBANK VIL.	DUTCHESS	UNION VALE
VERDOY	ALBANY	COLONIE
VERMILLION	OSWEGO	PALERMO

Alphabetical List of Cities, Villages and Hamlets
Showing Location by County and Town
PART TWO

NAME	COUNTY	TOWN
VERMONTVILLE	FRANKLIN	FRANKLIN
VERMONTVILLE STA.	FRANKLIN	FRANKLIN
VERNAL	WYOMING	ATTICA
VERNON CTR.	ONEIDA	VERNON
VERNON V.	ONEIDA	VERNON
VERNON VALLEY	SUFFOLK	HUNTINGTON
VERONA	ONEIDA	VERONA
VERONA BCH.	ONEIDA	VERONA
VERONA MILLS	ONEIDA	VERONA
VERONA SPGS.	ONEIDA	VERONA
VERONA STA.	ONEIDA	VERONA
VERPLANCK	WESTCHESTER	CORTLANDT
VERSAILLES	CATTARAUGUS	PERRYSBURG
VESPER	ONONDAGA	TULLY
VESTAL	BROOME	VESTAL
VESTAL CTR.	BROOME	VESTAL
VETERAN	ULSTER	SAUGERTIES
V.A. HOSP. CASTLE PT.	DUTCHESS	WAPPINGER T
V.A. HOSP. MONTROSE	WESTCHESTER	CORTLANDT
V.A. HOSP. NORTHPORT	SUFFOLK	NORTHPORT
V.A. MEDICAL CENTER	ERIE	BUFFALO C.
V.A. MEDICAL CENTER,ALBANY	ALBANY	ALBANY C.
V.A. MEDICAL CENTER,BATAVIA	GENESEE	BATAVIA C.
V.A. MEDICAL CENTER,CANANDAIGU	ONTARIO	CANANDAIGUA T
VETERANS MT. CAMP	ST.LAWRENCE	PIERCEFIELD
VETSBURG	TOMPKINS	ITHACA
VICTOR STA.	ONTARIO	VICTOR
VICTOR V.	ONTARIO	VICTOR
VICTORIA	CHAUTAUQUA	NO. HARMONY
VICTORY	CAYUGA	VICTORY
VICTORY LAKE	DUTCHESS	HYDE PARK
VICTORY MILLS V.	SARATOGA	SARATOGA
VIENNA	ONEIDA	VIENNA
VIEWMONTE	COLUMBIA	GERMANTOWN
VILL. OF THE BRANCH V.	SUFFOLK	SMITHTOWN
VILL. OF THE LANDING	SUFFOLK	SMITHTOWN
VILLENOVA	CHAUTAUQUA	VILLENOVA
VINCENT	ONTARIO	BRISTOL
VINE VALLEY	YATES	MIDDLESEX
VINTONTON	SCHOHARIE	FULTON
VIOLA	ROCKLAND	RAMAPO
VIRGIL	CORTLAND	VIRGIL
VISCHER FERRY	SARATOGA	CLIFTON PARK
VISTA	WESTCHESTER	LEWISBORO
VOLNEY CENTER	OSWEGO	VOLNEY
VOLUSIA	CHAUTAUQUA	WESTFIELD
VOORHEESVILLE V.	ALBANY	NEW SCOTLAND
VOREA	OSWEGO	ORWELL
VORHEES	OSWEGO	PARISH

-W-

NAME	COUNTY	TOWN
WACCABUC LAKE	WESTCHESTER	LEWISBORO
WADDINGTON V.	ST.LAWRENCE	WADDINGTON
WADHAM MILLS	ESSEX	WESTPORT
WADHAM MILLS STA.	ESSEX	WESTPORT
WADHAMS	ESSEX	WESTPORT
WADING RIVER	SUFFOLK	BROOKHAVEN
WADING RIVER	SUFFOLK	RIVERHEAD
WADSWORTH	LIVINGSTON	YORK
WAHMEDA	CHAUTAUQUA	CHAUTAUQUA
WAINSCOTT	SUFFOLK	E. HAMPTON
WAINSCOTT	SUFFOLK	SOUTHAMPTON
WAITE SETT.	TIOGA	OWEGO
WAITS	TIOGA	NICHOLS
WAITS	CHAUTAUQUA	SHERMAN
WAKE	BROOME	WINDSOR
WALDEN	ERIE	CHEEKTOWAGA
WALDEN V.	ORANGE	MONTGOMERY
WALDENVILLE	SCHOHARIE	WRIGHT
WALES	ERIE	WALES
WALES CTR.	ERIE	WALES
WALES HOLLOW	ERIE	WALES
WALESVILLE	ONEIDA	WHITESTOWN
WALKER	MONROE	HAMLIN
WALKER MILLS	COLUMBIA	LIVINGSTON
WALKER VALLEY	ULSTER	SHAWANGUNK
WALKERS	FRANKLIN	SANTA CLARA
WALKERS	WYOMING	CASTILE
WALLACE	STEUBEN	AVOCA
WALLACE HILLS	CLINTON	PLATTSBURG
WALLIN'S CORS.	MONTGOMERY	AMSTERDAM
WALLINGTON	WAYNE	SODUS
WALLKILL	ULSTER	SHAWANGUNK
WALLKILL CORRECTIONAL FAC.	ULSTER	SHAWANGUNK
WALLOOMSACK	RENSSELAER	HOOSICK
WALMORE	NIAGARA	WHEATFIELD
WALRATH HOLLOW	HERKIMER	DANUBE
WALSH HILL	LEWIS	TURIN
WALTON DEPOT	DELAWARE	WALTON
WALTON V.	DELAWARE	WALTON

NAME	COUNTY	TOWN
WALWORTH	WAYNE	WALWORTH
WALWORTH STA.	WAYNE	MACEDON
WAMPSVILLE V.	MADISON	LENOX
WANAKAH	ERIE	HAMBURG
WANAKENA	ST.LAWRENCE	FINE
WANGO	CHAUTAUQUA	VILLENOVA
WANTAGH	NASSAU	HEMPSTEAD
WAPPASENING	TIOGA	NICHOLS
WAPPINGERS FALLS	DUTCHESS	POUGHKEEPSIE
WAPPINGERS FALLS V.	DUTCHESS	POUGHKEEPSIE
WAPPINGERS FALLS V.	DUTCHESS	WAPPINGER
WARDNER	FRANKLIN	BRIGHTON
WARDWELL	JEFFERSON	ELLISBURG
WARNERS	ONONDAGA	CAMILLUS
WARNERS	ONONDAGA	VAN BUREN
WARNERS LAKE	ALBANY	BERNE
WARNERVILLE	SCHOHARIE	RICHMONDVILLE
WARREN	HERKIMER	WARREN
WARRENS CORS.	NIAGARA	CAMBRIA
WARRENS CORS.	NIAGARA	LOCKPORT
WARRENSBURG	WARREN	WARRENSBURG
WARSAW	YATES	BARRINGTON
WARSAW V.	WYOMING	WARSAW
WARWICK SCHOOL FOR BOYS	ORANGE	WARWICK
WARWICK V.	ORANGE	WARWICK
WASHINGTON	ORANGE	BLOOMING GR.
WASHINGTON	DUTCHESS	WASHINGTON
WASHINGTON HGHTS.	ORANGE	WALLKILL
WASHINGTON HGHTS.	SULLIVAN	THOMPSON
WASHINGTON HOLLOW	DUTCHESS	PLEASANT VALLEY
WASHINGTON HOLLOW	DUTCHESS	WASHINGTON
WASHINGTON MILLS	ONEIDA	NEW HARTFORD
WASHINGTON PARK	JEFFERSON	LORRAINE
WASHINGTONVILLE V.	ORANGE	BLOOMING GR.
WASHINGTONVILLE V.	ORANGE	NEW WINDSOR
WASSAIC	DUTCHESS	AMENIA
WASSAIC DEVELOPMENTAL CTR.	DUTCHESS	AMENIA
WATER ISLAND	SUFFOLK	BROOKHAVEN
WATER MILL	SUFFOLK	SOUTHAMPTON
WATER VALLEY	ERIE	HAMBURG
WATERBORO	CHAUTAUQUA	POLAND
WATERBURG	TOMPKINS	ULYSSES
WATERFORD JCT.	SARATOGA	WATERFORD
WATERFORD V.	SARATOGA	WATERFORD
WATERLOO MILLS	ORANGE	MINISINK
WATERLOO V.	SENECA	WATERLOO
WATERLOO V.	SENECA	FAYETTE
WATERPORT	ORLEANS	CARLTON
WATERPORT STA.	ORLEANS	CARLTON
WATERTOWN C.	JEFFERSON	WATERTOWN C.
WATERTOWN CTR.	JEFFERSON	WATERTOWN
WATERTOWN JCT.	JEFFERSON	WATERTOWN
WATERVALE	ONONDAGA	POMPEY
WATERVILLE	MONTGOMERY	CANAJOHARIE
WATERVILLE	JEFFERSON	LORRAINE
WATERVILLE V.	ONEIDA	MARSHALL
WATERVILLE V.	ONEIDA	SANGERFIELD
WATERVLIET C.	ALBANY	WATERVLIET C.
WATKINS GLEN ST. PK.	SCHUYLER	DIX
WATKINS GLEN STA.	SCHUYLER	READING
WATKINS GLEN V.	SCHUYLER	DIX
WATKINS GLEN V.	SCHUYLER	READING
WATSON	LEWIS	WATSON
WATSONVILLE	SCHOHARIE	FULTON
WATT FLATS	CHAUTAUQUA	HARMONY
WAVERLY	CATTARAUGUS	OTTO
WAVERLY V.	TIOGA	BARTON
WAWARSING	ULSTER	WAWARSING
WAWAYANDA STA.	ORANGE	WAWAYANDA
WAWBEEK	FRANKLIN	HARRIETSTOWN
WAWBEEK CENT. STA.	FRANKLIN	HARRIETSTOWN
WAYLAND	STEUBEN	WAYLAND
WAYLAND V.	STEUBEN	WAYLAND
WAYNE	SCHUYLER	TYRONE
WAYNE CTR.	WAYNE	ROSE
WAYNE FOUR CORS.	STEUBEN	WAYNE
WAYNEPORT	WAYNE	MACEDON
WAYVILLE	SARATOGA	STILLWATER
WEAVER HOLLOW	COLUMBIA	GALLATIN
WEBB MILLS	CHEMUNG	SOUTHPORT
WEBSTER CORS.	ERIE	ORCHARD PARK
WEBSTER CORS.	OTSEGO	ROSEBOOM
WEBSTER CROSS	LIVINGSTON	SPRINGWATER
WEBSTER STA.	MADISON	CAZENOVIA
WEBSTER V.	MONROE	WEBSTER
WEDGWOOD	SCHUYLER	DIX
WEDGWOOD STA.	SCHUYLER	DIX
WEED MINES	COLUMBIA	COPAKE
WEED MINES	COLUMBIA	ANCRAM
WEEDSPORT V.	CAYUGA	BRUTUS
WEGATCHIE	ST.LAWRENCE	ROSSIE
WELCOME	OTSEGO	NEW LISBON
WELLS	CHEMUNG	SOUTHPORT
WELLS	HAMILTON	WELLS
WELLS BRIDGE	OTSEGO	UNADILLA

NAME	COUNTY	TOWN
WELLS SETT.	JEFFERSON	LYME
WELLS STA.	CHEMUNG	SOUTHPORT
WELLSBRIDGE RIVER RD	DELAWARE	SIDNEY
WELLSBURG V.	CHEMUNG	ASHLAND
WELLSVILLE V.	ALLEGANY	WELLSVILLE
WELLWOOD	OSWEGO	MEXICO
WELSH HILL	LEWIS	TURIN
WELTONVILLE	TIOGA	CANDOR
WEMPLE	ALBANY	BETHLEHEM
WENDE	ERIE	ALDEN
WENDELVILLE	NIAGARA	PENDLETON
WESLEY	LEWIS	DAYTON
WEST	CATTARAUGUS	ELLICOTTVILLE
W. ALABAMA	GENESEE	ALABAMA
W. ALBANY	ALBANY	COLONIE
W. ALDEN	ALLEGANY	ALLEN
W. ALDEN	ERIE	ALDEN
W. ALMOND	ALLEGANY	W. ALMOND
W. AMBOY	OSWEGO	AMBOY
W. AMHERST	ERIE	AMHERST
W. AMITYVILLE	SUFFOLK	BABYLON
W. ASHFORD	CATTARAUGUS	E. OTTO
W. ATHENS	GREENE	ATHENS
W. BABYLON	SUFFOLK	BABYLON
W. BAINBRIDGE	CHENANGO	BAINBRIDGE
W. BANGOR	FRANKLIN	BANGOR
W. BARRE	ORLEANS	BARRE
W. BEEKMANTOWN	CLINTON	BEEKMANTOWN
W. BELLMONT	FRANKLIN	BELLMONT
W. BERGEN	GENESEE	BERGEN
W. BERNE	ALBANY	BERNE
W. BETHANY	GENESEE	BETHANY
W. BLOOMFIELD	ONTARIO	W. BLOOMFIELD
W. BRANCH	ERIE	NO. COLLINS
W. BRANCH	ONEIDA	LEE
W. BRIGHTON	MONROE	BRIGHTON
W. BRIGHTON	RICHMOND	NYC
W. BROOK	DELAWARE	WALTON
W. BROOKLYN	KINGS	NYC
W. BROOKVILLE	SULLIVAN	MAMAKATING
W. BROOKVILLE	ORANGE	DEER PARK
W. BURLINGTON	OTSEGO	BURLINGTON
W. BUTLER	WAYNE	BUTLER
W. CAMBRIDGE	WASHINGTON	CAMBRIDGE
W. CAMDEN	ONEIDA	CAMDEN
W. CAMERON	STEUBEN	CAMERON
W. CAMP	ULSTER	SAUGERTIES
W. CANDOR	TIOGA	CANDOR
W. CARTHAGE V.	JEFFERSON	CHAMPION
W. CATON	STEUBEN	CATON
W. CHAZY	CLINTON	CHAZY
W. CHENANGO	BROOME	CHENANGO
W. CHESTER	BRONX	NYC
W. CLARKSON	MONROE	CLARKSON
W. CLARKSVILLE	ALLEGANY	CLARKSVILLE
W. COLESVILLE	BROOME	COLESVILLE
W. CONESVILLE	SCHOHARIE	CONESVILLE
W. COPAKE	COLUMBIA	COPAKE
W. CORNERS	BROOME	UNION
W. CORNWALL	ORANGE	CORNWALL
W. CORNWALL STA.	ORANGE	CORNWALL
W. COXSACKIE	GREENE	COXSACKIE
W. CRAIGVILLE	ORANGE	BLOOMING GR.
W. CRAIGVILLE STA.	ORANGE	BLOOMING GR.
W. DANBY	TOMPKINS	DANBY
W. DAVENPORT	DELAWARE	DAVENPORT
W. DAVENPORT STA.	DELAWARE	DAVENPORT
W. DAY	SARATOGA	DAY
W. DAYTON	CATTARAUGUS	DAYTON
W. DELHI	DELAWARE	DELHI
W. DRYDEN	TOMPKINS	DRYDEN
W. DURHAM	GREENE	DURHAM
W. EATON	MADISON	EATON
W. ELLERY	CHAUTAUQUA	ELLERY
W. ELMIRA	CHEMUNG	ELMIRA
W. ENDICOTT	BROOME	UNION
W. EXETER	OTSEGO	EXETER
W. FARMINGTON	ONTARIO	FARMINGTON
W. FARMS	BRONX	NYC
W. FAYETTE	SENECA	FAYETTE
W. FORT ANN	WASHINGTON	FORT ANN
W. FOWLER	ST.LAWRENCE	FOWLER
W. FULTON	SCHOHARIE	FULTON
W. GAINES	ORLEANS	GAINES
W. GHENT	COLUMBIA	GHENT
W. GILBOA	SCHOHARIE	GILBOA
W. GILGO BEACH	SUFFOLK	BABYLON
W. GLENS FALLS	WARREN	QUEENSBURY
W. GLENVILLE	SCHENECTADY	GLENVILLE
W. GRANBY	OSWEGO	GRANBY
W. GRANVILLE	WASHINGTON	GRANVILLE
W. GRANVILLE CORS.	WASHINGTON	GRANVILLE
W. GREECE	MONROE	GREECE
W. GREENFIELD	SARATOGA	GREENFIELD
W. GREENVILLE	GREENE	GREENVILLE
W. GREENWOOD	STEUBEN	GREENWOOD
W. GROTON	TOMPKINS	GROTON
W. HAMBURG	ERIE	HAMBURG
W. HARPERSFIELD	DELAWARE	KORTRIGHT
W. HAUPPAUGE	SUFFOLK	SMITHTOWN
W. HAVERSTRAW V.	ROCKLAND	HAVERSTRAW
W. HEBRON	WASHINGTON	HEBRON
W. HEMPSTEAD	NASSAU	HEMPSTEAD
W. HEMPSTEAD	MONROE	HENRIETTA
W. HENRIETTA	MONROE	HENRIETTA
W. HENRIETTA STA.	MONROE	HENRIETTA
W. HERKIMER	HERKIMER	HERKIMER
W. HILLS	SUFFOLK	HUNTINGTON
W. HOLLOW	ONTARIO	NAPLES
W. HOOSICK	RENSSELAER	HOOSICK
W. HURLEY	ULSTER	HURLEY
W. IRVING	CHAUTAUQUA	HANOVER
W. ISLIP	SUFFOLK	ISLIP
W. ITALY	YATES	ITALY
W. JUNIUS	ONTARIO	PHELPS
W. KILL	GREENE	LEXINGTON
W. KILNS	CLINTON	BLACK BROOK
W. KORTRIGHT	DELAWARE	KORTRIGHT
W. LAURENS	OTSEGO	LAURENS
W. LEBANON	COLUMBIA	NEW LEBANON
W. LOCKPORT	NIAGARA	LOCKPORT
W. LOWVILLE	LEWIS	LOWVILLE
W. MACEDON	WAYNE	MACEDON
W. MARTINSBURG	LEWIS	MARTINSBURG
W. MEREDITH	DELAWARE	MEREDITH
W. MIDDLE PATENT	WESTCHESTER	NO. CASTLE
W. MILTON	SARATOGA	MILTON
W. NECK	SUFFOLK	HUNTINGTON
W. NEW BRIGHTON	RICHMOND	NYC
W. NOTCH	ALLEGANY	WIRT
W. NUNDA STA.	LIVINGSTON	NUNDA
W. NYACK	ROCKLAND	CLARKSTOWN
W. ONEONTA	OTSEGO	ONEONTA
W. PARISHVILLE	ST.LAWRENCE	PARISHVILLE
W. PARK	ULSTER	ESOPUS
W. PATTERSON	PUTNAM	PATTERSON
W. PAWLETT	WASHINGTON	HEBRON
W. PAWLING	DUTCHESS	PAWLING
W. PAWLING STA.	DUTCHESS	PAWLING
W. PERRY	WYOMING	PERRY
W. PERRYSBURG	CATTARAUGUS	PERRYSBURG
W. PIERREPONT	ST.LAWRENCE	PIERREPONT
W. PLATTSBURG	CLINTON	PLATTSBURG
W. POINT	ORANGE	HIGHLANDS
W. POINT STA.	ORANGE	HIGHLANDS
W. POTSDAM	ST.LAWRENCE	POTSDAM
W. RICHFORD	TIOGA	RICHFORD
W. RICHMONDVILLE	SCHOHARIE	RICHMONDVILLE
W. RIVER	YATES	ITALY
W. RUSH	MONROE	RUSH
W. SAND LAKE	RENSSELAER	SAND LAKE
W. SAUGERTIES	ULSTER	SAUGERTIES
W. SAYVILLE	SUFFOLK	ISLIP
W. SCHUYLER	HERKIMER	SCHUYLER
W. SENECA	ERIE	W. SENECA
W. SENECA DEVEL. CENTER	ERIE	W. SENECA
W. SHELBY	ORLEANS	SHELBY
W. SHOKAN	ULSTER	OLIVE
W.S. & L.V. JCT	MONROE	HENRIETTA
W. SHORE GREENWOOD LAKE	ORANGE	WARWICK
W. SOMERS	WESTCHESTER	SOMERS
W. SOMERSET	NIAGARA	SOMERSET
W. SPARTA	LIVINGSTON	W. SPARTA
W. SPARTA STA.	LIVINGSTON	W. SPARTA
W. STEPHENTOWN	RENSSELAER	STEPHENTOWN
W. STOCKHOLM	ST.LAWRENCE	STOCKHOLM
W. STONY CREEK	WARREN	STONY CREEK
W. TAGHKANIC	COLUMBIA	TAGHKANIC
W. THERESA	JEFFERSON	THERESA
W. TIANA	SUFFOLK	SOUTHAMPTON
W. TOWNSHIP	ALBANY	KNOX
W. TROUPSBURG	STEUBEN	TROUPSBURG
W. UNION	STEUBEN	W. UNION
W. VALLEY	CATTARAUGUS	ASHFORD
W. VALLEY FALLS	RENSSELAER	SCHAGHTICOKE
W. VIENNA	ONEIDA	VIENNA
W. WALWORTH	WAYNE	WALWORTH
W. WATERFORD	SARATOGA	WATERFORD
W. WEBSTER	MONROE	WEBSTER
W. WINDSOR	BROOME	WINDSOR
W. WINFIELD V.	HERKIMER	WINFIELD
W. YORKSHIRE	CATTARAUGUS	YORKSHIRE
WESTBURY	CAYUGA	VICTORY
WESTBURY	WAYNE	BUTLER
WESTBURY V.	NASSAU	N. HEMPSTEAD
WESTDALE	ONEIDA	CAMDEN
WESTERLO	ALBANY	WESTERLO
WESTERNVILLE	ONEIDA	WESTERN
WESTFIELD V.	CHAUTAUQUA	WESTFIELD
WESTFORD	OTSEGO	WESTFORD
WESTHAMPTON	SUFFOLK	SOUTHAMPTON

NAME	COUNTY	TOWN
WESTHAMPTON BCH. V.	SUFFOLK	SOUTHAMPTON
WESTMERE	ALBANY	GUILDERLAND
WESTMINSTER	JEFFERSON	ALEXANDRIA
WESTMINSTER PK.	JEFFERSON	ALEXANDRIA
WESTMORELAND	ONEIDA	WESTMORELAND
WESTON	SCHUYLER	TYRONE
WESTON MILLS	CATTARAUGUS	PORTVILLE
WESTOVER	BROOME	UNION
WESTPORT STA.	ESSEX	WESTPORT
WESTPORT V.	ESSEX	WESTPORT
WESTTOWN	ORANGE	MINISINK
WESTVIEW	LIVINGSTON	OSSIAN
WESTVILLE	FRANKLIN	WESTVILLE
WESTVILLE	OTSEGO	WESTFORD
WESTVILLE CTR.	FRANKLIN	WESTVILLE
WETHERSFIELD SPGS.	WYOMING	WETHERSFIELD
WETMORE	LEWIS	MARTINSBURG
WEVERTOWN	WARREN	JOHNSBURG
WEYS CROSSING	DUTCHESS	RHINEBECK
WHALEY LAKE	DUTCHESS	PAWLING
WHALLONSBURG	ESSEX	ESSEX
WHARTON	OTSEGO	BURLINGTON
WHEATLAND	MONROE	WHEATLAND
WHEATLAND CTR.	MONROE	WHEATLAND
WHEATVILLE	GENESEE	ALABAMA
WHEATVILLE STA.	GENESEE	ALABAMA
WHEELER	OSWEGO	HANNIBAL
WHEELER	STEUBEN	WHEELER
WHEELER CTR. STA.	STEUBEN	WHEELER
WHEELER HOLLOW	ERIE	CONCORD
WHEELERTOWN	HERKIMER	RUSSIA
WHEELERVILLE	FULTON	CAROGA
WHIG HOLLOW	CLINTON	BEEKMANTOWN
WHIPPLEVILLE	FRANKLIN	MALONE
WHIRLPOOL ST. PARK	NIAGARA	LEWISTON
WHITE CHURCH	TOMPKINS	CAROLINE
WHITE CITY	MONROE	IRONDEQUOIT
WHITE CREEK	WASHINGTON	WHITE CREEK
WHITE CREEK STA.	RENSSELAER	HOOSICK
WHITE HOUSE	HAMILTON	WELLS
WHITE HOUSE	CATTARAUGUS	PORTVILLE
WHITE LAKE	SULLIVAN	BETHEL
WHITE LAKE	ONEIDA	FORESTPORT
WHITE LK. CORS.	ONEIDA	FORESTPORT
WHITE LK. STA.	ONEIDA	FORESTPORT
WHITE MARTINDALE CORS.	WASHINGTON	WHITE CREEK
WHITE MILLS	COLUMBIA	CHATHAM
WHITE PLAINS C.	WESTCHESTER	WHITE PLAINS C.
WHITE STORE	CHENANGO	NORWICH
WHITE SULPHUR SPGS.	SULLIVAN	LIBERTY
WHITEFACE	ESSEX	NO. ELBA
WHITEHALL CORS.	WESTCHESTER	SOMERS
WHITEHALL V.	WASHINGTON	WHITEHALL
WHITELAW	MADISON	LENOX
WHITEPORT	ULSTER	ROSENDALE
WHITES	MONROE	CHILI
WHITES	CAYUGA	FLEMING
WHITES CORS.	MADISON	EATON
WHITESBORO V.	ONEIDA	WHITESTOWN
WHITESIDE CORS.	SARATOGA	GALWAY
WHITESIDES	CHAUTAUQUA	ELLERY
WHITESTONE	QUEENS	NYC
WHITESTOWN	ONEIDA	WHITESTOWN
WHITESVILLE	ALLEGANY	INDEPENDENCE
WHITESVILLE	JEFFERSON	RODMAN
WHITFIELD	ULSTER	ROCHESTER
WHITFORD CORS.	JEFFERSON	RODMAN
WHITMAN	DELAWARE	MASONVILLE
WHITNEY	HAMILTON	LONG LAKE
WHITNEY CROSS	ALLEGANY	BURNS
WHITNEY PT. V.	BROOME	TRIANGLE
WHITNEYS	HAMILTON	LONG LAKE
WHITTEMORE	OSWEGO	VOLNEY
WHITTEMORE	TIOGA	OWEGO
WHITTEMORE HILL	TIOGA	OWEGO
WICCOPEE	PUTNAM	PUTNAM VALLEY
WICCOPEE	DUTCHESS	E. FISHKILL
WICK	ST. LAWRENCE	PARISHVILLE
WICKAPOGUE	SUFFOLK	SOUTHAMPTON
WICKHAM VILLAGE	ORANGE	WARWICK
WIEDMAN	FRANKLIN	SANTA CLARA
WILBERS STA.	CHENANGO	SMYRNA
WILCOXVILLE	JEFFERSON	LYME
WILEYVILLE	STEUBEN	W. UNION
WILHELM	ERIE	LANCASTER
WILLARD	SENECA	OVID
WILLARD PSYCHIATRIC CTR.	SENECA	OVID
WILLARD PSYCHIATRIC CTR.	SENECA	ROMULUS
WILLARD STA.	CHENANGO	GREENE
WILLET	CORTLAND	WILLET
WILLET	CAYUGA	LEDYARD
WILLET PT.	QUEENS	NYC
WILLIAMS BRIDGE	BRONX	NYC
WILLIAMS CORS.	MADISON	EATON
WILLIAMSON	WAYNE	WILLIAMSON
WILLIAMSTOWN	OSWEGO	WILLIAMSTOWN
WILLIAMSVILLE V.	ERIE	AMHERST
WILLIS POND	FRANKLIN	ALTAMONT
WILLISTON	ERIE	MARILLA
WILLISTON PK. V.	NASSAU	N. HEMPSTEAD
WILLOW	ULSTER	WOODSTOCK
WILLOW BROOK	DUTCHESS	STANFORD
WILLOW BROOK	RICHMOND	NYC
WILLOW CREEK	TOMPKINS	ULYSSES
WILLOW GLEN	TOMPKINS	DRYDEN
WILLOW GLEN	SARATOGA	STILLWATER
WILLOW GROVE	ROCKLAND	STONY POINT
WILLOW GROVE	ROCKLAND	HAVERSTRAW
WILLOW PT.	BROOME	VESTAL
WILLOWEMOC	SULLIVAN	NEVERSINK
WILLOWVALE	ONEIDA	NEW HARTFORD
WILLSBORO	ESSEX	WILLSBORO
WILLSBORO PT.	ESSEX	WILLSBORO
WILLSBORO STA.	ESSEX	WILLSBORO
WILLSE FOUR CORS.	HERKIMER	STARK
WILLSEYVILLE	TIOGA	CANDOR
WILMINGTON	ESSEX	WILMINGTON
WILMURT	HERKIMER	OHIO
WILMURT CORS.	HERKIMER	OHIO
WILNA	JEFFERSON	WILNA
WILNA FARGO	JEFFERSON	WILNA
WILNA STA.	JEFFERSON	WILNA
WILSON CORS.	CAYUGA	MORAVIA
WILSON V.	NIAGARA	WILSON
WILTON	SARATOGA	WILTON
WILTON DEVELOPMENTAL CTR.	SARATOGA	WILTON
WINDECKER	LEWIS	HARRISBURG
WINDHAM	GREENE	WINDHAM
WINDOM	ERIE	ORCHARD PARK
WINDSOR BEACH	MONROE	IRONDEQUOIT
WINDSOR V.	BROOME	WINDSOR
WINFIELD JCT.	QUEENS	NYC
WING	WYOMING	EAGLE
WINGDALE	DUTCHESS	DOVER
WINONA	JEFFERSON	LORRAINE
WINONA LAKE	ORANGE	NEWBURGH
WINTERTON	SULLIVAN	MAMAKATING
WINTHROP	ST. LAWRENCE	STOCKHOLM
WIRT CENTER	ALLEGANY	WIRT
WISCOY	ALLEGANY	HUME
WISNER	ORANGE	WARWICK
WITHERBEE	ESSEX	MORIAH
WITHEY	ALLEGANY	AMITY
WITTENBERG	ULSTER	WOODSTOCK
WOLCOTT V.	WAYNE	WOLCOTT
WOLCOTT V.	WAYNE	BUTLER
WOLCOTTBURG	ERIE	CLARENCE
WOLCOTTVILLE	NIAGARA	ROYALTON
WOLF CREEK	ALLEGANY	GENESEE
WOLF HILL	ALBANY	NEW SCOTLAND
WOLF POND	FRANKLIN	BELLMONT
WOLF RUN	CATTARAUGUS	ELKO
WOLF SWAMP	FRANKLIN	FORT COVINGTON
WOOD FALLS	CLINTON	MOOERS
WOOD ROW	RICHMOND	NYC
WOODBOURNE	SULLIVAN	FALLSBURG
WOODBOURNE CORR. FAC.	SULLIVAN	FALLSBURG
WOODBRIDGE CORS.	ST. LAWRENCE	CANTON
WOODBURY	ORANGE	WOODBURY
WOODBURY FLS.	ORANGE	WOODBURY
WOODBURY STA.	ORANGE	WOODBURY
WOODFORD	DELAWARE	WALTON
WOODGATE	ONEIDA	FORESTPORT
WOODHAVEN	QUEENS	NYC
WOODHAVEN JCT.	QUEENS	NYC
WOODHULL	ONEIDA	FORESTPORT
WOODHULL V.	STEUBEN	WOODHULL
WOODLAND	ULSTER	SHANDAKEN
WOODLAND BEACH	ERIE	HAMBURG
WOODLANDS	WESTCHESTER	GREENBURGH
WOODLAWN	ERIE	HAMBURG
WOODLAWN	SCHENECTADY	ROTTERDAM
WOODLAWN	BRONX	NYC
WOODLAWN BEACH	ERIE	HAMBURG
WOODMERE	NASSAU	HEMPSTEAD
WOODMERY	QUEENS	NYC
WOODRIDGE V.	SULLIVAN	FALLSBURG
WOODS	ST. LAWRENCE	CANTON
WOODS	JEFFERSON	WILNA
WOODS CORS.	STEUBEN	TUSCARORA
WOODS CORS.	CHENANGO	NORWICH
WOODS MILL	CAYUGA	SCIPIO
WOODS MILLS	JEFFERSON	WILNA
WOODS MILLS	CLINTON	SCHUYLER FALLS
WOODS OF ARDEN	RICHMOND	NYC
WOODS SETT.	JEFFERSON	WILNA
WOODS STA.	CHENANGO	NORWICH
WOODSBRIDGE	WESTCHESTER	SOMERS
WOODSBURGH V.	NASSAU	HEMPSTEAD

NAME	COUNTY	TOWN
WOODSIDE	ERIE	CONCORD
WOODSIDE	QUEENS	NYC
WOODSTOCK	ULSTER	WOODSTOCK
WOODVILLE	JEFFERSON	ELLISBURG
WOODVILLE	LIVINGSTON	W. SPARTA
WOODVILLE	ONTARIO	SO. BRISTOL
WOODVILLE P.O.	JEFFERSON	ELLISBURG
WOOGLIN	CHAUTAUQUA	CHAUTAUQUA
WORCESTER	OTSEGO	WORCESTER
WORTH	JEFFERSON	WORTH
WORTH CENTER	JEFFERSON	WORTH
WORTHINGTON	WESTCHESTER	GREENBURGH
WORTHVILLE	JEFFERSON	WORTH
WRECK LEAD	NASSAU	HEMPSTEAD
WRIGHT	TIOGA	CANDOR
WRIGHT	WASHINGTON	PUTNAM
WRIGHT CORS.	WYOMING	MIDDLEBURY
WRIGHT CORS.	NIAGARA	LOCKPORT
WRIGHT SETTLEMENT	ONEIDA	ROME C.
WRIGHT STATION	WASHINGTON	PUTNAM
WRIGHTS	NIAGARA	LOCKPORT
WRIGHTS CORS.	HERKIMER	LITTLE FALLS
WRIGHTS CORS.	NIAGARA	NEWFANE
WRIGHTSON	OSWEGO	PARISH
WURTEMBURG	DUTCHESS	RHINEBECK
WURTSBORO V.	SULLIVAN	MAMAKATING
WYANDALE	ERIE	CONCORD
WYANDANCH	SUFFOLK	BABYLON
WYCKOFF	CAYUGA	FLEMING
WYCKOFF STA.	CAYUGA	FLEMING
WYNANTSKILL	RENSSELAER	NO. GREENBUSH
WYOMANOCK	RENSSELAER	STEPHENTOWN
WYOMING STA.	WYOMING	MIDDLEBURY
WYOMING V.	WYOMING	MIDDLEBURY

-Y-

YAGERVILLE	ULSTER	ROCHESTER
YALEVILLE	ST. LAWRENCE	POTSDAM
YALEVILLE	CHENANGO	GUILFORD
YANKEE LAKE	SULLIVAN	MAMAKATING
YAPHANK	SUFFOLK	BROOKHAVEN
YATES CENTER	ORLEANS	YATES
YATESVILLE	MONTGOMERY	ROOT
YATESVILLE	YATES	JERUSALEM
YEAGER JCT.	CATTARAUGUS	RED HOUSE
YONKERS C.	WESTCHESTER	YONKERS C.
YORK	LIVINGSTON	YORK
YORK	ST. LAWRENCE	CANTON
YORK CORS.	SARATOGA	GALWAY
YORKSHIRE	CATTARAUGUS	YORKSHIRE
YORKTOWN	WESTCHESTER	YORKTOWN
YORKTOWN HGTS.	WESTCHESTER	YORKTOWN
YORKVILLE V.	ONEIDA	WHITESTOWN
YOST	MONTGOMERY	MOHAWK
YOUNG HICKORY	STEUBEN	TROUPSBURG
YOUNG'S CAMP	ST. LAWRENCE	HOFKINTON
YOUNG'S CROSSING	HERKIMER	COLUMBIA
YOUNGPORT	SUFFOLK	ISLIP
YOUNGS	DELAWARE	SIDNEY
YOUNGSTOWN V.	NIAGARA	PORTER
YOUNGSVILLE	SULLIVAN	CALLICOON
YULAN	SULLIVAN	HIGHLAND

-Z-

ZABRISKIE	SARATOGA	EDINBURG
ZELLIF MILL	CATTARAUGUS	RED HOUSE
ZENA	ULSTER	WOODSTOCK
ZOAR	ERIE	COLLINS
ZOAR	CATTARAUGUS	OTTO
ZOAR	JEFFERSON	RODMAN
ZURICH	WAYNE	ARCADIA

Part Three

The Formation and Origins of New York's Present-Day Sixty-Two Counties

(with Appendix)

Source: John H. French, *Historical and Statistical Gazetteer of New York State*, Syracuse, NY, 1860.

ALBANY COUNTY - Formed November 1, 1683. An original county. Counties taken off: Tryon County and Charlotte County (now Montgomery County and Washington County respectively), March 12, 1772; Columbia County, April 4, 1786; Saratoga County and Rensselaer County, February 7, 1791; portion of Schoharie County, April 6, 1795; portion of Greene County, March 25, 1800.

ALLEGANY COUNTY - Formed April 7, 1806 from Genesee County; portion of Steuben County annexed March 11, 1808. Counties taken off: portion of Livingston County, February 23, 1821, and all of Wyoming County, May 14, 1841.

BRONX COUNTY - Formed 1914 from New York County.

BROOME COUNTY - Formed March 28, 1806 from Tioga County. Towns of Berkshire and Owego annexed March 21, 1822 to Tioga County.

CATTARAUGUS COUNTY - Formed March 11, 1808 from Genesee County.

CAYUGA COUNTY - Formed March 8, 1799 from Onondaga County. Counties taken off: Seneca County, March 29, 1804, and a portion of Tompkins County, April 17, 1817.

CHARLOTTE COUNTY - see Washington County.

CHAUTAUQUA COUNTY - Formed March 11, 1808 from Genesee County.

CHEMUNG COUNTY - Formed March 29, 1836 from Tioga County. Portion of Schuyler County taken off April 17, 1854.

CHENANGO COUNTY - Formed March 15, 1798 from Herkimer County and Tioga County. Town of Sangerfield taken off to Oneida County, April 4, 1804. Madison County taken off March 21, 1806.

CLINTON COUNTY - Formed March 7, 1788 from Washington County. St. Lawrence County provisionally annexed 1801 and taken off 1802. Counties taken off: Essex County, March 1, 1799, and Franklin County, March 11, 1808. (See Lisbon note under ONEIDA COUNTY entry.)

COLUMBIA COUNTY - Formed April 4, 1786 from Albany County.

CORTLAND COUNTY - formed April 8, 1808 from Onondaga County.

DELAWARE COUNTY - Formed March 10, 1797 from Otsego County and Ulster County.

DUTCHESS COUNTY - Formed November 1, 1683. An original county. Provisionally annexed to Ulster County and first represented separately in the General Assembly in 1713. Livingston Manor annexed to Albany County, 1717. Putnam County taken off June 12, 1812.

ERIE COUNTY - Formed April 2, 1821 from Niagara County.

ESSEX COUNTY - Formed March 1, 1799 from Clinton County. A portion annexed to Franklin County in 1808. Small portion annexed from Franklin County, March 22, 1822.

FRANKLIN COUNTY - Formed March 11, 1808 from Clinton County. Small portion annexed to Essex County, March 22, 1822.

FULTON COUNTY - Formed April 18, 1838 from Montgomery County.

GENESEE COUNTY - Formed March 30, 1802 from Ontario County. Counties taken off: Allegany County, April 7, 1806; Cattaraugus County, Chautauqua County, and Niagara County, March 11, 1808; portions of Livingston County and Monroe County, February 23, 1821; Orleans County, November 11, 1824; and all of Wyoming County, May 14, 1841.

GREENE COUNTY - Formed March 25, 1800 from Albany County and Ulster County. Portions annexed to Ulster County, May 26, 1812.

HAMILTON COUNTY - Formed February 12, 1816 from Montgomery County. "[B]ut its independent organization has never been fully completed (as of 1860). This territory was included in Herkimer County 16 Feb 1791 but was re-annexed to Montgomery County 31 Mar 1797. It can complete its organization when it has a sufficient population to entitle it to a member of Assembly. It remained annexed to Montgomery County until 1838 when it was annexed to Fulton on the erection of the latter county. Courts were established in 1837."

HERKIMER COUNTY - Formed February 16, 1791 from Montgomery County. Onondaga County was taken off March 5, 1794. Oneida County and a portion of Chenango County were taken off in 1798. Parts of Montgomery County were annexed April 7, 1817 and parts of the towns of Richfield and Plainfield, Otsego County were annexed in forming Winfield, April 17, 1816. (See HAMILTON COUNTY entry and end note under ONEIDA COUNTY entry).

JEFFERSON COUNTY - Formed March 28, 1805 from Oneida County. A portion of the town of Rodman was set off to Lewis County in 1809. A portion of the town of Wilna was formed from Leyden (Lewis County), April 2, 1813.

KINGS COUNTY - Formed November 1, 1683. An original county. "From 1665 to 1683 this county was a part of the 'West Riding of Yorkshire, England.'" (See related note under the QUEENS COUNTY postings).

LEWIS COUNTY - Formed March 28, 1805 from Oneida County.

LIVINGSTON COUNTY - Formed March 28, 1821 from Genesee County and Ontario County. One portion of Allegany County was annexed in 1846 and another portion in 1856.

MADISON COUNTY - Formed March 21, 1806 from Chenango County. Portion of the town of Stockbridge formed from parts of Augusta and Vernon (both in Oneida County) in 1836.

MONROE COUNTY - Formed February 23, 1821 from Genesee County and Ontario County.

MONTGOMERY COUNTY - Formed from Albany County, March 12, 1772 in the name Tryon County with name changed April 2, 1784. Counties taken off: Ontario County, January 27, 1789; Herkimer County, Otsego County and Tioga County, February 16, 1791; Hamilton County, February 12, 1816 (see note under HAMILTON COUNTY entry); Fulton County, April 18, 1838 (see end note under ONEIDA COUNTY entry).

NASSAU COUNTY - Formed 1899 from Queens County.

NEW YORK COUNTY - Formed November 1, 1683. An original county.

NIAGARA COUNTY - Formed March 11, 1808 from Genesee County. Erie County taken off April 2, 1821.

ONEIDA COUNTY - Formed March 15, 1798 from Herkimer County. Lewis County and Jefferson County taken off in 1805 and a portion of Oswego County, 1816. Portions annexed to Clinton

County, 1801 and to Madison County in 1836. Town of Sangerfield transferred from Chenango County to Oneida County, April 4, 1804. Note: Montgomery County, Herkimer County, and Oneida County originally extended in long, narrow strips northward to the St. Lawrence River. In 1801 Lisbon, then an immense town upon the north border, was annexed to Clinton County.

ONONDAGA COUNTY - Formed March 5, 1794 from Herkimer County. Cayuga County taken off March 8, 1799; Cortland County, April 8, 1808; portion of Oswego County, March 1, 1816.

ONTARIO COUNTY - Formed January 27, 1789 from Montgomery County. Steuben County taken off March 18, 1796; Genesee County, March 30, 1802; portions of Livingston County and Monroe County, February 23, 1821; Yates County and part of Wayne County, February 5, 1823; strip annexed from Montgomery County west of Seneca Lake, February 16, 1791, and a small tract in the fork of Crooked Lake from Steuben County, February 25, 1814.

ORANGE COUNTY - Formed November 1, 1683. An original county. Rockland County taken off February 23, 1798 and a portion was annexed from Ulster County in that same year.

ORLEANS COUNTY - Formed November 11, 1824 from Genesee County. Town of Shelby annexed from Genesee County, April 5, 1825.

OSWEGO COUNTY - Formed March 1, 1816 from Oneida County and Onondaga County.

OTSEGO COUNTY - Formed February 16, 1791 from Montgomery County. Part of Schoharie County taken off April 6, 1795 and part of Delaware County, March 10, 1797.

PUTNAM COUNTY - Formed June 12, 1812 from Dutchess County.

QUEENS COUNTY - Formed November 1, 1683. An original county. Note: "By a convention held at Hempstead, Long Island in 1665 Staten Island (now Richmond County) and a part of Westchester County were erected into a shire called 'Yorkshire' for the purpose of holding courts and administering justice. This was subdivided into 'Ridings' known as 'East Riding' (Suffolk County), 'West Riding' (Kings County, Staten Island and Newtown), and 'North Riding' (Queens County except Newtown)."

RENSSELAER COUNTY - Formed February 7, 1791 from Albany County.

RICHMOND COUNTY - Formed November 1, 1683. An original county. "It includes Staten Island, Shooters Island and the islands of the meadow in Staten Island Sound." See the note under QUEENS COUNTY.

ROCKLAND COUNTY - Formed February 23, 1798 from Orange County.

ST. LAWRENCE COUNTY - Formed March 3, 1802 from Clinton County and parts of Montgomery County and Herkimer County.

SARATOGA COUNTY - Formed February 7, 1791 from Albany County.

SCHENECTADY COUNTY - Formed March 7, 1809 from Albany County.

SCHOHARIE COUNTY - Formed April 6, 1795 from Albany County and Otsego County.

SCHUYLER COUNTY - Formed April 17, 1854 from Chemung County, Steuben County, and Tompkins County.

SENECA COUNTY - Formed March 29, 1804 from Cayuga County. Part of Tompkins County taken off in 1817 and part of Wayne County, 1823.

STEUBEN COUNTY - Formed March 18, 1796 from Ontario County. Parts annexed to Allegany County, March 11, 1808; Ontario County, February 25, 1814; Livingston County, February 15, 1822; Schuyler County, April 7, 1854.

SUFFOLK COUNTY - Formed November 1, 1683. An original county. See note under QUEENS COUNTY.

SULLIVAN COUNTY - Formed March 27, 1809 from Ulster County.

TIOGA COUNTY - Formed February 16, 1791 from Montgomery County. Part of Chenango County taken off March 15, 1798, all of Broome County, March 28, 1806, part of Tompkins County, March 22, 1822, and all of Chemung County, March 29, 1836.

TOMPKINS COUNTY - Formed April 17, 1817 from Cayuga County and Seneca County. Three towns from Tioga County annexed March 22, 1822 and part of Schuyler County taken off in 1854.

TRYON COUNTY - see Montgomery County.

ULSTER COUNTY - Formed November 1, 1683. An original county. Part of Delaware County taken off March 10, 1797, part of Greene County, March 25, 1800, and all of Sullivan County, March 27, 1809. Town of Catskill annexed from Albany County, April 5, 1798.

WARREN COUNTY - Formed March 12, 1813 from Washington County.

WASHINGTON COUNTY - Formed from Albany County, March 12, 1772 as Charlotte County with name changed April 2, 1784. Clinton County taken off March 7, 1788; eastern segment ceded to Vermont in 1790; southern strip annexed from Albany County, February 7, 1791; Warren County taken off March 12, 1813. February 7, 1791, towns of Cambridge and Easton annexed from Albany County.

WAYNE COUNTY - Formed April 11, 1823 from Ontario County and Seneca County.

WESTCHESTER COUNTY - Formed November 1, 1683. An original county. See the note under QUEENS COUNTY.

WYOMING COUNTY - Formed May 14, 1841 from Genseee County. Towns of Eagle, Pike, and a part of Portage were annexed from Allegany County in 1846.

YATES COUNTY - Formed February 5, 1823 from Ontario County.

APPENDIX TO PART 3

The following illustrates the complications caused by rapid expansion in New York, roughly 1790-1850, concerning the formation of counties and towns.

Assume that there is a searcher whose family notes indicate only that his or her ancestor John Doe married Mary Roe in the late 1850's in Schuyler County, New York and that John's Doe ancestors reportedly had lived continuously in that county "from earliest times". Assume further that this searcher initially scans New York's U.S. Census indexes for any Does in Schuyler County from 1850 back through 1790 inclusive without exception. As quickly revealed in Part 3, this person is doomed for total failure. There was no Schuyler County as early as 1850. If this searcher opts to pursue his Doe ancestry through these NY Census indexes he might well quickly jot down from postings in Part 3 here, prior to index scannings, a note similar to the following concerning counties to be reviewed periodically:

> For the former Chemung County segment of Schuyler County check these county indexes: Chemung 1850, 1840; Tioga 1830, 1820, 1810, 1800; Montgomery 1790.

> For the former Steuben County segment of Schuyler County check these county indexes: Steuben 1850 back through 1800 inclusive; Ontario 1790.

> For the former Tompkins County segment of Schuyler County check these county indexes: Tompkins 1850 back through 1820 inclusive; Cayuga 1810, 1800; Herkimer, 1790; also (from the Seneca County branch of Tompkins County) Seneca, 1810.

Summary: To check census records 1790 through 1850 for families thought to have been living continuously from earliest times "just anywhere" within the territory of present-day Schuyler County the searcher may need to scan census indexes for as many as nine different counties.

The above illustration is, of course, an extreme one. However, New York-concerned searchers, particularly those seeking ancestors in the pre-1850 period who were then settled in central or western New York, are advised, before proceeding, to check county-related information in Part 3 here and town-related information in French's *Gazetteer* of previous reference here, where warranted. As an extreme illustration town-wise assume that the above John Doe had been seeking the same ancestors who were thought to have been living continuously in the town of Huron in present-day Wayne County. French's *Gazetteer* statements <u>town-wise</u> and county-wise lead the searcher to post the following notes pertaining to census scannings:

> Huron, Wayne Co., 1850, 1840; Port Bay, Wayne Co., 1830; Wolcott, Seneca Co., 1820, 1810; Washington, Cayuga Co., 1800; reportedly an unsettled region in 1790.

TOWNS AND FAMILIES OF ONTARIO

COUNTY, NEW YORK - 1790*

by Fred Q. Bowman

It took New York (first settled in 1624 in today's Albany area) no fewer than 232 years (1683-1914) to form its present-day sixty-two counties. In 1683 this colony was divided into ten counties with Albany, the largest one, then spanning an area equivalent to that of New Hampshire, Massachusetts, Rhode Island, Connecticut, New Jersey, Delaware and Maryland combined. Within the interval 1683 through census-time 1790 five additional counties were formed from within Albany's original bounds with Ontario, the county of present concern, formed last of all (January 27, 1789). This newest and most westerly county then covered an area 20% larger than that of Massachusetts and Rhode Island combined. Within the period 1791 through 1841 forty-four counties of various sizes were struck off from the existing ones statewide. Within the span 1854 through 1914 the final three counties were formed in this state.

If the over-all rate of county formations in New York is viewed as relatively casual (Massachusetts, in contrast, acquired its fourteen counties within the period 1643-1812 and Connecticut its eight within the span 1666-1785) then its rate of town formations must be interpreted as super casual. Throughout the colonial period local areas, as revealed on maps and land records, were most frequently defined as manors and patents. In the 1700's several local areas in various counties were formed into precincts. Within the period roughly 1770 to 1800 several of the counties, including Ontario, were sub-divided into districts. Relatively seldom found in colonial New York were references to towns. Most of these were widely scattered with their boundaries in most cases not clearly drawn.

It was not until 1788, the year New York gained statehood, that for the first time all the land in this state was carved into towns - 120 in number. In size, most of these bore little resemblance to their counterparts throughout New England. For example between 1788 and 1796 Palatine, then the second largest town, extended in a swath more than twenty miles wide straight north from the Mohawk River more than 130 miles to the Canadian border. Whitestown, the largest town, reportedly covered all of New York lying to the west of the present-day city of Utica (see Julia Boyer-Reinstein's map, "120 Towns of New York State in 1788", Cheektowaga, 1957, available in the State Archives). J.H. French (*Historical and Statistical Gazetteer of New York State*, Syracuse, 1860, pg. 471) states that "Whitestown...originally included an indefinite amount of territory extending westward, at the present time forming several counties."

In 1790 the assigned census enumerator, Amos Hall of Genesee, could find in all of Ontario County a total of only four of what he then called districts (not towns as specified in *Heads of Families* for New York, pg. 138) with a *cumulative* population of 1075 persons. Fifty years later those enumerators of the 1840 census whose cumulative assignments spanned the area of this original Ontario County were able to find 480,000 persons living in 230 towns spread across thirteen counties.

This rapid increase in this state in the numbers of towns and counties formed within the period roughly 1790 through 1840 can cause complications for the New York-concerned searcher. The following insert covers most points in this regard (the town of central concern, Huron, abuts on the northeast corner of the original Ontario County):

Assume that a person presently living in California writes as follows to a genealogist living in Lyons, Wayne County, New York: "Our undocumented family notes indicate that three generations of my ancestors in the uncommon surname STANDFAST lived continuously in one house on one plot in Huron, Wayne County *from the close of the Revolutionary War through 1840 minimally*. If you are

* This article is reprinted with the publisher's permission.
Bowman, Fred Q. 1993. Towns and Families of Ontario County, New York - 1790. *Heritage Quest*, (46):54-57.

willing to abstract for me in your hometown county seat of Lyons any and all land and probate records you can find in the above surname but confined within the bounds of Huron within the time period underlined above, please send me a rough estimate of the total cost involved." The hypothesized genealogist might fairly respond thus: "In order to complete this surface-seeming straightforward assignment I must travel round trip 270 miles. Along the way I must conduct twelve sub-searches spread across six counties (in seven names) with my cumulative scannings confined to no fewer than six residence-town names as illustrated within the following outline (data from J.H. French, *Historical and Statistical Gazetteer of New York State*, Syracuse, 1860). (See Illustration #1 on next page.)

At census time 1790 the eastern boundary of Ontario County was a north-south line (the earlier-formed "Old Preemption Line") which extended from Lake Ontario to the Pennsylvania line and passed immediately to the west of the present site of Geneva (formed as an incorporated village April 4, 1806). Dividing this mammoth sized county roughly in half east to west is the Genesee River which flows north from the Pennsylvania line to empty into Lake Ontario near the present city of Rochester. Orsamus Turner (*History of the Settlement of Phelps and Gorham's Purchase and Morris' Reserve*, Rochester, 1851, pg. 480) in his summary of the 1790 census for Ontario County indicates that only 23 of the 204 family heads identified in total countywide by census-enumerator Amos Hall then lived anywhere west of this mid-line Genesee River. These family heads then reported cumulatively in their households (including themselves) 69 males, 54 females and 4 free black persons. A summary concerning Hall's county-wide census postings, by district of report, follows. (See Illustration #2 on next page.):

As will be seen the 465 residents of the Canandaiguay district were then living within an area which by census time 1790 had acquired at least six towns and which by 1838 would contain at least six additional ones.

The section of Ontario County which lay to the west of the Genesee River remained relatively unsettled until after 1800 (Turner's *Pioneer History of the Holland Purchase of Western New York*, Buffalo, 1850, 670 pages). The first town within this region (Batavia) was not formed until 1802 (French, pg. 324). In contrast, as early as census-time 1790 there were formed in this county east of this river no fewer than twenty towns (according to French) although Hall at census time 1790 was able to find settlers in only eleven of these communities.

Sources tapped for the town-centered postings to follow include Hall's original 1790 census report on microfilm, French's Gazetteer (primarily to determine dates of formations of towns and counties), Tuner's Phelps-Gorham book, especially pages 479-480, (to note his redistributions of the Hall-defined family heads within 29 specially titled sub-regions formed in 1788-89 within Ontario County), and George E. Lookup's 286-page *Index to the Pioneer Settlement of Phelps and Gorham's Purchase and Morris Reserve*, Newark, NY, 1973(?) (to convert Turner's sub-region postings to present-day towns through use of Lookup's charts found in the foreword to his book).

The sequence of name postings (on pages 91 and 92) is precisely that found on Hall's original census report. For example, Benjamin Tuttle of the town of Seneca and John D. Robinson of the town of Phelps are reported by Hall simply as "next door neighbors" in the district of Canandaiguay. The letter C, E, G or J symbolizing Canandaiguay, Erwin, Genesee or Jerusalem and found to the left of the name of each town of report, reflects the name of the original but no longer extant district within the bounds of which the town of reference now lies. The numbers found to the right of the family heads' names reflect males age 16 or older, males under age 16, females all ages and, where applicable, free black persons and slaves respectively.

Illustration #1

Date span to be covered in twelve sub-searchs	Town name to be sought	County within which the town then lay	Town where search must be conducted (County Seat)
End of War (1782)-4/1/1784	r.u.r.*	Tryon**	Fonda
4/2/1784-2/15/1791	r.u.r.*	Montgomery**	Fonda
2/16/1791-3/4/1794	r.u.r.*	Herkimer	Herkimer
3/5/1794-3/7/1799	Romulus	Onondaga	Syracuse
3/8/1799-3/13/1800	Ramulus	Cayuga	Auburn
3/14/1800-2/11/1803	Washington	Cayuga	Auburn
2/12/1803-3/28/1804	Junius	Cayuga	Auburn
3/29/1804-3/23/1807	Junius	Seneca	Waterloo
3/24/1807-4/10/1823	Wolcott	Seneca	Waterloo
4/11/1823-2/24/1826	Wolcott	Wayne	Lyons
2/25/1826-3/16/1834	Port Bay	Wayne	Lyons
3/17/1834-12/31/1840	Huron	Wayne	Lyons

*reportedly an unsettled region
**Montgomery County was formed March 12, 1772 in the name Tryon. Its name was changed to Montgomery April 2, 1784.

My total cost estimate:

270 miles of travel (Lyons to Fonda and return) at 20 cents per mile	$54.00
New York State Thruway tolls round trip	$8.60
Parking garage fee (Syracuse center city)	$5.00
6 hours travel time (Thruway speed limit 55 mph) at $7.00 per hour	$42.00
Overnight lodging	$45.00
12 hrs of search (2 hrs per county-seat search site) at 20 dollars per hour	$240.00
Total cost estimate	$394.60

If the entire search could have been confined to Lyons, as you had originally visualized, the total cost would have been between $40 and $60 probably..."

Illustration #2

Name of district	Number of family heads	Number of males	Number of females	Number of free blacks	Number of slaves	Total number of persons
Canandaiguay	89	351	111	1	2	465
Erwin	31	92	69	0	7	168
Genesee	68	214	122	5	2	343
Jerusalem	16	59	40	0	0	99
Totals	204	716	342	6	11	1075

The updated residence towns of Ontario County's families of 1790 here follow.

C-Seneca (Ontario Co.) formed Jan. 1789:
Latty, James 4 3 4
Benton, David 2 2 1
Wheeton, Samuel 6 0 4
Rice, (given name lacking) 5 0 0
Smith, David 3 0 0
Pierce, Phineas 2 1 2
Forsyth, Easther 2 3 2
Smith, Thomas 2 3 2
Smith, Harry 3 1 2
Barden, Thomas 1 0 0
Reed, Seth, Esq. 12 3 3
Whitney, Jonathan 5 0 1
Warner, Solomon 3 0 0
Okes, (given name lacking) 3 0 0
Kilbourn, Joseph 3 1 6
Whitcomb, John 2 0 2
Tuttle, Benjamin 2 1 4

C-Phelps (Ontario Co.) formed Jan. 1789:
Robinson, John D. 2 3 4
Granger, Pierce 2 0 0

C-Potter (Yates Co.) formed 4/26/1832 from Middlesex:
Briggs, Francis 1 2 2
Pierce, Michael 1 3 1
Tibbet, Benjamin 1 0 2
Hall, William 2 0 0
Potter, Arnold 1 3 1 0

C-Hopewell (Ontario Co.) formed 3/29/1822 from Gorham:
Gates Daniel 2 0 0
Sweets, (given name lacking) 3 0 0
Warren, Thomas 2 0 0
Chapin, Israel, Junr. 1 0 0 1 0
Platt, (given name lacking) 3 0 0
Day, (given name lacking) 1 1 0

C-Manchester (Ontario Co.) formed 3/31/1821 in the name Burt:
Sweet, (given name lacking) 2 0 0
Phelps, Ezra 2 0 0

C-Canandaigua (Ontario Co.) formed Jan. 1789:
Gorham, Nathaniel Jr., Esqr 5 0 0
Sanbourne, Nathaniel 10 0 4
Feilows, John 10 0 1
Smith, Joseph 5 0 3 0 1
Fish, James D. 3 2 2
Chapin, Israel (Genl.) 9 0 1
Dudley, Martin 3 1 3
Bates, Phinias 2 0 0
Walker, Caleb 6 0 1
Colt, Judah, Esq. 2 0 0
Barlow, Abner 2 2 4

Brainard, Daniel 1 2 1
Holcomb, Seth 3 0 0
Brocklebank, James 2 0 0
Castle, Lemuel 1 0 0
Wells, Benjamin 3 1 3
Freeman, John 2 1 0

C-Farmington (Ontario Co.) formed Jan. 1789:
Lapum, Abraham 6 0 0
Hathaway, Isaak 3 2 1
Harrington, Nathan 2 0 0
McCumber, John 1 2 3
Harrington, Joshua 1 2 3
Smith, Elijah 2 0 0
Pane, John 1 2 2
Smith, Jacob 2 0 0
Russel, John 7 0 2
Comstock, Nathan 3 1 0
Reed, Israel 2 1 2
Allen, Reuben 2 0 0

C-Macedon (Wayne Co.) formed 1/29/1823 from Palmyra:
Webb, Herard 4 1 3
White, (given name lacking) 2 0 0
Comstock, Daniel 2 0 0
Smith, Jerome 2 0 0

C-South Bristol (Ontario Co.) formed 3/8/1838 from Bristol:
Wilder, Gamaliel 9 0 2
Wilder, Ephraim 3 0 0
Rice, Aaron 4 0 0
Spencer, Aaron 2 0 0

C-Bristol (Ontario Co.) formed Jan. 1789:
Goodwin, James 2 0 1
Goodwin, William 2 4 1
Fisher, Nathaniel 3 0 0

C-Town not here known (either Bristol or East Bloomfield:
Fellows, John (Gen.) 7 0 1

C-East Bloomfield (Ontario Co.) formed Jan. 1789 in the name Bloomfield:
Rew, Ephriam 6 1 2
Rew, Lot 2 2 3
Hubble, Matthew 2 0 4
Barns, John 1 0 2
Chapin, Oliver 2 0 2
Norton, Nathaniel 7 0 0
Addams, John 7 0 1
Rogers, Michael 2 0 0
Sage, Allem 2 3 5

C-Victor (Ontario Co.) formed 5/26/1812 from Bloomfield:
Boughton, Seymour 3 0 0

Boughton, Gerard 5 2 2
Norton, Zebulon 3 0 0
Taylor, Elijah 2 0 2

E-Corning (Steuben Co.) formed Jan. 1789 in the name Painted Post:
Lamphear, Abel 1 2 3
Henshaw, William 1 1 7
Rowley, Ezra 5 0 1
Calkins, Frederick 2 0 1
McCormick, Henry 3 4 3
Patterson, Ephraim 4 1 5
Patterson, Ichabod 1 2 1
Eaton, Benjamin 1 0 0
Mead, Eli, Esqr. 103
Goodhue, George 3 1 2

E-Lindley (Steuben Co.) formed 5/12/1837 from Erwin:
Lindley, Eleazer, Esqr. 3 0 5 0 6
Lindley, Samuel 1 2 1
Daniels, (given name lacking) 1 0 1
Mumpford, Ezekiel 1 3 2 0 1
Sealy, John 1 2 1

E-Canisteo and Hornellsville combined (Steuben Co.) former formed Jan. 1789 and latter 4/1/1820 from Canisteo:
Headly, James 1 1 2
Baker, William 2 1 1
Stevens, Jedediah 2 2 4
Stevens, Uriah 2 3 1
Stevens, Uriah, Junr. 1 1 3
Stevens, John 1 1 2
Crosby, Richard 3 0 3
Bennett, Solomon 3 2 3
Bennett, Andrew 1 1 2

E-Erwin (Steuben Co.) formed 1/27/1826 from Painted Post:
Curph, Henry 2 2 5
Auar, William 1 0 1
Youngs, Martin 3 2 3
Gordon, Peter 1 0 1
Erwin, Arthur 2 2 0
Lindley, Eleazer, Jr. 1 0 2
Jameson, James 1 0 0

Concerning the postings under the towns of Benton and Milo to follow: Since Turner did not specify any numbered town codes for the district of Jerusalem the source here tapped for the town determinations in this district (J) has been French's town postings of names of "pioneer Settlers".

J-Benton (Yates Co.) formed

2/12/1803 from Jerusalem in the name Vernon:
Hough, Zephaniah 1 2 6
Benton, Levi 6 3 5
Taylor, Samuel 3 1 1
Spencer, Truman 3 0 3
J-Town not here known (either Benton or Milo):
Hathaway, Richard 4 1 4
J-Milo (Yates Co.) Formed 3/6/1818 from Benton:
Dayton, Abraham 3 1 4
Brown, Daniel, Jr. 2 2 2
Lawrence, John 1 2 3
Sherman, Thomas 2 2 2
Hunt, Addam 3 0 0
Nichols, Isaac 2 4 1
Briggs, John 3 1 0
Briggs, Elizabeth 0 0 2
Briggs, Peleg 1 0 4
Briggs, Peleg, Jr. 1 2 2
Townsen, Hezekiah 2 1 1
G-Richmond (Ontario Co.) formed Jan. 1789 in the name Pittstown:
Pitts, Gideon 2 0 0
G-West Bloomfield (Ontario Co.) formed 2/11/1833 from Bloomfield:
Gardner, Benjamin 3 1 5
Gardner, Peregrine 2 1 1
Hall, Amos 3 0 0
Thayer, Sylvanius 3 0 0
Miller, Samuel 1 2 0
Alger, John 2 0 0
Sears, Jasper P. 3 0 0
G-Mendon (Monroe Co.) formed 5/26/1812 from Bloomfield:
Ball, Jonathan 4 0 0
Moore, William 1 3 2
G-Pittsford (Monroe Co.) formed 3/25/1814 from Smallwood:
Stone, Israel 1 1 2
Stone, Simon 1 1 1
Farr, Josial 1 2 5
Cleland, Thomas 1 0 1
Nye, Silas 2 0 0
Giminson, Josiah 2 0 0
Dunn, Alexander 2 0 0
Davis, David 5 0 0
G-Lima (Livingston Co.) formed Jan. 1789 in the name Charleston:
Minor, John 2 0 3
Burchel, Asa 4 2 1
Miles, Abner 3 1 6
Davison, (given name lacking) 1 2 1
G-West Sparta (Livingston Co.) formed 2/27/1846 from Sparta:

Niele, (given name lacking) 1 3 1
G-Geneseo (Livingston Co.) formed Jan. 1789:
Wadsworth, William 7 0 0 0 2?
Bates, Phinehas 1 0 3
Ross, Daniel 1 0 1
Brown, Henry 2 0 2
Noble, Enoch 1 1 2
Rosegrantz, Nicholas 1 1 0 1 0
Robbs, David 2 0 0
Furbanks, Nahum 1 2 3
G-"West of Genesee River" (Turner's terminology) - towns and counties not here known:
Berry, Gilbert r. 1 0 3
Havens, Darline 2 3 3
Bailey, David 1 4 4
Rice, William 1 4 5
Smith, Gershom 1 3 4
Carney, Hill 3 0 2
De Shays, Morgan 2 0 3
De Shays, William 1 1 2
G-(Towns and counties not here known):
Ganson, John 2 3 3
Windship, Philemon 2 0 1
Wilsey, Abel 3 0 1
Morgan, Elijah 2 2 2
Hoovey, Solomon 1 2 0
Morgan, John 6 0 2
Morgan, Joseph 2 0 2 (not mentioned by Turner)
Webber, Williams 1 3 6
Devons, Abraham 3 2 2
G-"West of Genesee River" (Turner's terminology):
Phillips, Nicholas 2 0 2
Phillips, Jacob 1 1 1
Forsyth, Calep 1 2 3
Schoonover, Jacob 1 2 4 (not mentioned by Turner)
Chapman, Nathan 1 3 4
Miller, Nicholas 1 0 1
Utley, Asa 1 3 4
Shafer, Peter 3 0 0
Walker, Jacob 2 0 2 (not mentioned by Turner)
Allen, Ebenezer 2 1 1 3 0
Dugan, Christopher 1 0 1 1 0
Jones, Horatio 2 2 3
Ewing, William 3 0 0
Fowler, Nathan 2 0 2
Gregory, Jeremiah 1 1 1
Skinner, Joseph 3 2 2
Harp, Edward 1 1 3
Marcum, William 6 0 1 (not mentioned by Turner)

Note: Hall on his summary sheet reflects a total of 2 slaves in the district of Canandaiguay. The photocopy of his original postings reflects only one in that district - owned by Joseph Smith as herein indicated.

Fred G. Bowman served sequentially, within the interval 1940-70, in New York as high school math teacher, guidance director and principal and as guidance associate and as planning consultant in the State Education Department. From 1971 onward he has conducted on-site genealogical searches in 24 states and in 58 of New York's 62 counties. Since 1983 he has compiled six books of New York-based genealogical records dated prior to 1856 and his articles have appeared in the *NYG&B Record*, the *NEGH Register*, and Neil D. Thompson's *The Genealogist*. In 1991 he became a certified genealogist.